Hunting the Way it Was

In Our Changing Alaska

LENORA CONKLE

PUBLICATION CONSULTANTS

We Believe In The Power Of Authors

PO Box 221974 Anchorage, Alaska 99522-1974

books@publicationconsultants.com—www.publicationconsultants.com

ISBN 1-888125-08-X
eBook ISBN 978-1-59433-190-9

Library of Congress Catalog Card Number: 96-70834

Copyright 1997 by LeNora Conkle
—First Printing 1997—
—Second Printing 2000—
—Third Printing 2005—

Manufactured in the United States of America.

Other Books by LeNora Conkle

Trail of the Eagle

Wind on the Water

This collection of stories is dedicated to my husband
—C. M. "Bud" Conkle—
who filled my years in Alaska with adventure.

A
L
A
S
K
A

Arctic Ocean

• Barrow

• Wainwright

• Coalville River Delta
(Hemrick's Place)

• Uniat

Brooks Range

Alaska
Canada

• Walker Lake
• Bettles

• Fairbanks
• Eagle Trail Ranch
• Paxon
• Slana
Gakona •
Wrangells
• Tanada Lake Lodge

• Palmer
• Tatitlek
• Cordova • Cape Yakataga
• Montague Island

Anchorage •
Bruin Bay •
• King Salmon

Gulf
of
Alaska

Chukchi Sea

• Landing strips
used by Bud Conkle
while hunting

North

Port Heiden •

Alaska Peninsula

7

Foreword

Polar bear hunting, with airplanes, was started in the early 1950s by sportsmen off the frozen shores of northern Alaska. Pilot/guides and their clients headquartered at various coastal villages: Barrow, Kotzebue, Point Hope and Wainwright were the popular ones. Gene Joiner, of Kotzebue, was the first to fly a small plane over the pack ice, land on an ice pan, (smooth, loose, drifting ice), and collect a polar bear. Gene has been gone now for many years.

By the late 1950s, polar bear hunting with Alaska's pilot/guides was popular big game hunts, very expensive, but desirable. In 1960, C.M. 'Bud' Conkle and C.B. 'Cleo' McMahan—both pilots/guides, started taking clients polar bear hunting out of Barrow, Alaska. They had many accident-free years of big-game guiding, flying Piper PA-18 Super Cubs. Short 'bush-pilot' airfields in the Copper River Basin were their departure points.

Weather permitting, it was a long 2-day flight, taking them over the beautiful jagged peaks of the Alaska and Brooks Ranges. They flew north and west over and between mountain peaks which averaged 8,000-foot MSL (mean sea level). Their flight took them through Isabel Pass to Fairbanks, then through Anaktuvuk Pass to cold, cold Umiat, squatting on the tundra of the Colville River. Barrow, the farthest-northern Native village on the North American continent—71'17" North, 156'46" West, was their staging area.

The popular sport, polar bear hunting by aircraft, was made illegal by the State of Alaska in 1971. The USSR banned polar bear hunting in 1956. In 1972, the U.S. Congress enacted the Federal Marine Mammal Protection Act, and took away the American sportsman's privilege of hunting polar bears. New regulations allowed only Alaska Natives (Eskimo) to hunt the big white bears. The International Union for the Conservation of Nature, and Natural Resources Polar Bear Agreement, signed by the USSR, Norway, Denmark, Canada, and the United States in 1973, became effective May 26, 1976. Alaska polar bear hunting, except by Natives, no longer existed after that date.

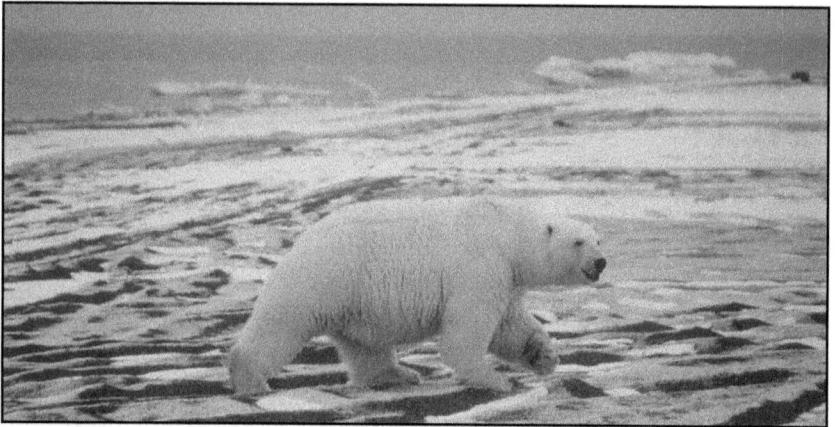

Polar bears, Thalarctos maritimus, are inhabitants of the treeless, icy wastes of the arctic. They may be as long as 11 feet and weigh more than 1,500 pounds. White fur provides excellent camouflage in their snowy environment and even have fur on the soles of their feet that keeps them from slipping on ice. Of all bears, the polar bear is the strictest carnivore. It eats seals, walrus, fish, caribou, and beached whales.   US Fish and Wildlife photo

Polar bear hunting with aircraft is no more. It was a brief era that will never return. Admittedly, it was uncontrolled and getting out of hand and all 'fair-chase' pilot/guides felt the same. Better supervision of hunting practices, study of the animal's population's territory, travels, and reproduction rates was a priority.

United States Fish and Wildlife Service (USFWS) started a polar bear study during the last three years Bud and his partners hunted for polar bear on the arctic pack ice. The agency hired pilots with Super Cubs to fly their Protection Officers out onto the pack ice to locate and study polar bears. Pilots flew low over the bears and the officers shot them with tranquilizing darts. They landed nearby and a radio-collar, bright red and easily spotted from the air, was put on the sleeping bear.

There wasn't much excuse for a collared-bear to be taken by a hunter. Fish and Wildlife agents asked all pilots/guides to tell their clients that these polar bears were not to be taken. But it did happen and the USFWS officers weren't happy when it did. Collared bears were taken when the bear's size proved too tempting for the guide or his client. Agents asked pilots to return the radio collar of a bear accidentally taken. Only one collar was turned in, accompanied by a plethora of excuses and apologies.

United States Fish and Wildlife Service biologists, along with scientists from other northern countries, have continued to do polar bear research in the arctic. Today, polar bear populations are stronger than they have been in recorded history and would support hunting. Bears have visited Alaska communities and had to be "rounded up" with helicopters to protect people. Bears, without fear of man, are a threat and have entered cabins and even killed people.   US Fish and Wildlife photo

One year, months after pilot/guides returned from the polar bear hunts, some were together drinking beer and convivially relating hunting experiences. One told about being a hundred miles out on the ice with a big name hunter and his wing mate. They came across a very big 'red bear' (the carcass of a skinned bear). A radio collar was laying on the ice nearby. The two planes quickly left the vicinity to avoid blame for shooting the bear. No one reported taking that bear. No pilot, even if he knew who was hunting in that area, would turn in another pilot for a violation. Being rescued in an emergency was paramount, and the pilot who flew over and saw his problem just might be the culprit. In that circumstance, one could consider himself very fortunate if that pilot landed to help, or even reported his position and sent help.

What bonded the pilot/guides, so closely, was excitement of the hunt. For the brave few, hunting the arctic pack ice with wings, was a new intoxicating sport, and a new frontier. There was a camaraderie among men who flew so far out on the vast, uncharted, ice-covered ocean in their frail aircraft with few instruments and limited-range radios. It was the most hazardous of all small airplane activities in Alaska, and unequaled since.

Men who flew airplanes, hunted polar bears, and wolves, had the freedom of this great land, enjoyed it. They weren't happy any place else and loved their aircraft and the great distances they traveled. They were willing to endure the cold, primitive conditions, and to care for an airplane to keep it safely flying. Wildness of Alaska and the animals, kept most of them excited—and conservationists.

Denied experience—one often has to invent knowledge, so this type of ingenuity reflects the resourcefulness of making due with what you have and know, and learning from it.

First Polar
Bear Hunt

Bud was alone on the arctic pack ice 150 miles north of Point Barrow, Alaska. He touched down. The big, white polar bear, not 50 feet away, was facing him. His Super Cub slid forward, even after killing the engine. While riding backward on the ski, he grabbed his faithful old 30.06 Model 70 Winchester guiding rifle stashed behind the pilot's seat, and jumped onto the smooth ice. He slammed a shell into the chamber. As he turned, there was the bear.

When he spotted the bear from the air, he was sauntering away. He expected the bear to be running in the opposite direction of his landing airplane, but the bear likely had no idea what an airplane was and held his ground to find out. A 10-foot polar bear is a really big bear and looks even bigger at close range—especially if it's planning a charge. Bud didn't take time to do much thinking. If his first shot didn't do the job, he knew that he or his Super Cub might not come out of the fracas in good shape.

His wing-mate, Cleo, was still circling above, and Bud heard him throttle back to land. Bud shot once, the bear dropped, but quickly got back up. There was red blood showing against his white fur, just behind the front shoulder.

Bud and Cleo had left their home-bases two days before, with an overnight stay in Fairbanks, they flew through Umiat on their way to Barrow. For both of them, it was their first year to hunt polar bear.

At Umiat, while they cooked their evening meal, they decided to get a polar bear for themselves—if they could. Their clients needed to know they had previous experience with the big bears. However, Bud and Cleo were confident in their ability because of years of experience with grizzly bears and brown bears. They didn't think polar bears would be much different.

Who got the chance at the first bear? Why not flip a coin? Bud won the toss that night. It was unusual for him to win anything, let alone the first chance at a big bear and both had a good laugh.

They flew over bear tracks, across rough ice, for two hours before sighting a bear on smooth ice. What luck to have it stay on a smooth ice floe with ample room for two Super Cubs!

The bear staggered up and over a pressure ridge, and Bud placed a second shot. Cleo's Super Cub came to a sliding stop close to Bud's. Still alive, the bear was waiting just over the ice ridge, and attempted to charge as the two men reached the top, but Bud's third bullet proved good. The beautiful white boar was Bud's.

The bear fell the last time, snagged by sharp ice, a few feet from the top. They rolled him down to the bottom, onto smooth ice, and skinned him. The green hide measured 9 feet 9 inches. The skull looked big enough to make North American Big Game Records, but, after it dried the required amount of time, it was a fraction short of scoring. The conservative skull, for so large a bear, made no difference to Bud.

Before, and after, skinning the bear, photographs, and 16mm movies were taken, of course! Both of them wrestled the slippery hide up the icy 8-foot pressure ridge and down the other side.

It was customary, when skinning a bear in the field, to leave the head and paws, cut off at the first joint, intact with the hide, then pay local Eskimo women $25 per hide to skin them out. This procedure added considerable weight to the hide and they became very frustrated with the slick, heavy pelt.

As they loaded it into the plane behind the pilot's seat, it slid out just as fast. They finally got the knack of getting the head and front paws in first, then pushing, shoving and poking in the rest. Bud and Cleo had lots of practice backpacking and loading grizzly and brown bear hides. But they skinned them clean, where they fell. It was generally warmer when skinning grizzly/brown bears, too!

Our home base, Eagle Trail Ranch, is near Mile 58 on the Tok Highway. (The original Valdez to Eagle telegraph line runs through the middle of our property.) At daylight on April 10, Bud took off

16

from mile-long, ice-covered Cobb Lake. He was to meet Cleo in Fairbanks. Then, weather permitting, they would fly their planes 700 miles through the Brooks Range to Umiat. They planned to overnight there before flying on to Barrow where they would meet their clients.

Cleo left for Fairbanks 2 days earlier to have minor repairs done on his Cub. The clients, booked for the polar bear hunt, would fly directly into Barrow on Wein Airlines, then the only commercial airline flying to Barrow.

Bud Conkle and Cleo McMahan with Super Cubs when wolf hunting on the south slope of the Brooks Range. Generally, they'd park Cleo's Cub and Bud would do the flying in his plane and Cleo would shoot from the back seat. Alaska Department of Fish and Game paid a bounty on wolf pelts and the fur traders paid top dollar for quality furs making hunting worth the risk.

Cleo is a well-known, longtime, Alaska outfitter and guide with a reputation as an excellent pilot. His home base is 50 miles southwest of us on the Tok Highway, in Gakona. Bud worked as an assistant guide, in 1950, with Cleo's big game hunting outfit at Meiers Lake, near Paxson Lake on the Richardson Highway. When Bud became eligible, Cleo recommended Bud to the Alaska Department of Fish and Game for a Registered Guide's License. They teamed up for the polar bear hunts in the Arctic, a new exciting big game hunt. Both men were in their late 40s, in excellent health, and mature in their hunting/guiding practices. The young bucks tried anything and their accident rate was high.

Bud and Cleo contended with a real variety of good and bad weather on the long flights to Barrow from our ranch. On his first morning, Bud got into turbulent weather. Icing conditions, snow, and wind, were hurled at him and the Super Cub. He wasn't sure he was going to get to Fairbanks, let alone Barrow. The Super Cub started developing carburetor ice so he landed on the Alaska Highway, a long straight stretch of icy highway, without traffic.

"Oh hell, Bud, you're a long way from Barrow, with lots of this kind of weather between it and you. How long you gonna sit here?" He mumbled to himself. After waiting a short while, he took a chance and took off. The snow was thinning and he followed the highway well enough. He could always land, if the need arose. It cleared near Big Delta and on into Fairbanks. Weather is always a contest for pilots, no matter where they're flying, but especially in the Arctic.

They had beautiful flying weather from Fairbanks and, near Bettles, Cleo called Bud on the radio, and reported spotting a wolf ahead. They landed on the hard, windblown, snow-covered tundra. After unloading everything packed behind the seat, Bud crawled into the back seat of Cleo's Cub. It didn't take long to catch up with the running gray wolf. Cleo came in for a low pass and the wolf dropped with the first blast of Bud's 12-gauge Model 97 Winchester shotgun and died instantly. The big, old fellow's stomach was filled with caribou meat and he wasn't running at top speed. The men didn't see the caribou kill. Likely, the wolf was heading away from a caribou kill to his favorite napping grounds to digest his groceries.

They skinned him on the spot and returned to Bud's parked plane, reloaded Cleo's gear, and

Cleo with 100 pound gray wolf shot on the Wind River. Wolves generally run in packs and it is unusual to find a lone wolf hunting in winter. Caribou are wolves main food source, but they are not above killing a cow or calf moose.

were on their way again. There was no room in the plane to poke the pelt, so Bud held the freshly skinned, smelly hide on his lap the rest of the way to Umiat. He was glad they didn't fill their Fish and Game permits and get more than one wolf.

It was -10° while flying across the Brooks Range and -20° when they landed at Umiat. A 20-knot wind dropped the chill factor to -70° Fahrenheit. The Wein Airlines agent had a Quonset-hut, with cots and

an oil stove, where various air travelers could stay, and his wife ran a small cafe. Bud and Cleo felt this courtesy was more than reasonable for such an isolated place and had a warm place to stay overnight.

The next morning, they followed the Colville River north. On the Colville River Delta, they dropped in on Bud and Martha Helmericks. Helmericks were home, preparing to take a client, who had arrived the evening before, out for a polar bear hunt. Jim 'Andy' Anderson, a pilot for Wein Airlines, from Bettles and Dr. Robert Rausch of the Arctic Health Research Center had landed a half-hour earlier. Bud and Cleo stayed long enough to drink three cups of Martha's good coffee, eat some of her homemade cookies, and exchange a few hunting and flying experiences.

After leaving, they flew 50 miles or so, out over the frozen Beaufort Sea, searching the sunlit ice for their first polar bear. "This sure is a barren, empty waste," Bud thought. Cleo and Bud simultaneously spotted a lone bear. It was so far away, Bud thought it was an arctic fox.

"73 Zulu," Bud called to Cleo on the radio, "I'm going down to have a better look. The ice-floe is small, maybe too small for two planes, so if you want to land and try for movies, I'll stay in the air. Otherwise, I'm going to try it. Seems like a very small bear to be out alone."

"64 Delta, go ahead and give it a try," Cleo decided.

The bear was small, and seemed confused by the noise of the engine. He just stood there, with his nose in the air, trying to figure out all the noise and no identifying smell. Bud cut the throttle, pulled on the flaps and made a bumpy landing on the rough ice. All he got for his trouble, though, was the little south end of a little north bound bear.

Cleo's cover plane droned in circles above him and as Bud took off, he knew Cleo was wondering if he would be airborne in time to clear the pressure ridge looming ahead. But Bud hadn't underestimated the weight he carried and the ability of its 150 horsepower Lycoming engine. All of those short landings and take offs on short fields during the past years had given him the experience to do it right.

At Barrow, they refueled and checked in at the hotel. One of their concerns was getting accommodations for themselves, and for their clients. They had no way of knowing how many pilot/guides, with clients, were hunting out of Barrow at the time, and had probably arrived before Bud and Cleo.

There is only one hotel—The Top of the World Hotel—and it was usually full. Phoning ahead for reservations did no good. They didn't take reservations.

"Just show up" they said. Luck was still with them, and when they 'showed up' they got a semiprivate room and didn't have to settle for the larger dormitory rooms upstairs.

Three pilot/guides already there, had filled their hunters' permits. The hunters had already left, and the pilot/guides were waiting for their next clients to arrive. There was quite a party in the hotel that night. Bud and Cleo joined in for a while, though they were weary from the long flight, they made big plans for a full day on the pack ice. After hearing the stories about hunters and their bears, they went to rooms with paper-thin walls and tried to rest.

Their first two hunters collected good bears and left for Fairbanks on an afternoon commercial flight. Bud and Cleo hoped the clear weather, -10° temperatures and unusually beautiful sunny days, continued during the next hunt.

Finding and taking a trophy polar bear on the arctic ice pack took a skilled pilot, knowledgeable guide, and a dedicated hunter—and a great deal of good fortune. Even after a bear was spotted from the air and identified as a trophy, landing and stalking him and being able to get a clean shot off was by no means guaranteed. US Fish and Wildlife photo

Their next client, Bill Van Houten, arrived on Wein Airlines from Fairbanks. Because the flight was late, they were unable to fly that day, so the guides got acquainted with Bill and his hunting background, and explained their hunting methods. They also decided who would be backup guide and who would be the photographer. Bill was a bow-and-arrow hunter and a member of North American Bow Hunters. Bud and Cleo hadn't met him before, but heard he was a professional hunter with bow and arrow for smaller game.

Cleo and Bud were still a bit apprehensive about this hunt and hoped for fortunate circumstances and a cooperative bear allowing them to get close enough for a kill. They came highly recommended to Van Houten and he had confidence in their ability, though Bud and Cleo had little experience with bow-and-arrow hunting. This hunt could prove interesting.

On the first day, they flew more than 100 miles over the pack ice without locating a lone bear. About 60 miles out, under overcast skies, with tracking impossible, they still hoped to catch up with a single, fair sized bear. They needed sunny skies and a moving white bear that could be seen. With a remote chance of locating the right bear that day, they flew on.

Along the return flight to Barrow, both planes landed on a long, wide, smooth ice-floe and unsuccessfully attempted taking movies of a small lone bear. The bear immediately lost interest in intently watching the dark water of an open lead, and galloped into the hazy distance. By the time they were airborne again, the bear was too far away, and the haze was too thick for movies from the air.

The third day on the ice, Cleo called Bud over the Cub's radio. "64 Delta, I see tracks ahead and they look like they belong to a fair-sized bear."

Polar bears are Alaska arctic's largest carnivore and taking one with a bow on the arctic pack ice was dangerous. The shot must be taken within 40 yards of the bear and even though the guide was there with a rifle, a mad, wounded bear could quickly cover that distance and kill both guide and hunter. It was hoped, that if the bear wasn't killed instantly, it would only move a short distance away and die.

Bud's hunter, riding in the back seat of the Cub, nodded yes, he'd take this bear, if it was a 6-footer or better. The sun was bright and tracking was good, and they passed on two other smaller bears.

The pilots followed the big tracks, for quite a distance, until both Super Cubs could land near a large ice floe slung with ridges. The bear was behind a 6-foot pressure ridge, and still there when the three men eased to the top and peeked over.

Cleo was back up guide and Bud took the movies. Both had their rifles at the ready. The unsuspecting bear was about 35 yards below them, deciding whether to settle down for a snooze or continue his way. Cleo gave the nod and Bill drew the bow. The first arrow hit the bear in the neck, but too low. Bill immediately let go a second arrow catching the bear in the rump as it whirled and tried to bite the first arrow. His third arrow hit in the chest, and the bear jumped across the ice, heading for an open lead. Cleo's rifle spoke and caught the bear in the front leg. Bill's fourth arrow hit the bear's chest simultaneously with Cleo's shot. This time, the bear sprawled and stayed down. Bill was using a 55-pound bow manufactured in Texas. His bear was a 7-foot bear weighing 600 pounds.

They were 85 miles north of Barrow, with -15° temperatures and a harsh wind. Bill believed the wind was a factor in deflecting his arrows. He said confidently that his first shot, at the angle and distance, should have killed the bear. The same wind had been to their advantage to get that close to the bear. Either, the bear hadn't heard the noise of their landing planes, or simply ignored it. The chest shot with the arrow proved to be the fatal one, but Bill couldn't officially claim the kill as a bow and arrow trophy, because it was also shot with a rifle. Cleo, of course, felt bad he had been obligated to shoot, but as dangerously close to thin ice, and an open-water lead, as the bear was, it might have been a lost bear if he hadn't shot. They'd heard tales from other guides about losing bears through thin ice. Bears will invariably try to make it to open water and swim under. They sink quickly, if wounded or dying.

Thin ice is rubbery feeling and often too thin for a man to crawl onto to retrieve a bear. Guides carried several lengths of rope and usually a rubber raft, in case the bear made for open water.

The next two hunters, from New York, each collected a trophy bear after a few days of flying the pack ice. They were really fine sportsmen and the hunt was enjoyable. On their last day, Bud and Cleo took them aerial wolf hunting a couple of flying-hours south of Barrow. But were unsuccessful locating the pack reportedly following a caribou band on the open flats.

Their last two hunters canceled their hunt because of business commitments in Tokyo. Bud and Cleo were notified by a telegram waiting for them at the hotel, on their return from the wolf hunt. It was a low blow. Although these men forfeited their deposits, it was too late to book two more hunters to replace them. So polar bear hunting was over for the year.

On the flight home, Bud and Cleo collected two big gray wolf pelts. As the men neared the Brooks Range they spotted the wolves sunning themselves on an open hillside. The planes were flying side by side with-out radio conversation. They spotted the two wolves simultaneously. Cleo's plane circled lower, then settled on a snow field near the base of the hill. Bud immediately followed. Cleo unloaded some gear and made sufficient room for Bud to jump aboard with his shotgun. The activity alerted the wolves, and they were running flat out. They had no place to hide and Bud tumbled the lead wolf on the first pass. The second wolf turned back in the opposite direction and Bud nailed him on the third pass.

It was a long hike to the wolves. By the time they left two carcasses for the ravens and hiked back to their airplanes, it was late afternoon. They needed to get airborne again and cross the Brooks Range before dark to be able to overnight in Bettles.

Back at home, the success of their hunts was noted in the local newspaper. 'Local' means Valdez, 200 miles away. They were hot stuff and enjoyed the publicity, although neither would ever admit it. At the time, they were the only pilot/guides from the Copper River Valley area that were doing this new type of hunting. Slana on the Tok Highway, where our home was, had just ten or twelve families in the community. Gakona, where the McMahan's lived, didn't have many more, so, of course, everyone knew the men.

Bud's beautiful polar bear rug-mount hung on the trophy room wall at Eagle Trail Ranch for many years.

For 25 winters I have hunted red fox and coyote in the midwest by tracking through the snow, herding them, and shooting while on the run with a .243 rifle. I now want to come to your state and hunt wolves in the same fashion. Perhaps you can assist me in getting the correct information which will enable me to arrange for a hunt this fall or winter. I will need a guide, transportation, and a place to stay. Can you send whatever other information is pertinent?
Truly yours,
Martin A.

Dear Mr. A. Thank you for your letter regarding a wolf hunt in Alaska. Until now, I have never taken a client on a wolf hunt by tracking on foot, as you described in your letter. That

method could understandably be called 'fair chase' with a capital
F. Wolves travel in a five-hundred-mile radius, claiming and
marking their territory. To track one down on foot, specially on
snowshoes, would take a better man than I am.

We used to hunt wolves from the airplane, using a
shotgun with buckshot. Even this method was tough at times,
but aerial wolf hunting has been banned since the early 1970s.

If you're interested, we could fly in my Super Cub
and locate wolves possibly traveling along a river, then I could
set you out a few miles away—hopefully downwind of them.
I would then come back, after a reasonable length of time, and
pick you up, with your trophy, if luck favored you.

February is the best time of the year for this type of
hunt. Wolves move around a lot and hides are in prime condition then. I would fly only during good flying weather since it
is just about hopeless to track wolves from the air in whiteout
conditions. Also, the safety factor rules out such flying. I can't
guarantee you will shoot a wolf, but I can guarantee you will
have some experiences you have never had before.
Sincerely:
Bud Conkle

I don't think I'll be coming to Alaska to hunt with you. I have
never flown in an airplane as small as a Super Cub and I am more
scared of that than flying in a big airplane. With my luck, the plane
would probably crash—because I'd be so scared that I would do
something rash like grab onto the pilot, or maybe get so airsick
that I would start yelling at the pilot to land and there would be
no place to land. I have suffered bad dreams, many times, and
the dream was always about flying in an airplane that crashed.
Truly yours,
Martin A.

Naturally, we didn't encourage this great fox hunter from the
mid-west to hunt wolf with us.

Tidbits of Hunting
Information

In 1960, Bud Conkle and Cleo McMahan started guiding polar bear hunts on the arctic pack ice, headquartering at Barrow. Many other pilot/guides temporarily based there, but there were others who maintained bases in other coastal villages. Few pilot/guides lived year-round in these remote villages, because there weren't many other kinds of game. They flew in at the end of the dark, sleepy winter, flew from an established base and stirred up the villages for a couple of months. When they went home, the villages quieted down again.

Cleo and Bud always flew their planes in a buddy system, mainly for safety reasons. If one plane went down while on the ice pack, pilots could leave extra gas cans and survival gear near the downed plane, crowd into the other plane, and fly back to base. The two aircraft never ventured far from land with a passenger in each plane because two-seated planes won't carry four people. It was hard enough to squeeze the smallest person into the cargo area behind the passenger seat, when flying three people. It was also very cold for that person—the heat never reached that far back!

Piper PA-18, and Super Cubs, were the most popular aircraft for this type of hunting, although a few of the pilot/guides flew one or two other model tail draggers. The Cubs were lightweight, easily equipped with skis or wheels, carried good loads, and got decent mileage with the standard 150 HP engines. They allowed the use of very small landing fields and were easy to care for in the arctic adverse weather conditions. The design and paint on Bud's were standard Piper colors (red over white). Cleo's was the same colors, but a different design.

It was customary to take one client at a time, and either pilot could fly the other plane, at his choice. Each client had his own favorite pilot. Some felt they would be safer if they flew with the guide who booked them. Others took turns between the two planes. Still others flew with the pilot they were most comfortable with, in terms of temperament and personality.

The plane with the client, always landed first on a suitable ice floe, large enough for both planes to land if possible. The cover plane could land just behind the client's plane, when circumstances allowed. If it looked like the second plane's landing would scare the bear away, the cover plane remained airborne until the bear was down.

Bud with a client's polar bear and his and Cleo's Super Cubs in the background. Special equipped Cubs, most often white with red trim, took polar bear hunters far out on the ice pack. This bear was taken over 100 miles from Point Barrow on the Arctic Ocean. A polar bear is not pure white. It has a yellow cast to its hair and has a black nose.

All of the planes used to hunt polar bears were radio-equipped to maintain contact with each other. At the time, it was considered an added expense of polar bear guiding, because most of the pilot/guides operated independently the rest of the year and rarely, if ever, needed to talk to another aircraft.

The planes were known by their last three alphanumerics and each pilot/guide quickly became familiar with other plane's call signs. Our Cub was N8464D—which was reduced to six-four-Delta. Cleo's plane, N3673Z, became seven-three-Zulu.

March and April were the best months for polar bear hunting. The weather was milder and the daylight hours longer. Some pilot/guides however, started their hunts in mid-February, when the daylight hours were considerably shorter. However, it curtailed the number of flight/

hunt hours each day. By mid-March, the sun was up for almost 12 hours each day. The sun doesn't shine in Barrow from mid-November until mid-January, then by late-May, the sun doesn't set at all.

Barrow is 335 miles north of the Arctic Circle, situated on the coast of the Arctic Ocean. In 1960, Barrow was one of the largest Eskimo settlements in North America, with a population of close to 1,500 people. A short distance north of the village was the Arctic Naval Research Laboratory, operated by the University of Alaska, under contract to the U. S. Navy at the time. The center engaged in a wide range of arctic studies.

Named for Sir John Barrow, an English geographer, Point Barrow, 10 miles north of the village, is the northernmost point of Alaska, and subsequently of the United States.

Most small planes used the ice-covered Elson Lagoon as an airfield and parking area. It was much closer to Barrow and the hotel than the much larger commercial airfield. Most pilot/guides don't want to be too far from their aircraft. Weather conditions changed suddenly and erratically and tie-downs need to be checked during high winds. Sometimes, each airplane had to be physically turned around to face into the wind.

Polar bear hunters, and pilot/guides, referred to the local hotel as the Barrow Hilton. It definitely wasn't a first-class hotel by Lower 48, or even by less-rigid Alaska standards. One didn't have much choice, though, it was the only hotel in town. It was comfortable enough, under the circumstances, and at the top of the world, the hotel provided a glimpse of refreshment. The few semiprivate rooms downstairs were occupied on a first come first served basis. There were eight, if memory serves me right. When they were full, everyone else bunked in the dormitory upstairs. All of the rooms downstairs were small and each had two cots. There were no locks on the doors of the dormitory rooms and no showers or toilets in any of the rooms. The walls were thin and the only heat in the dormitory came up the stairwell from the lower floor.

In the winter months, the hotel's entire water supply came from ice blocks, cut and stacked outside alongside the building. They were melted in large containers on the big kitchen range. When the water level was low, another block of ice was added. Cooking water, dishwater, personal wash water, and even drinking water came from the same big containers. It wasn't uncommon to see yellow streaks running down the sides of the blocks stacked on the bottom level, within reach of loose dogs. After all, there was a total absence of fire hydrants and trees. Yellow ice, as it was commonly called, was undisturbed the entire winter.

There wasn't a restaurant in the hotel and everyone ate their meals at Al's Cafe, located about two blocks from the hotel. Al's was the only eating place available while the bear guides were based there.

When the evening meals were over, the planes taken care of, and all of the pilot/guides were in from the ice, it was time for talking. Pilots love to regale each other with tales of their daily happenings. One story leads to another, the storyteller often adding a bit of bravado to embellish the story when he has rapt and admiring listeners. The story tellers and their tales, fascinated the Cheechakos.

Polar bear hunts were expensive and not every avid hunter could afford it, no matter how he planned or saved. His air fare from his home to Barrow, his hotel and meals while there (expenses not included in the price of the hunt paid to the guide), the taxidermy and shipping charges for his full-mount trophy, or rug, added considerably to the total cost. A hunter paid his pilot/guide for a trophy-size bear whose hide measured eight feet or more. The hunt lasted until they got the bear, or until the hunter ran out of personally allotted time. After he had his bear, and if there was time before the next clients arrived, he had the privilege of going on a free aerial wolf hunt. Some hunters were delighted with a chance of collecting a wolf pelt. If more than one wolf was taken, the pilot/guides kept them.

Resident hunters paid a lower fee for the hunt and were allowed 10 days to get a bear of 6-feet or better. They were, however, obligated to wait if a nonresident client was still hunting. A resident hunter paid a set fee to hunt wolves and wolverine. There was no guarantee of getting an animal. Sow bears with cubs were not fair game to any hunter, and all of the pilot/guides respected this rule.

Aviation gas was bought in Barrow or was shipped there. All pilot/guides used many 55 gallon barrels of aviation-gas. When they hunted wolves, they all knew where the government left drums of gas. After the DEW Line, (a line of Distant Early Warning radar stations, 100 miles apart, near the 70th parallel) was built, the gas drums were abandoned. They helped themselves. Many drums of aviation-gas were also left behind when the U.S. Navy explored for oil in the areas north of the Brooks Range.

The Super Cub is not noted for unlimited load space but has amazing load-carrying capacity. Loaded by an experienced pilot who can expertly gauge its allowed poundage, it never fails. By the time the pilots loaded their planes with necessary gear for arctic hunts, they were hard pressed to find room for themselves and their bulky clothing.

Much of their equipment was shipped, or mailed, north, and most of the pilots carried the same list of standard supplies. They carried emergency rations, cooking utensils, a down sleeping bag made for temperatures as low as -50°, and a duffle bag of dry winter clothing. Winter clothing and sleeping bags took considerable available space, but didn't add much to the weight.

There had to be room for insulated engine and wing covers, a catalytic heater that fit inside the engine cowling for maintaining overnight warmth, a couple of 5-gallon cans of aviation-gas and a gallon of Blazo (white gas) for the catalytic heater. Two quarts of engine oil and a container to hold drained oil when the plane was parked overnight, or any length of time. The important, always handy, chamois-covered gas funnel, was well protected near the top of the load. All pilots religiously poured their gasoline through a filter to keep out water and/or dirt. There also had to be room in the gear for backup rifles and ammo. A shotgun and several boxes of #1 and #4 buckshot were packed for wolf hunts. Outside temperature gauges were taped to the left lift strut. Snowshoes, an absolute must, during the winter months, were tied to the left strut as well. The Cub's single door opens on the right side. The window lifts out and latches onto the bottom of the wing, the lower door drops down beside the fuselage. Items were tied to the left lift strut, where they are out of the way.

Bud and Cleo's Cubs had the flight controls removed from the rear seat and a protective box built over the place where the stick was attached. Their Cubs had stick control instead of wheel controls, and of course, tandem seats. Flexible heater-hose, connected to the engine for interior heat, was used to clear frost from the interior of the windshield. The passenger in the rear seat could have the heat hose only when the windshield was clear. Despite the cold, or the wealth of the hunter, the windshield had priority! There was no other heat in the Super Cub, so the warm air this hose funneled to the face, fingers and toes, was always enthusiastically welcomed.

Much preparation went into polar bear hunts. The airplanes had to have the required 100-hour and/or annual inspections and licensing. Bud and Cleo had additional navigation instruments installed, besides their radios. After 2 years of polar bear hunting, they had VHF radios, better compasses and automatic direction finders (ADF) installed.

These instruments were expensive, cash-wise, but paid off in terms of safety for the hours they flew over distances and unmarked landscapes.

Fuel tanks in each wing held 36 gallons of aviation gas, and provided an average of 6 hours flying time. Sometime later, Cleo had a 30-gallon belly tank installed on his Cub thus extending his flying hours.

Ralph Marshall sold Bud an ELT (Emergency Locator Transponder). They were battery-operated and triggered automatically during a wreck. This wasn't the more expensive or better one on the market a year or so later, but Bud thought it was fine. I was thankful we never had to use it. It was a good feeling having it aboard. Most Alaska pilots bought them when they were available. Later their installation became mandatory.

There were no reliable weather forecasts at the time polar bear hunting guides flew north of the Brooks Range. They did their own forecasting—mainly by looking out the window. Umiat was an important gravel, or snow-packed, air field, 175 miles east-southeast of Barrow where many pilots landed, coming and going from Barrow. It was easy to locate on the vast expanse of unmarked tundra, by following the Colville River to it's angle northward to the sea.

It was a policy of all the pilot/guides to arrive in Barrow ahead of their clients. Weather decided the hours and/or days it took them to arrive after leaving home base. This didn't count the additional time they spent wolf hunting along the way. Pilot/guides carried wolf hunting permits issued by the Fish and Wildlife. Each pilot was allowed to take a certain number of wolves on this permit. Besides the $50 bounty the State paid as a predator-control measure, the hides brought a fair price when sold (as much as $500), and it was considered a great sport.

Only a few of the pilot/guides, Cleo and Bud among them, took their clients on wolf hunts, when time and weather allowed. Wolf hunting proved to be some interesting story telling in the far north. There wasn't any noticeable depletion in the wolf population during the years they made these hunts.

Clients were told what temperatures to expect, that guides didn't fly if the weather wasn't right, and that they might have to wait 2 or more days without hunting. The clients paid for their own meals and hotel and knew what the cost might be. They were given a list of clothing to wear, and bring, and what type of sleeping bags were recommended. Cautions about personal medicines and those they may require were given.

As a rule, most clients preferred to bring their own heavy outer wear, but we furnished parkas and the white canvas covering if the client didn't have one. One client didn't take our advice about having his camera degreased and the only photographs he had to show of his hunt were what Cleo and Bud took with their cameras.

Once, Bud heard another pilot/guide make some uncomplimentary remarks about a client who was already on the plane winging its way south. It seems they flew many hours locating a 'bragging-size' bear. Their cover pilot stayed in the air because the ice floe was too small for both planes. The man's gun froze and he nearly broke the trigger pulling on it, while the bear galloped away. The guide almost clipped the pressure ridge with a ski on takeoff and he was really ticked off, after all of the effort he put into getting this guy into a position to collect a real trophy.

The guide had no intention of handing the man his own rifle. At base he told the man to be sure to degrease his rifle. Later, the hunter apologized, said he had just been too busy getting ready to leave and had forgotten. Now, how could a dedicated hunter ever forget to do that? That client went home without a bear.

Bud didn't blame the guide, but he surely wasn't pleased with his remarks in the lobby that evening. Bud and Cleo always tried to practice good manners and courtesy. They loved to tell stories about hunting and flying but they were never unkind.

Another year, we booked a man from Texas, who didn't read the list we sent, or he didn't believe it was all necessary. When he arrived in Barrow, he was wearing a very large cowboy hat, leather cowboy boots and an unlined denim jacket and matching blue jeans. His ears were as red as lobsters by the time they walked the half-mile to the hotel in -30° temperatures. It surely didn't take him long to shuck his summer clothes and dig into his duffle bag for warm gear. He grudgingly gave up his cowboy hat and replaced it with a monstrosity of a fur cap. He was going to show Alaskans just how tough Texans were. Naturally, the Alaskans weren't impressed. No pilot/guide would take a hunter out until he was properly equipped with the right clothing.

The pilot/guides walked out to the airport when they had hunters arriving and helped carry their luggage back to the hotel. There were no taxies for transportation in Barrow in those days.

Fantastic displays of northern lights, nature's incredible night show, impressed the clients from Outside. One year they were overpowering. A few of the clients, at various times, saw the displays when in

Fairbanks. Occasionally they were in vivid colors. It is impossible to witness this phenomenon without being deeply moved with the mystery and awe. Clients, lucky enough to witness such a display, expressed their appreciation and were often overwhelmed and speechless. Some hunters saw the northern lights in their northeastern home states, but never like the ones in the far north.

On nights when shafts of lights dance across star-filled skies, it excites the imagination and is a new show every time. When a diaphanous veil is waved by an unseen hand, whether in color or misty white, the sight is never forgotten.

Some polar bear hunters wanted to try fishing the Eskimo way. As soon as the fish comes out of the water and hits the ice, it is immediately flash frozen. Charlie Edwardson fishing through the arctic ice for tom cod. A hole is cut about 12 inches in diameter through 2 feet of ice. Lines unwound from sticks held in each hand are artfully used to bring up the small fish.

Ice fog—commonly called 'sea smoke' is the telltale sign of a large system of open leads on the pack ice. This phenomenon results when moisture rises from cracks in the sea ice and condenses as thick vapor. It hangs dark and uninviting, and rises high in the air across the distance of open water. It freezes whenever it contacts something else, making hoarfrost or solid ice. The planes avoided ice fog if possible.

'White out' is similar to ice fog, but of different origin. It's very serious, especially for pilots. A white out generally occurs on a cloudy, gray day when sunlight doesn't cast shadows or define shapes. 'White out' occurs too, during a falling snow or ice fog and critically limits vision.

In the northernmost areas of the state, the total absence of trees plus myriads of snow-covered pothole lakes makes a definitive horizon very important. Sudden storms and cloud cover can be very dangerous for a pilot. In these cases, the pilot tries to either climb above the clouds or drop below them, hoping to find a creek or lake with tall bushes to guide them. If necessary, they land in the first suitable place and wait for conditions to improve.

Polar bears are pale yellow, not pure white. Their hollow, heat-reserving hairs have a light yellow tint. Therefore, they are easier to spot against the snow-white background. They have a black nose, eyes, and a dark interior ear. They are easier to spot when they are up and moving, but when they are asleep with a paw over their nose and their eyes shut, it's easy to fly right over them without seeing them. A pilot/guide could, under favorable circumstances, tell by the size of the bear's track if it is a trophy bear and worth following further.

Guides are required to be very knowledgeable to pass their guide exams. Among other things, they are required to know the different parts and names of basic camera equipment, know different kinds of light and how to get the best camera shots. The photographs and movies are a very important part of the hunter's experience. Often unbelievable, hunting stories are proven with movies and pictures. Guides become very competent photographers, just from the sheer number of photos they take.

Green bear hides, freshly skinned, untanned hides, are measured from nose-tip to the end of the tail. Green hides are very heavy, quite slippery and hard to handle under any circumstance, but more so when the handler has cold hands and is bundled in multiple layers of bulky clothing. Skulls are measured with more complicated techniques. Bear records are taken once the hide and skull are dried, because taxidermy can effect the size of the hide. Tanning and mounting processes shrink and deform the hide to a small degree.

Hides were fleshed and cleaned by local Eskimo women. To rinse the blood off, a hole was cut in the sea ice, a rope securely tied to the hide, then the hide was dipped up and down in the salt water. They beat the water out with a smooth wooden paddle, then laid it on the snow, and walked on it with their mukluks, thus the snow absorbed the moisture. The hide was turned over and the process repeated. Most of the pilot/guides took care of the salting of the hides and packing them for transport. Hides were generally shipped, by the guide, to whichever taxidermist the client chose. It often took a year before the hunter received his trophy, depending on how he wanted it mounted. Although some had their trophies made into standing life-size mounts, rug-mounted hides, hung on a large wall, were favorites.

I am reminded of the outfitter from Canada who exclusively used horses for his hunts. A couple of our clients hunted very successfully with his outfit and spoke highly of his hunting and guiding abilities. We met this man at a North American Sheep Conventions and were impressed with his reputation as a capable guide and outfitter. He seemed fearless, an outdoorsman. He and Bud corresponded frequently for 2 years about a trade hunt. He would hunt polar bear with Bud and Bud would then hunt with him in the Yukon Territory for Stone or Fanin Ram. The dates were all arranged for his hunt with us in late February, then Bud would take his Canadian hunt after our fall hunts ended.

Less than a month before this man was to arrive in Barrow, we received a telegram from him, which said to call him "collect" immediately. Thinking some disaster had happened to him or his family, Bud put forth extra effort to get to a distant phone. He apologized and told Bud he wasn't going to make the polar bear hunt. Then in lengthy detail he recounted a dream he had while hunting. In the dream, Bud's plane had crashed and he was killed in the vast arctic, in such an isolated area that his dear wife had a nervous breakdown before his body was found and brought home. His wife talked him out of going on the polar bear hunt. Then, during the same phone call, he said he would change his mind if we could hunt with horses.

Was he kidding? Hunt polar bears on pack ice and snow with horses? How did he expect us to get horses to Barrow? And how would we feed them? Airline freight charges would have been outrageous for bales of hay and bags of feed, let alone the horses. How comfortable would he have been riding hundreds of miles in -30° temperatures? It all left us wondering.

Elderly Man,
Small Boy

Bud and Cleo planned, for some time, to take their 9-year-old sons to Barrow, and let them shoot their own polar bear. The year, 1961, was the opportune year to take them, since the men's schedule allowed extra time to spend with their sons. Bud was forced to leave his son, Colin, down with a bad case of the flu, at home. Hotel accommodations in Barrow, and the Arctic itself, was no place for anyone feeling under par. Cleo's son, Harley, was well and eager.

The two men left together from the Gakona airfield. One plane carried Harley sitting high a top duffle bags and sleeping bags in the Super Cub's passenger seat. It was a very long ride to Barrow, especially for a squirmy young boy. They stopped in Fairbanks only long enough to top off the fuel tanks, stretch their legs and eat their lunch. They stayed overnight in Bettles. The weather held them there for 2 days. On the third morning they started for Barrow. Bud telephoned and reported they flew all the way to Bettles from Fairbanks, dodging heavy fog patches. They sneaked through chinks in the fog and arrived in Bettles a bit before dark.

"The lodge rooms and meals cost us plenty," Bud said. "But it sure beat camping in a snow bank all night."

They fought flying snow, and freezing rain, from Bettles to Barrow. Conditions at Barrow weren't the best either. There was no avgas in Barrow. They immediately ordered seven barrels from Fairbanks, hoping Wein Airlines would deliver them soon. Wing-mates, Pete

Merry and George, were almost finished with their hunts and they lent Bud and Cleo two barrels of avgas so they could start hunting while the flying weather was favorable.

Bud and Cleo had only two nonresident hunters booked for the season, Fred Patterson, from one of the eastern states and Chester Rose, a 71-year-old Californian. Chester and Cleo had hunted big game together in previous years. They also had deposits for two resident hunters from Fairbanks.

There was always the chance of taking out clients booked by other guides, when, frequently, weather delayed a hunt or the client's va-

Whiteouts, wind, and ice fog are part of polar bear hunting and flying in the arctic. Many hunting days are lost due to weather. On one occasion, Bud and Cleo McMahan were grounded in a whiteout for 3 days while returning from their polar bear hunt at Point Barrow.

cation time was running out. Besides, pilot/guides had other hunters arriving, so they were pleased to pay any of the idle pilot/guides. It took more than two nonresident's checks during the hunting season to meet Bud and Cleo's expenses so they counted on extra clients. Chester was one of those pleasant hunters who never complained and Bud said he was an enjoyable man to have on a hunt. Flying weather favored them for two days and they flew over a lot of ice-covered ocean. The first day, they flew all morning without seeing as much as a single bear track. They flew back to Barrow to fuel up and eat lunch, then back out over the ice in a different direction. Tracking conditions weren't the best, but they finally picked up tracks and located the wandering bear. He wasn't trophy size and seemed confused about which way to run. Cleo flew his plane low enough for the hunter to take photographs through the opened side window.

By late afternoon of the third day, Chester had a polar bear whose freshly skinned hide measured 10 feet.

He said. "My usual good luck worked when we came across that old boar concentrating on a fur seal he was eating for lunch." They were able to land both planes on a smooth ice pan far enough away that it didn't disturb the bear, and they stayed out of his sight until they were within 175 yards. His back was toward them, but he apparently sensed something was wrong, sat up, and turned his head toward them. Three quick, well-placed shots, was all it took. Photos taken, the bear's fur-covering was removed. The warm hide was carried, lifted, poked, and shoved into Bud's plane and then the carcass was left for little arctic fox. The men were back in Barrow in time for an early steak dinner.

Using a pressure ridge as a background, Bud is photographed holding Jim Dieringer's trophy polar bear.

Word got around. The client always bought steak dinners for his pilot/guides, after he got his bear. Chester had passed on the offer to take him on a wolf hunt and was on the scheduled Wein flight the following day. Ten years later, while Harley was guiding for his father, Cleo, Chester Rose died in their camp of a sudden heart attack.

Resident hunters from Fairbanks, Jim Dieringer, and Dennis Long-fellow, each collected a bear during the following 4 days of good flying weather. Jim's was an 8-footer and Dennis' was 7-feet, and a few inches.

The weather started changing, becoming hazy and looking like snow when it was 9-year-old Harley's turn to hunt for a bear. In the late afternoon the previous day they hadn't located any bear. So instead of trying to hunt, in adverse weather, the three of them walked a mile out on the pack ice where Jonah Leavitt and another Eskimo man were fishing through the ice for Tom Cod.

A hole was cut about 12 inches in diameter through 2 feet of ice.

They fished hour after hour. They sat patiently on stools brought with them. Lines unwound from sticks held in each hand were artfully used to bring up the small fish. When a fish took the tiny chunks of meat they used for bait, they brought it to the surface by deftly winding the line from one stick to the other.

Bud, Cleo and Harley enjoyed their afternoon watching this activity, talking with the two men and taking movies. The fish they caught, favorite of the Eskimo, were only four inches or so in length, and it took many of them to make a meal. It was an interesting way to spend an afternoon. Harley was promised a chance to hunt again, after the next hunter departed.

Fred Patterson arrived on Wein Airlines the following day. It was too late to fly, so he was initiated into the activities at the cafe and an evening in the Barrow Hilton, listening to the variety of stories related by the other pilot/guides and their hunters.

Bud and Cleo flew the following day with Fred, but couldn't follow any of the fresh bear tracks they picked up. Wind drifted the light snow and tracking conditions weren't good. The second day, Fred flew in Bud's plane and Cleo was cover-pilot. Fred spotted a bear at the same instant his pilot/guide did, and at that moment Cleo called.

"64 Delta, bear in open lead ahead and to my right!"

Both planes slid in for a landing on an ice-floe, behind a pressure ridge, out of the bear's sight. With cameras and rifles in hand, the three men climbed the 5-foot ice ridge, and peeked over the edge. They saw the bear gracefully exit the far side of a nearby open lead, then vigorously shake himself, throwing showers of sea water into the sparkling afternoon sun. Fred kept the camera running during the bear's action. There was never a lack of interest or excitement in seeing one of those free, roaming bears, no matter their size or activity.

The bear stood for a minute, looking in their direction, where the only sound was the whirring of the movie camera and the fast clicking and winding of Bud's 35mm camera. The bear let out a roar, and with a disgusted shake of its head, crossed to another open lead, slid into the water, and swam away. He looked like he was no more than a 4-year-old enjoying an isolated existence.

They flew another hour with no success. Then, on the third day, they flew 110 miles east of Barrow and located a 9-foot bear. The bear was very cooperative. He watched both planes land on the expansive ice floe where he was snoozing, then just stood up.

Fred was very excited with his trophy and didn't want to wait to go on a wolf hunt. Weather was looking like it wanted to change for the worse. He telephoned home, and his family, and the office crew, was eager for him to come home and tell them all about the great white bear; the one he talked about and planned to get for such a long time. They had to be satisfied with his photographs for many months, until the hide was rug-mounted and shipped to him from the taxidermist.

With 3 days of good flying weather, Bud and Cleo took two of Bob Cooper's nonresident hunters and they went home happy with their hunts and their bears. Both were easy hunts. The tracking and places they landed were good, and the hunters shot with deadly aim and without assistance from the backup guide. One 8 and 1/2-foot bear put on quite a growling and thrashing display before a third bullet put him down. The other man's bear, a 9-1/4-foot-er, lay without moving after the second bullet slammed into a vital spot.

All of the planes were grounded for the next two days. When they could fly

Nine-year-old, Harley McMahan, with his polar bear.

again, it was Harley's turn to fly for a bear. He spent the intervening days doing school work he brought with him and playing with local children after school was out for them.

Northeast of Barrow, about 75 miles, with a light wind and -20°, Harley collected a 9—foot polar bear. His bear was almost identical, in size, to the one Cleo had taken for himself the year before. Harley's story, Nookup-pak Nannok puk (little boy, big bear) was published in the Alaska Sportsman magazine in the February, 1963 issue. It was also reprinted, with permission, in my first book—Trail of the Eagle. An edited version of Harley's story follows:

"We ate lunch and I got my warmest clothes on. We walked down to the airplane and tried out Mr. Rose's .338 magnum to see if it kicked too much for me. I was glad to find out that it was just right. We took off the motor cover and loaded up. Last of all I was packed in and my seat belt fastened. We took off and flew northeast about 75 miles. We flew along an open lead about 3 miles wide. Along the lead we saw a lot of oogruk seals which the polar bears feed on. They eat other kinds of seals, too, such as the ribbon seal and the hair seal.

"After about one hour of flying we saw where a bear had been waiting at a seal hole. We followed the bear tracks a little way until we got to broken ice. Then we had a real hard time tracking it. We went around in circles, down low, and almost straight up. Finally on a small piece of ice we saw the polar bear running along flapping its hind legs. You could see its heavy fur rippling as it lumbered along. As it crossed a freshly frozen lead, we landed about half a mile on the other side. I couldn't see anything so we walked in the direction we thought the bear should be. We finally saw it, walking broadside to us, so I ran over and climbed up on an ice and snow pile about 10 feet high. Just as I got to the icy top and got the crosshairs of the four-powered scope on the bear's front leg, I slid clear down to the bottom of the ice hummock!

"I kicked my toes into the ice and snow and climbed like that, but by the time I got to the top again, the bear was a good 200 yards away. I was so tense with excitement I didn't know if I could shoot straight or not, but I took quick aim and began firing. One of the shots got the bear in the rear end, then I had to stop because the gun was empty. After we reloaded, I ran as fast as my legs would carry me after the bear but I soon got tired and had to slow down. We caught up with it after walking about half a mile. It was floundering on the snow but managed to get up and start walking away. We didn't need to worry now, though, because the bear couldn't go far. Just the same I was in a hurry and I wanted to put him out of his misery. I ran about 25 more yards and started shooting and hit him three times, twice in the neck. That finally did it.

"We took movies and tried to take slides but the camera froze up. It was about -20°. We quit taking pictures and skinned the bear and dragged the skin and meat back to the airplanes. I really wanted that skin and I knew the Eskimo would like the meat. We had a pretty hard time loading it, too, as it was a 9—foot bear.

"We got back to the hotel that night at 8:30. After we got back from eating, there were two Eskimo boys waiting for me. We talked and they taught me some Eskimo words: two I remember were 'nookut-pak'—young boy, and 'nanook-puk'—big polar bear. I guess that makes me a 'nookut-pak'—and my bear was sure enough a real 'nanook-puk!'"

Harley's was the last hunt for that year, and it was time to package all the gear that wouldn't fit into the planes and mail it home. Cleo was obliged to mail most of his gear to/and from Barrow, since his son was taking up the space in the tandem seat.

Cleo had his polar bear made into a full standing-mount. It is an impressive sight in his Meiers Lake trophy room. Harley's bear was made into a beautiful rug-mount that graces a wall of his lovely log home in Gakona.

Colin, our son, never did get to go polar bear hunting with Bud. The following years were either fully booked or Colin was unable to go. Of course, he heard his father and Cleo tell their stories many, many times and he says, "Maybe the stories, told in warm comfortable environments, are better than actually being there!"

One of our Native guides was held overnight on a mountain, by a snowstorm, during a sheep hunt. "White men pay for dangers and discomforts that us poor Indians can't afford." Jake said. "White man build big fire and stay warm getting wood. Indian build small fire and stay warm sitting close." He sat by the fire and watched a client bring in enough wood to supply a huge fire.

Bud had a polar bear hunter out on the ice one year, who was so fascinated with seeing polar bears in the wild that it was the fifth day of his hunt before he could talk himself into shooting a bear. He told Bud and his partner not to worry if he went home without a bear, as he had been on many hunts and left without a trophy. He was what all big game guides and outfitters call a true sportsman.

"Whether I take the bear or not, the sight of a big, white polar bear alone on this vast expanse of white wilderness where it's at home, is an unforgettable experience." It had to be a trophy that would have a special meaning to him, or he wouldn't take it. Where he shot it, what it was doing at the time, how it was hunted, and who he was with were his main criteria for taking an animal.

Arctic Wolf and Other Exciting Hunts

Inn March of 1964, Bud and Cleo loaded their Super Cubs to the limit with emergency and arctic gear, and left from the Gakona airfield.

The Gakona airfield, from which Bud and Cleo had many hours flying time, was a gravel strip 900 feet long. It had barely enough clearance between the tree—lined sides for the lengthy wingspan of the Cubs. There was ample length for take off the average loaded Super Cub, but a pilot better not misjudge his aircraft's ability to clear the trees at the northeast end.

Colin, now 11 years old, and Cleo's sons, 11 year—old Harley, and Chuck, age 9, were excused from their morning classes at the Gakona School, situated near the airfield, so they could watch their fathers leave for the two months away from home. The three boys stood on the edge of the airfield as the men did their last minute preflight checks. I remember thinking, "The boys look like statues, standing motionless, side by side, each lost in his own thoughts."

Cleo's Cub engine revved up, and showered the boys with snow. The plane gained speed and left the ground, clearing the trees by a generous margin. Through all the boys didn't move, but raised their heads a bit to follow the plane's course, as it disappeared into the distance.

Bud started his own take off run as his partner's plane disappeared. Right at lift off, a cow moose ran out from the trees on his right. Running all out, her ears laid back, she crossed to the opposite side in front of his aircraft just as it left the ground. Too late for Bud to abort he pulled back on the stick, throttling that last fraction, the Cub responded, lifting off the ground nearly shaving the hair from the moose. All of us took a deep breath after the plane cleared the moose's back with just inches to spare!

"Whew, I could just see our good old Super Cub hitting that moose and landing on its back and in a heap." Colin commented when he'd caught his breath.

"Keep your eyes on the lookout for a cow moose with ski tracks across her back, near the Gakona airfield," Harley told the class when he returned to school.

"All I could think about was 'I sure do hope we can get my dad out of the wreckage and to the hospital quick enough,' added Colin."

A couple of months later, when Bud was home again and the take off was mentioned, he said. "I didn't have those thoughts until after I was fully airborne. Right at the time I was saying, 'Lift, lift, lift! Come on, you can do it'. . ."

Good flying weather allowed the two pilots to fly to Fairbanks, where they landed only long enough to fuel the planes and eat lunch. In the air again, they winged their way north to Bettles to spend the night.

Flying weather held and they were out at 6:30 AM, preparing the airplanes. They followed the Johns River, through Anaktuvuk Pass to the treeless tundra of the North Slope. They saw small, scattered herds of Barren ground caribou, laying sunning themselves or leisurely pawing the snow for the grass and lichens underneath. Where there are caribou, it's likely you'll find wolves. They thrive on caribou.

While on a heading for Umiat, Cleo called on his radio.

"64 Delta. Wolves ahead and to my right."

Bud's plane was far to the left of Cleo's as he scouted the tundra in that direction. The planes landed at the base of the rolling hills of Outpost Mountain, within sight of the meandering, willow-lined Chandler River. Both pilots tried to feather their Cubs onto the crusted, wind-driven snow as quietly as is possible, and at a distance from the wolves, which were trotting away from them. Planes with metal skis make too loud a noise on crisp snow.

It was a quiet, windless day, and not too cold. When the rattling, scrunching noises, of the planes stopped, they exited the cockpits and donned snowshoes. All they got from the mile-long snowshoe hike over brushed hills was lots of exercise. The area where Cleo first sighted the wolves was vacant and only the tracks of seven running wolves

44

were proof of their existence. Apparently, those wary wolves had completely disappeared on hearing the noisy landing. They couldn't be flushed from the low bushes or willows where they took refuge.

After landing and refueling at Umiat—the one and only time they were there when it wasn't -20°, or colder—they ate a cold lunch and took off for Barrow.

While flying over the seemingly endless expanse of snow-covered pothole lakes, both pilots spotted, far in the distance, a big gray wolf leisurely trotting along. There was no caribou in sight and there was no way of knowing his plans, but his plans certainly didn't include being on the open tundra with no place to hide.

Bill Etchells' and Bud's Super Cubs on Cobb Lake on their return from Barrow with wolves collected on their way. Bud loved to guide polar bear hunters, but he lived to hunt wolves. He took wolves on nearly every trip to and from Barrow.

They landed and set out most of the gear from the passenger seat of Cleo's plane, then Bud climbed in with his 12-gauge Model 97 Winchester loaded with #4 buckshot. Cleo flew behind and a few feet above the panicked, fleeing wolf. Bud tumbled the big dog wolf on the first pass. It didn't take either of them long to skin the wolf, and, were soon back to the other Cub, with the green hide. They reloaded the gear left sitting on the snow and were airborne again.

The Alaska grey wolf averages 100 pounds, with big males ranging upwards to 135 pounds, and some in the arctic region are known to reach 175 pounds. They figured this one weighed at least 150 pounds. Most wolf hides stink. Bud shot this one, so he was obliged to put the prime pelt into his airplane, along with the accompanying aroma.

Eskimo always wanted good wolf hides and paid a good price for them. Guides roughly skinned the hides at the time they shot them, then Natives finished the cleaning job. They tanned the hides themselves or sent them to be tanned professionally. Wolf hide was used for parka ruffs, trim for mukluks and mittens, and crafts sold in the Native craft store to summer tourists. The hides were also sold to pilot/guides and their hunters.

Eager Eskimos waited near the lagoon when planes arrived, knowing pilots may have wolf pelts to sell. Pilots, who had been in Barrow awhile, with no hunters to take out, were asked by the Eskimo, "When you going wolf hunting?"

Bud made a trade with an elderly Eskimo lady. He gave her a wolf hide and she made him a wolf hide parka with a beaver fur lined hood. She also made him a white canvas covering he could wear inside or outside. The white cover was usually worn outside the parka during polar bear hunting. It was warm clothing to wear while on the pack ice, especially if a wind was blowing. She also made him mukluks. Bud wore them during those years in the arctic and for many years afterwards. They surely beat the army surplus down parka and foot gear he wore the first 2 years while he was getting started.

Elson Lagoon had plenty of room for their aircraft when they arrived in Barrow. They busied themselves preparing tie downs by getting the catalytic heaters filled and placed under the engine cowlings, putting wing covers on, and fueling both wing tanks, and doing other important chores before leaving the planes overnight. Natives helped carry their sleeping bags and personal gear to the hotel.

Cleo and Bud always looked forward to arriving at the hotel, and learning who was there ahead of them, how the hunts were going, whose hunters had scored and what size bear they found.

Bill Ellis and Ralph Marshall, wing mates, were still out for the day. Bob Cooper and his wing mate landed while Bud and Cleo were still working at their planes. Cooper's hunter didn't get a bear, but they had seen two good keepers and had to let them go because there was no place to land. Chuck Gray and LeRoy Schebal's hunter had scored. He had an 8-foot 1/2-inch bear. They had been in from the ice long enough to eat and relax in the lobby.

The next 2 days of bad weather kept all of the planes grounded. Impatience to get flying is an enemy. But none of the pilot/guides there were tempted to challenge terrible weather. Pilots each have memories of times they crowded the weather, which favors none. Clients who say things like, "Oh, this won't last much longer and just think how much bigger that bear is getting each day out there in this storm. A bear is comfortable in a storm, but it surely isn't good for flying machines," are very much appreciated.

Spots on playing cards wore thin. The theater filled every night, regardless of how ancient the movie. Stories eventually lost momentum and drinking and parties in the hotel increased. Rational, excited, activity filled a morning when the wind abated, the sun shone, and the lagoon was soon bare of airplanes. Airplanes, carrying excited hunters, winged their way far out over the frozen sea in all directions.

Cleo's two clients were not due for a couple days, so he and Bud took two resident hunters booked by another guide. They had no problem in locating bear, and they didn't have to fly as far as they usually did. Bear were all out on a hunting foray after the storm. They flew one full day for the first man's bear. The second man had his bear just one hour after they left Barrow.

Hunting wolves with the J-3 Piper Cub. The J-3 didn't have the power of a Super Cub, but the side windows opened to allow the hunter to shoot, the plane could fly slow, and it was light for landing in deep snow.

With a long afternoon to fill, Bud and Cleo flew both planes to Liberator Lake, near the headwaters of the Colville River. They looked for gas caches but hoped to fill wolf permits as well. Rumors were plentiful about wolf packs in that area. Various pilots reported seeing scattered bands of caribou but they had no luck in either finding wolves or gas caches. The whole trip, though fruitless was far more interesting than killing time in Barrow.

Pilot/guides didn't commit to taking a client on an aerial wolf hunt until they were sure of his attitudes and abilities. They judged by the way he shot his bear, how he handled his gun, if he were the excitable type, or inclined to get airsick. If the pilot/guide had no confidence in the hunter, he was a master of excuses about not being able to fly or locate wolves to shoot. Airplane repairs cost a lot more money than what could be earned on a wolf hunt!

The pilot had to have full confidence in the gunner sitting behind him. The pilot's skill in handling the plane during low level flight over scattering wolves was of primary concern and he couldn't be fumbling with an inept client.

Flying demands priority and full concentration. Even experienced pilots had some close calls in the heat of an exciting chase. They were caught up, too, in watching the wolf and worrying about the gunner, instead of paying full attention to flying.

The gunner, also, had to have full confidence in the pilot's ability to put him in position to shoot. Ignoring the pilot's twisting maneuvers, to put him in a position to shoot, he had to keep his eye on the wolf or he'd not make a kill.

Prior to a wolf hunt, the inexperienced gunner was briefed to be ready when the pilot opened the door. "Keep your seat belt fastened because I'll tip the plane to give you a good angle. Be ready, but don't shoot if the prop or a lift strut is in the direction you're aiming!"

Or he told him, "Please don't shoot the prop or a lift strut because it doesn't help the airplane one bit. Remember, too, aiming requires a negative lead because the plane is flying faster than the wolf is running. Wolves and coyotes are tricky critters and seldom run in a straight line. They can be difficult targets for the approaching aircraft's gunner. If several wolves are running in a straight line, shoot the lead wolf first."

I think most pilots have had more than one flight when the gunner couldn't hit a wolf, no matter how many passes the pilot made. Many gallons of fuel were burned and many shells expended with no wolves shot. It just scared the hell out of the wolves and made them wiser. It scared the hell out of the pilot, too!

Always, when a bunch of pilots were together and remembering times of close calls, one told of a gunner in his plane shooting at the wrong target or letting the gun go off at the wrong angle, giving both of them a lot of extra, unappreciated excitement. One joker had all of the stories topped when he told about his wife. She talked him into letting her fly with him as his gunner. He agreed against his better judgment. He very carefully went through the entire procedure with her before they left the ground. He figured he must have just forgotten to tell her to never put a round into the chamber of the shotgun until she pointed it out the door. The wife was just as shook up as he was, but they landed without incident. He didn't have to have any buckshot removed from the back of his head, but the Plexiglas covers on top of the airplane needed to be replaced! She didn't ask to go wolf hunting with him ever again.

Bud had a variety of gunners during the years he hunted wolves, but he never had one shoot him down. He did that to himself! It was the 1950s and the second year we had the J-3 Cub. He was wolf-hunting without much experience and without a gunner.

"Believe me, once you've been shot down, or walked away from an emergency landing with undamaged self and plane, it brings out the caution in you," he commented about the incident. "I was alone, cruising around on a sunny day in late March, flying near the headwaters of the Copper River." I spotted two big, gray wolves traveling together. I circled some distance from them, hoping they would work their way into open country, away from the try, away from the sparsely scattered stunted spruce. But they had their mind set to travel in a different direction. I watched them disappear into thick timber.

Hunter with a wolf collected on the slopes of the Brooks Range. Bud would only take his clients wolf hunting who had proven themselves while on a polar bear hunt.

"I then made a direct heading for Copper Lake, but was delayed while circling and watching a wolverine trying to catch a caribou in deep snow. I never fail to feel a special privilege in observing, without disturbing, the participants in such natural dramas. Several caribou in a herd of 10 weren't taking the determined wolverine very seriously. The wolverine scattered snow 3 feet in the air as it bounded through deep snow. After a few minutes, it realized it had no chance for a meal from the one he was chasing. The wolverine retraced its trail and started after another caribou, standing, seemingly enjoying the game. A third caribou took off from the herd, in a different direction and the wolverine began chasing it. The first one returned to stand with the others and watch. After the third caribou outdistanced the short-legged wolverine, he gave up on getting a meal from that alert group. I sure had to give him credit for trying.

"As I neared the western end of 6-mile-long Copper Lake, I spotted a lone black wolf as he trotted from the shore out toward the middle of the lake. This unlucky wolf was a goner. I figured I had the $50 bounty already spent as I swung around in a wide turn, throttling back almost to a stall. I leveled out at 30 feet above the ice and lined up with the unsuspecting, trotting, wolf. But, instead of shooting the wolf, I shot myself down.

"The J-3 has a stick instead of a wheel, and I was wearing a pair of heavy flight pants made of a slick nylon material. When shooting from the plane, alone, I held the stick between my knees. Opening the right-hand door, I latched the top half up and dropped the lower half open. Then, with both hands, I held the shotgun, a Model 97 Winchester, out the side, pointed in the direction of the wolf. I waited to get a bit closer. The loaded shotgun was cocked. Apparently this wolf hadn't been shot at from an airplane before, or perhaps the wind drowned out the sound of my approaching plane, because it didn't swerve.

"'It's the end of the trail for you, old fellow'" I said. A strong wind gust jolted the plane sideways, slam-banging the gun barrel against the fuselage. With my finger still on the trigger, the gun went off with a spine-chilling Kaboom. Just then, the stick slipped from between my knees and the right wing dropped. I immediately forgot the wolf, and with my left hand, worked to recover the angle of the plane. That loud bang, immediately followed by vibrations from the engine, alerted me to what every pilot hopes will never happen.

"'Oh, oh, I got the prop!' I yelled. "I initially gave it more throttle to level out and to head, hopefully, for a smooth surface farther ahead. I was afraid the engine would pull off the mounts because of the severely vibrating propeller. I had no choice other than cut the power, pull back on the stick to keep the nose up. As I did so, the skis hit a hard snow hump. I'm sure the plane bounced 10 feet, then connected hard again with the uneven, crusted snow. After the third bounce, the plane came to a halt without further aerobatics.

"I jumped out, shotgun in hand, ejected the spent shell and popped another #4 in the chamber. Dropping to one knee, I took a parting shot at the wolf as it busily put distance between it and my roaring monster. The wolf put too much distance between us for the buckshot to be effective, but I thought I saw it hump and move faster.

"The last glimpse I had of the fleeing dark figure, as it disappeared into the timber, was a backward glance over its shoulder; and I just imagined hearing a 'raspberry' sound. He wasn't such an unlucky wolf after all. I was the unlucky one. A new metal propeller was gonna cost much more than what the bounty and sale of his prime wolf hide.

Three inches of the tip of Bud's prop was shot off when he was aerial wolf hunting without a gunner. Bud got excited and shot himself down.

"The ragged tip of the metal prop was missing by 3 inches and was the cause of my unplanned descent into 2-feet high, crusted snow drifts. It was definitely not a place I wanted to land. I considered myself lucky I hadn't ended up with the plane on its back and that I still had several miles of lake ahead of me. The landing gear was weakened and the spread between skis was a bit wider than normal, but not as bad as it could have been.

"I figured there was a reasonable chance, which I was willing to take, that I could make one more landing, if I landed on a smooth surface with no unnecessary weight in the plane. The thermometer read -20° and I wasn't exactly excited about camping there overnight. "Well, it was too cold and windy to stand around fuming at my misfortune. I unlaced the snowshoes from the lift strut, dug the hatchet out from under the gear, hiked over to the closest timber along the shore and dragged two heavy, downed trees back and tied down the plane. I snowshoed the 5 miles of unbroken trail to our cabins at Tanada Lake, brewed myself a quick cup of tea on the Coleman stove, and ate some crackers. I took an old wooden souvenir propeller off the trophy room wall where it had hung for the past 2 years, and snowshoed back to the Cub. I removed the damaged prop, fit the wooden prop on the extended bolts, and to my dismay, the holes lined up okay, but weren't counter sunk enough for the nuts to fasten on the bolts.

"Now why didn't I think of that while I was at the cabin where the tools are?" I asked myself and shook my head at being so dense. "Tired, exasperated, and in the dark now, I retraced my five-mile trail back to the cabin. The days were still short in March and I was out in the dark, scrounging enough wood to get the kitchen range going to warm up the cold room for a few warm hours of sleep.

"I now had another exasperating situation to fume about. There was no wood or kindling. The three young men I had let stay for 6 weeks during November and December, while running a trap line, left no wood for the next person. I hadn't had occasion to check it after they'd left.

"Leaving a wilderness cabin without replacing the supply of firewood and kindling was serious business and does not make the culprits very popular. It's an old, established courtesy, as well as a survival necessity, to freely use a wilderness cabin, but to replace the wood supply, and, if possible, the used groceries.

"I finally went to sleep, thankful those young men were far out of my reach, because I felt I could whip all three right then. I slept until daylight, about 9 o'clock, gathered just enough wood to leave for another emergency fire, carried the brace and bit with me, and then, without breakfast, followed the trail back to the Cub. The trail was frozen, so I didn't need the snowshoes and I felt pretty tough trotting right along.

"After setting the fire pot to start warming the Cub engine, I undertook the cold, finger-freezing-job of counter sinking the holes on that wooden prop. I wanted no play in the substitute prop, but I didn't have the tools to get an accurate measurement. I used my store of bailing wire on the landing gear for added strength, then started the engine. The prop didn't fly off, so I figured I could make it home. The morning was well spent and I wanted to get home before somebody notified Cleo I was missing.

"I never liked having to be rescued and told everyone, 'Give me time enough to walk out, if or when I am overdue.' LeNora wasn't worried that I hadn't returned before dark, and hoped I had stayed overnight at Tanada Lake.

"I feathered the plane's prop, as gently as possible, and drifted onto the smooth stretch of the Slana River, near our temporary winter cabin at Mile 68 on the Tok Highway. I held my breath, waiting for the gear to collapse or to hear the sound of the prop splintering as it hit the ice. I cut the power when the danger of nosing over was past.

"I knew the landing gear was spread wider than normal, allowing the longer blades of the substitute prop to spin even closer to the ground. I patted the side of my J-3 Cub and expressed thanks we were both home again—a bit more experienced—even without the prime black wolf hide.

"LeNora stood waiting, while I drained the oil and checked the wider spread of the landing gear, then said, "'I heard you fly straight on in without buzzing the cabin. I can see now why the Cub sounded differently. That prop surely looks strange, but it sounded like it was flying okay, What's the story?'"

A hunter, shooting from a moving airplane subject to wind currents and tight turns, and taking a running wolf, knows the thrill of the hunt that will never again come to Alaska.   US Fish and Wildlife photo

"It's always a worry for wives whose pilot-husbands enjoy aerial wolf hunting. She's home with the kids wondering who's going to win, the pilot and his aircraft, or the wolf. The wiley old wolf has been known to even the score by damaging airplanes or killing pilots. More than once, a pilot and gunner 'bought the farm' while hunting wolves with airplanes.

"While hunting one day in early April, in 1951, on the open rolling hills above Copper Lake, I shot a black wolf. When I was skinning it out, I found two #4 buckshot pellets just under the hide on the rear end. The buckshot had penetrated the hide and a little into the flesh without doing any serious damage and the wounds had fully healed. No doubt in my mind, this was the same wolf I had been after when I shot the tip of my prop. The wolf was an unusually large male with the extra long nose and tail I had noticed when flying above it the first time. It was old and had very badly broken teeth. I hope I did him a favor by ending his struggle for survival with his hunting days nearly over. He was probably a loner that had been rejected by the pack.

"The hide was rug-mounted on the trophy-room wall. It hung alongside the metal prop with the three inch tip missing and the wooden prop. Those two props, hanging side by side, never failed to bring instant notice from pilots who saw them. Most guessed the cause of the metal prop's ragged tip. Those props were real conversation pieces. The pilots who hunted wolves from the air invariably shared their own interesting experiences with degrees of humor and advice. And they invariably suggested the tip of the other blade could be shot off, then filed smooth to fly the plane home. I heard of a couple of pilots who did just that.

"It never ceased to amaze me that many people who were not familiar with wolves would mistake this big wolf hide for a black bear, without remembering that a bear doesn't have a long tail.

"I would like to think this old dog wolf, which, I'm sure, lived a happy life, was as happy displayed in our trophy room being admired by so many people. Better, I think, than disappearing into nothingness."

Bud had two very wealthy clients on a Brown bear hunt, out of Cordova, one year. They sat on a hillside, shivering in a cold, windy rainstorm, and watched Bud start a fire. "I'm paying big money to be this miserable," one guy laughingly remarked. That thought cheered everyone up, including Bud!

Record Flight
to Barrow

There are five separate but interactive weather patterns in Alaska. Weather is always a major factor in flying to and from Barrow, and in hunting the area. Bud and Cleo were grounded for 3 days, on some of their trips to and from Barrow.

In the early 1950s, however, they made an all-time record flight (for them) of 11 hours from the Gakona airfield to Barrow, with fully loaded Super Cubs. Ideal flying weather and strong tail winds blessed them after crossing the Brooks Range. They stopped in Fairbanks, and again at Bettles, to top-off the gas tanks. While they were in the air they washed down homemade sandwiches with lukewarm coffee from their thermos. After leaving Bettles, they climbed to a much higher altitude than usual, about 8,500 feet MSL. At that altitude, in the absence of the usual winds or low clouds, they didn't have to follow the bends of the John River through Anaktuvuk Pass. Their airspeed, helped by a good tail wind, hovered around 110 MPH and their groundspeed was as high as 125 MPH which is fast for a Super Cub.

They left Gakona at 7:30 AM and landed on the Elson Lagoon at Bar-row about 6:45 PM, right on the edge of darkness. Both men were stiff, tired, hungry and thankful they hadn't given in to a tempting wolf hunt. They might have been forced to camp on the snowbound tundra. After their arrival, a snow blizzard with 40 knot winds kept them, and the rest of the pilot/guides and their hunters, grounded for nearly 2 days.

Life is so different for the clients while in the arctic. They generally killed time playing cards or sleeping. If their hangover wasn't too bad from the night before, they toured the tiny village-town of Barrow.

In Barrow there was an Alaska Native Services hospital, a couple of churches, a cafe, bakery, grocery store, and the village store where Native crafts were sold. Most of the hunters liked to spend time browsing for gifts made by the locals. Furs, mukluks, carved ivory, and jewelry were always favorites. There was only one theater—The Polar Bear Theater. Locals and visitors killed time there, no matter how old the movies—mostly cowboy shows. A hero is always a hero.

Round-faced, dark-eyed Eskimo children from the village liked to have their pictures taken. Most hunters took movies or 35 MM slide pictures of kids dressed in colorful clothing of fur parkas, (the fur worn on the inside). Bright, floral cottons covered the parka and generous hood ruffs of wolf or wolverine fur framed their shiny faces.

The pilot/guides and their hunters carried candy in their pockets and were always assured of a good following. Eskimo kids never begged for candy, but like kids everywhere, they seemed to appear out of nowhere when a pilot/guide or hunter showed up.

In one of his letters home, Bud wrote: "The hotel is fairly full. Bob Cooper's two hunters have their bears and will be leaving on the Wein flight today. He has two more hunters arriving on the same flight. Chuck Gray and LeRoy Schebal got a bear for their hunter yesterday and they have two more men waiting to go hunting. Pete Merry and George Theil are here and they have two hunters waiting to go.

"Two men from the Arctic Research Station came to the hotel each evening to join in our conversations. They desperately want to fly out and get a bear. They say they'll be ready to go whenever two of us are available. We gather, from the conversations, the ice is really rough. Everyone is doing a lot of flying and sighting bears, but without places to land, they keep on flying."

Bert Klineburger, a well-known taxidermist from Seattle, Bud Piper, and Ernest Jower arrived while Bud and Cleo were out with a hunter, and they settled in the hotel lobby. They were hunting with Pete Merry and George Theil. Jower, an English hunter from the African Sudan, was a fascinating conversationalist. Endless stories of his African hunts, told in his strong British accent, kept the room full of captivated listeners. He was a right likeable guy with a terrific sense of humor." Whenever these men were in the lobby, it was soon crowded and the stories lasted late into the night. The pilot/guides who flew the next morning were usually the first to reluctantly leave and hit the sack. We always regretted not having a small recorder to document those stories. The stories, and sadly, the men who made them happen, will soon be forgotten. Alaska is swiftly changing, and as its early history dims, the younger generation, our own sons and daughters are making different history.

After hearing the African hunting stories, our client got all primed for an African Safari, and talked about taking Cleo and Bud with him, expenses paid. It was just talk, most likely, considering all of those drinks he downed. He had the money and Bud would have jumped at the chance to go. He always wanted to see that country and its game. He was especially fascinated with the big cats there and dreamed of hunting them.

Part of the guide's training, skills, and duties were to take pictures of the hunt for the hunter. The real work for the guide begins when the kill is made. He must cape out the bear and prepare the hide for the taxidermist. A hunter who has taken a polar bear has been to the end of the world.

Cleo booked a client from Italy, so he was riding in Cleo's plane. The ice was rough below them and Cleo was skimming along with Bud flying below him. He picked up, but soon lost, the tracks of a traveling bear and followed. The hunting party was ready to head back when Cleo picked up another bigger track and circled to get a closer look.

"64 Delta, do you read me?" came in loud and clear on Bud's radio.

"Go ahead, 73 Zulu."

"64 Delta. This Italian yahoo is pukin' all over everything in back and I'm landing as soon as I can find smooth ice. Fly on, to the west a ways, and maybe you'll catch up with that bear. The tracks look fresh. Then call me."

Cleo's plane settled slowly and gently onto the ice while Bud kept vigil above. He found and lost the tracks again. Not wanting to get too far away and out of radio contact, he flew back to circle and wait. Bud detected a high degree of annoyance in Cleo's voice when he called to say they were taking off again. Using snow, Cleo had energetically cleaned the bright orange engine cover previously tucked into the gear.

"This guy's drinks from the night before aren't as welcome today as they were last night at the hotel." Cleo grumbled. Both planes flew back to Barrow early. Flying all of the following day—with an ample supply of sick-sacks and explicit instructions about where they were kept and what to do with them, he collected an 8-foot bear.

Bud said this bear didn't care much for life. He stood his ground about 500 yards beyond the taxiing planes, and accommodated them by being on an extra large, smooth ice floe. He continued to stand in the same open area and watch, with interest, as the two men in their white covering crept within 350 feet of him. He finally got restless and decided they weren't something to eat. He was down and dead before finding out for sure. Bud stayed near the closest plane and got the whole thing on film with the hunter's 16mm movie camera with telephoto lens. He wrote later and said the film showed all of the action of his hunt, and he was delighted.

Bud flew several different hunters who occasionally 'saw their breakfast twice.' He maneuvered a lot, circling and quickly dipping the wings to look on one side or the other and concentrating on handling the plane. He kept within the safety margin above the ice and didn't give a thought to the man in the seat behind him.

He didn't mind it when the guy used the sick-sack, then asked him to open the side window so he could toss it. What scared the hell out of him as a pilot, though, was when a guy unfastened his seat belt, reached up and opened the side window himself, to lean out and let go. I knew of no one who lost a hunter this way, but it could have happened and Bud sure didn't want it to happen to anyone flying in his airplane.

He often opened the side window to let a hunter take pictures, but always warned him to keep his safety belt tightly fastened. Once, he had a tall lanky hunter lean a bit too far out and his expensive mink cap went sailing off into the blue yonder. Another client unfastened his seat belt to lean forward to let Bud know he was feeling sick. He timed it just right and let go down Bud's shoulder, front, and back. Bud's own breakfast almost came up too. They made an immediate landing on rough ice and spent considerable time gathering the scarce snow to clean up as best they could. He never found a way to get the entire smell out of an airplane. This did, however, teach Bud to carry a roll of paper towel in his plane at all times.

It's a good thing the FCC (Federal Communications Commission) wasn't active in Alaska during those years. Some conversations between pilots got a bit carried away. Pilots knew the guy in the back seat couldn't hear what was said because of the engine noise. Quite often, pilots heard conversations between planes that wouldn't bear repeating anywhere. Cleo's name for a hunter who didn't use the sick-sack was milder than Bud's. His was unprintable and would have been worse if he had damaged the landing gear when he made unscheduled landings.

One year, Cleo booked two men from the East. One of them I'll call him Gus, owned a popular restaurant and he told everyone his specialty was spaghetti. His hunting partner said it was a high class restaurant and noted the spaghetti was made from a recipe handed down from an uncle in Italy. Gus brought plenty of his spaghetti and all of the ingredients necessary for making more. He insisted on making it himself in the kitchen at Al's Cafe, and made enough for the pilot/guides and hunters who were eating at the time. Bud wasn't fond of spaghetti any time, and didn't think it was so special, but he ate it to be polite. Gus bought drinks, and drank way too much himself, for whoever spent time listening to great accomplishments in his chosen career, as well his tremendous feats on big game hunts, including those in Africa.

After these two men arrived all of the pilots were grounded for two days, waiting on flying weather. Gus was a short, well-nourished gentleman in his late 40s and liked to tell everyone within hearing distance that his financial status was not to be taken lightly. He had a way of dominating conversations and gave the impression he was used to giving orders and being obeyed. Of course, he wanted a braggin sized bear. Both hunters were becoming noticeably irritated by the living conditions in the hotel and started asking the questions a pilot/guide dreads.

"When are we going hunting? The weather doesn't look too bad to me." Bud could see they were beginning to annoy Cleo. He had booked them though, so he stuck around and explained why they couldn't fly or hunt. Cleo could always find more interesting places to be whenever they showed up.

Few pilot/guides will let their client push them into flying when they know better, but there have been times when an eager pilot will chance the weather, be lucky, and return with a happy client and his trophy. It makes the rest of the pilots, safely sitting it out, look like amateurs. They recognize their clients' questioning looks, but have the satisfaction of knowing first hand, and from past experience, what could happen.

There is also the client who lets his pilot/guide know he appreciates his good judgment. Knowing they are thinking of his welfare, he is perfectly content to wait with the others, sitting around swapping hunting stories or playing cards. Liquor flows freely, the hotel gets lively, and by morning, no one is too eager to be up and about very early.

On a dry, snow-dusted morning lit by a hazy arctic sun, they took Gus out for his bear. It wasn't a good day for tracking, but there was always a chance of locating a moving bear. Cleo and Bud both hoped the first one they saw would be a keeper. They knew he wouldn't be satisfied with less.

They hadn't been in the air long the next day, and Cleo had been doing the usual tilting, circling and banking to pick up tracks. Suddenly, his voice crackled loud and clear in Bud's ear, and he knew Cleo had blown his cool.

"64 Delta. This spaghetti-eatin' son of a bitch is pukin' his specialty all over me and the back seat. I'm landing. I don't give a damn how rough the ice is. I just hope I don't wipe out the gear."

Cleo had a way of handling his airplane that few pilots ever achieved. I've heard it expressed as 'his plane wrapped around him.'

Bud stayed in the air as a close observer and watched Cleo's Super Cub settle lightly across rough ridges and uneven snow. As it slid to a stop, Cleo disembarked in his easy way, checked the landing gear, then gave Bud the signal they had ridden it out okay. He began tossing things out as soon as Gus had clumsily exited. Bud flew around looking for bear while they used loose snow to clean as best they could.

This guy got a 10-foot bear in an easy place on their way back. More deserving hunters than he went home with smaller bears.

Gus' hunting partner, who wasn't one of their favorite hunters either, got his bear 2 days later, after a mile-long hike from where they landed. His bear was 2 inches over the 8-foot size considered a decent trophy for a nonresident.

He was slow and clumsy walking that distance, and dead tired when they returned to the hotel. The hunters were happy to be on the plane heading for home the next day. Bud and Cleo were happy they hadn't made plans to take them on a wolf hunt.

With extra time and ideal tracking conditions, Bud and Cleo took a hunter out for his contracted guide. He was flown out just 60 miles and had his 8-foot 1-inch bear by 4 PM. They were all at the cafe by 6 PM and digging into good, newly arrived, beef steaks.

Many polar bears, having no natural enemies, showed little fear of hunters or their flying machines. They'd just give them the eye and saunter off behind an ice ridge or swim the nearest open lead. US Fish and Wildlife photo

Also this year, Fred and Ralph Space—father and son mink ranchers from New Jersey went hunting with Bud and Cleo. They had hunted on a fall hunt, earlier, with the McMahans at Meiers Lake. Both men were real sportsmen and it was a pleasure to hunt with them. It was left up to clients, who came together on booked trips, to decide who flew in the lead plane. Since Cleo booked these two, they chose to ride in his plane and Bud flew as cover pilot.

Cleo revved the engines as Ralph settled into Cleo's passenger seat. Both planes were headed out for the day's hunt by the time northern sun was lighting the day. It turned out to be a very exhausting day. The temperature was only -10°, but hazy conditions made it difficult to judge landing sites. They passed on a bear that looked like a keeper and headed back to Barrow to refuel and eat lunch, hoping the weather condition would clear later in the afternoon.

Later that afternoon, perhaps 80 miles out, Cleo spotted a bear ambling aimlessly on a large ice floe and signaled Bud that he was landing. The ice floe was long enough for both planes and looked smooth enough from the air, but it was rougher than they had judged in the hazy conditions. The planes rattled and bounced to a stop. The bear heard them landing and was soon loping away into the mist. They never knew if he was trophy size. They felt lucky the landing gear on both planes were still intact after such a harsh landing. They faced getting off the rough ice without damaging the landing gears. Ordinarily, Bud stayed in the air until Cleo's plane landed. This hunt looked like a cinch and he was supposed to take movies for the hunter—if and when he shot a bear. All of them worked at knocking off the sharp ridges of ice and make a counterfeit runway long enough to get into the air again. A ridge with a hard, frozen top can catch the front of a ski and flip a plane on its back really easy. Cleo experienced just that thing when flying the mail to an isolated lake village. They were the last planes into Barrow that day, but shortly behind those ahead of them. No worry.

Ralph got a bear, but Fred didn't. He made plans to come back the next year to try again. Weather held them down a day in Barrow, then they went on a wolf hunt in the low hills between the Anaktuvuk and Nanushuk Rivers. They collected four big grays. The hunters flew from Barrow to Fairbanks. Bud and Cleo equipped their planes with tundra tires and met them a few days later in King Salmon on the Alaska Peninsula and went spring brown bear hunting.

It was one of those cold, windy days common to the arctic slope. They had flown over the pack ice all day and hiked quite a distance to take movies of polar bear cubs playing next to their mother as she snoozed.

The millionaire hunter had gotten chilled, then became even colder while flying back in the Cub with its limited heat supply. The dormitory rooms, upstairs in the 'Barrow Hilton,' were always chilly compared to lower floors, and were unusually cold this night. The hunter thought he would acquire a warmer room on the second floor the following night, after the two guys who currently had the room were gone. But they had decided to stay over another day and wouldn't budge from the room they had—Bud's client just had to survive the cold night where he was.

"The essence of big game hunting is discomfort in such lavish proportions that only the wealthy can afford it," Bud's client observed, as he huddled further into his down parka, dry wool socks on his feet and blankets wrapped around his shoulders, he sat shivering on his cot in the cold hotel dormitory. "Here I am, a wealthy man, and I can't buy us a warm room or bribe anyone to give up their room downstairs."

Accidents Are Bound to Happen

Arctic polar bear hunts had an element of danger; there was no doubt about it. Surprisingly, there were only a few tragedies during the years Bud and Cleo hunted out of Barrow.

The knowledge of dangers, preparations for the hunt, experience in winter flying, the care of the aircraft were significant reasons for so few accidents. Still, thinking back about the years we hunted Alaska's big bears, there were dangerous circumstances.

Ward Carroll, a well-known pilot/guide from Anchorage, and the hunter with him, were the only fatalities while polar bear hunting during the years that Bud hunted. However, all of the pilots had close calls. Some pilots with engine trouble, or gear problems on the ice, were lucky to find their planes again after they had left them and had flown back in with a wing mate.

Bill Ellis' and Ralph Marshall's Maule (an expensive aircraft for that day and time) developed engine trouble and was left many miles out on the ice. They, along with all of the local pilots, found the plane after five days of searching. It had drifted many miles. It was only by sheer chance that it was found. It was patched up and flown back to land for extensive repairs.

Wally Rochester had to leave his Super Cub on the ice not far from Barrow but dangerously close to an open lead. Bill Ellis, noted for his ability to do all types of repairs, took the necessary parts out and repaired it. The ice pan hadn't moved far and the plane was still the same distance from the open lead.

Ward Carroll and the hunter with him, died when Carroll's Super Cub didn't clear a pressure ridge on takeoff. They accumulated too much weight when they put a freshly skinned, green hide aboard. Both men died on impact. Carroll's wing mate, pilot/guide, Pete Merry had a passenger in his plane and couldn't bring the bodies home. He zipped the bodies into their sleeping bags and put them back inside the wrecked Cub, hoping the polar bears and foxes wouldn't disturb them. He flew back to Kotzebue to get help. Every pilot available flew for days, searching the pack ice in all directions and many miles from land, but neither the plane nor the bodies were ever found.

The Russian government protested frequently when polar bear hunting pilots flew closer than was strictly legal. Many stories circulated that the ice floe, where Carroll and his hunter went down, drifted over near Russia. It's unlikely we will ever know what really happened to Ward Carroll and his client. His plane, with the two bodies, is probably at the bottom of the Chukchi Sea or the Arctic Ocean.

Ward Carroll flew in Alaska for many years and had a reputation as an excellent pilot. Did he misjudge the height of the pressure ridge? Or did his aircraft fail to perform? A hunter who had flown with Carroll often in previous years wrote the following tribute to Carroll. It was published in Alaska Sportsman magazine.

A Tribute to Ward Carroll
by George X. Sand
Farewell

"I hesitated when the mailman handed me the red-blue bordered airmail envelope postmarked Anchorage. Too many such envelopes have arrived lately in the names of old friends—but written in their wife's handwriting. I opened it there by the mailbox and suddenly the Florida sun was no longer warm and cheerful against my hands and neck. Not Ward Carroll! No . . . if there was one bush pilot in all Alaska I'd least expect to crash . . . I'd watched him fly his little yellow plane across the tawny skies with all the majestic grace and sureness the Creator normally reserves for eagles with feathers . . .

I recalled the happy hours we'd spent in that plane, flying throughout the silent Alaska Range he loved. Moose standing like lazy dark brown cattle among the fir trees below . . . the morning we'd awakened in camp at Lake Chelatna to discover sometime during the night God had whitened everything with the approaching winter's first snow.

He'd chuckled when he caught me trying to cast for trout, not realizing in cheechako fashion that the temperature had dropped so low that the line was frozen fast inside the rod guides. He loved to chuckle, this tireless, soft spoken outdoorsman whose name I'd heard spoken respectfully from Juneau to Barrow.

Ward. Quiet. Competent. Courteous always. A man born to the woods and waters and sky. When you looked into his weather browned, friendly face you sensed the whole vast expanse of this Great Land he was so much a part of, grim grandeur and human compassion, roaring fireplaces and bleak, frozen reaches of moonlit silence. The fierce wild freshness of bursting spring and the listless dead heat of breathless summer. Those eyes had often watched the flashing, leaping approach of a thousand silver salmon. The ears had listened proudly to the majestic crescendo of Alaska's song. The heart had beaten in quick, strong acceptance of the challenging tempo set by those who'd gone on ahead over these Far Northern trails.

Here was a man. Here was an Alaskan.

He'd invited me to return this last spring as his guest, this dear friend, to hunt together the great white bear on the Arctic ice. How I would have loved to accept, had time allowed. And now the belated word, coming 4,000 miles on its tireless wings of sadness. February 19th, near Kotzebue . . . while flying cover for a second plane in the usual manner . . . Ward and his hunter apparently struck a pressure ridge while attempting a landing. No one actually saw what happened . . . Good-by, Ward Carroll. I have been enriched by our brief friendship. We break camp now, but I look forward to meeting you again later—a bit farther along the trail."

Lee Holen, a well known and capable pilot with years of flying experience, ran out of gas and set his Piper PA-18 down on an ice floe of the frozen Chukchi Sea, while hunting 100 miles northwest of Point Hope. He figured he was lucky to have a favorable looking ice floe within range of his remaining fuel supply. But while landing, there was a sickening crash, as the new ice, hidden under a light covering of snow, gave way and the plane sank to the wings. Lee and his hunter, 58-year-old George Baumann, barely had time to exit, as the 28° sea water rapidly filled the interior. Then they were alone on the vast expanse of Arctic ice.

Holen's wing-mate, Warren Johnston, and Gordon Eastman, the famous photographer, was low on fuel, too, and had already turned back, thinking they were following Lee. Too far apart for radio contact, they didn't know the other plane was down. They didn't make it back to land, either and made an emergency landing on the ice. Kotzebue received their radio message, with position and needed fuel. They were easily rescued, and by dark reported their other plane as overdue.

Lee Holen was a 43 year old, tall, attractive man, an interesting conversationalist, with a tanned, outdoors look. He was known for his flying skills. His ability to walk away from unplanned landings in difficult places, usually with minimal damage was well known. He could repair a plane and fly out of a place that looked quite impossible. His motto should have been, "If it looks impossible, do it anyhow." This time down on the ice was a classic example of his ability to survive with skill and ingenuity.

The pilot/guides hunting out of Point Hope, Kotzebue, and Barrow, searched for the missing men and their airplane. The constantly moving ice floes, and changing weather, hampered the search and no one could find them. After five days of dedicated flying, they were given up for dead. Was it possible they could survive this long in the intense arctic cold without shelter? Did a polar bear wound or kill them? Did they drown? Why couldn't any of the searching planes pick up a radio signal from their plane's ELT?

Six days after their plane went down, Lee and George, a general contractor from Missouri, were found walking on the beach by a group of Natives hunting caribou with dog teams. They camped that night by their first campfire. The following morning, they arrived in Kivalina, and this was the first news of their survival. Bob Baker, an Alaska Airlines bush pilot, stopped at Kivalina on his mail run, and flew the two men to Kotzebue. They were in good condition and needed no hospitalization.

"Heavy winds blew us off course" explained Lee. "I was too low on gas to attempt facing a headwind, so I found the best place I could and landed. The plane sank immediately, barely giving us time to cut the fuel tanks out of the wings with our pocket knives. All of the tools and our emergency gear went down with the plane. With the fuel tanks to buoy us, we floated across an open lead, about a mile wide, from thin ice to solid ice. We stayed in that area for three days, waiting to be rescued. Then we started walking."

They lost all of their clothing except what they were wearing. They had no gloves. Their canvas mukluks kept their feet fairly dry. One of them had managed to grab the two sleeping bags loaded near the top of the gear in back. The only food they had was Pilot Bread (hard, flat biscuits) and moose sausage. Their water was snow melted in their mouths.

"I'll bet I ate 1500 snowballs," Lee told a reporter. "For three days, all we did was walk. If we slept at all, it was in wet sleeping bags. We were wet all night and sorta dried off during the day while we walked. We started with coughs and runny noses, but soon got over them."

"We both have a few blisters on our feet after all that walking," When he was told temperatures had ranged from 0° to -20° the past six days, Holen laughed and said "Piece of cake."

Lee Holen died of a stroke in Tucson, Arizona in April 1993.

Colin was the assistant guide for Orville Kuester from Montana. The two men camped for two days by a small, high mountain, lake in caribou country. Orville had already collected a Dall ram and a bull moose in different camps and Bud had set them out on this lake to fill his caribou tag. He flew over them a day later. They had just taken a caribou about three miles from their camp. Colin had the cape removed from the animal and was starting to separate the meat into quarters for backpacking. Bud was through flying that day, so he landed his float plane, tied it to the shore, then hiked over to help pack meat and antlers back to the plane.

Weather was deteriorating. He knew it could keep a plane on the ground much longer than planned and decided it would be wise to get the meat and the three of them back to the base camp on Wolf Lake quickly. It was only a half-hour flight.

In the last mile, to the tethered Super Cub, they followed a rough game trail along a steep hillside. Colin was in the lead carrying the front quarters, neck and smaller pieces. Orville had the cape and antlers of the big bull. Both carried rifles. Bud had both hindquarters with the backstrap still attached. They weighed much more than he generally carried, and he could backpack more than the average man.

"I never weigh a loaded pack." Bud said. "If I knew what it really weighed, I wouldn't pack it."

The weather was pushing him. He was in a hurry. It was starting to snow. He thought they could get it all back to the plane in one trip, then make two flights to Wolf Lake before dark. Bud told Colin to go on ahead and not to wait for him.

"Fly Orville and the meat you have, to Wolf Lake." He said. "If the weather gets worse. I'll camp here overnight and wait until you can come back for me."

Orville and Colin were quite a distance ahead of Bud as they struggled on the roughest part of the trail. Colin stopped and looked back to see if Bud was close enough to ask a question. He turned just in time to see Bud, and his loaded pack, tumble head over heels. Then he disappeared.

Bud carried many a pack board loaded with game meat off mountains in steep, dangerous places and across loose shale slides. Had he slipped, he would have rolled or fallen hundreds of feet.

When he slipped this time, it was a real surprise to him.

Colin expected to find his father, then 66 years old, in a mangled heap at the bottom of the steep, rocky, hillside. Bud had rolled nearly 200 yards before a rock outcropping snagged him. He couldn't remove himself from the pack board. He was pinned, face down, and suspected his left arm was broken. It didn't hurt much, but the angle of his arm under the pack frame was suspicious.

Colin and Orville shucked their own packs and scrambled down to him. Colin said he knew his dad was alive when he could hear language worthy of an old ex-Marine sergeant. Blood was running down his father's face when Colin worked the pack off his back and helped him turn over. The cuts and bruises were the least of the worries. In sheep and goat country, he was as surefooted as the animals he hunted, but this day he had stepped on deceptive shale.

Once Bud was free of his pack, he made it back up to the trail under his own power. He carefully held his injured left arm, and muttered all the way. Colin made two trips getting the hindquarters back up the hill. They stashed them under a pile of brush and heaped rocks on top to keep it safe from bears.

Orville was the youngest of the big game hunters we catered to, and I doubt if he weighed even 150 pounds, so he crawled into the baggage space behind the passenger seat. Colin helped his father into the back seat, then climbed in and flew the short hop to the main camp at Wolf Lake.

Colin immediately flew to Grace Lake near the Alaska/Canada border along the Alcan Highway. He called me from a public telephone at the U.S. Customs Station and told me to come and get Bud. We kept a small travel trailer parked at Scotty Creek, so Colin ate a dinner from the supplies left there, then bedded down for the night. It was too dark to fly back to Wolf Lake.

The camps cook at Wolf Lake, looked at Bud's arm and found it sore to the touch, but not visibly bruised. She wanted him to wear a sling but he refused. He did the best he could to avoid using his arm, and tried not to let anyone catch him grimacing when he bumped it.

The camp bedded down for the night, but his arm throbbed when he lay down, so he sat at the kitchen table most of the night.

"How could I be so clumsy?" He grumbled repeatedly. "And just how am I going to manage flying and guiding for the rest of the hunting season?"

The next morning, Colin flew to pick up the meat they had stashed, then back to Wolf Lake. The meat was lifted into the high cache and Bud was loaded into the Cub. He had argued against leaving camp at all, the day before, but after suffering the pain all night, he was willing to concede that his arm might be broken. They flew back to the highway, with Bud yelling 'just in case' instructions into Colin's ear for the entire 30 minute flight.

Bud backpacking a trophy moose rack across rough tundra.

When I arrived at the trailer, Colin, in his usual droll way, said, after telling about the fall, "It really didn't do much improve Dad's temper, his language, or his face."

Bud's arm was ex-rayed at the small hospital in Glennallen, 275 miles away. It doesn't appear broken." The doctor said. "Unless it's a hairline fracture already hidden by the bruises and damaged muscles. I'll give you some pain medicine to take while it's healing."

As a guide, Bud was required to be physically in camp at all time, so he drove back the following day and Colin flew him in to Wolf Lake. Bud felt quite good by the time he got back. He got out of backpacking jobs for the rest of the season.

We were fortunate to have good, capable, guides and horse wranglers, and our pilot son to fill the gaps. Colin was as capable a pilot as his dad, likely better. At least he thought so!

We were fortunate and never had a hunter get seriously hurt in our camps. Bud was constantly instructing, almost to badgering, his guides and horse wranglers in safety practices. One common instruction was to not follow too closely behind each other when climbing where rocks could fall on the guy below. A client Bud was guiding on a sheep hunt didn't take his advice, however.

Dr. Modisett, from Madison, Indiana, was climbing right behind Bud up a steep, rocky cliff high in the sheep hills. They were after a ram they had been glassing and were determined to collect. They needed to get above it, though, and this was the only route they could take to remain out of its sight, downwind, and within shooting range.

They maneuvered some difficult terrain on their climb, and were nearly to the edge of the grassy knoll where the ram lay chewing its cud. Bud looked back to alert Doc about some loose rocks. Doc wasn't far enough behind him, and as Bud turned, a fair-sized rock under his foot broke loose and loosened two more on its way down. Doc managed to dodge two of them, but moved his head into the path of the bigger one.

"Want to go back down?" Bud asked quietly. There was a long silence. Doc was leaning into the bank, with his arm over his head, holding on with the other hand. Bud was concerned about how badly he was hurt, but there was no way he could get down to him without knocking Doc off balance. He waited.

"I'm okay. Keep going and let's get that ram. No pebbles are going to keep me from filling my sheep tag." He said jokingly. The doctor collected the ram, but only after Bud used snow to wipe blood from Doc's eyes so he could see to shoot.

Back in their spike camp, a day later, Doc was showing the horse wrangler how thin he could cut kindling with the sharp double-bitted ax. He had some dry pieces of firewood set up on the chopping block and had cut four sticks of good thin kindling already. Apparently, though, he forgot to keep his fingers out of the way, and after the next chop, he had a bloody forefinger on his left hand. Fortunately, only the tip was missing and it didn't shorten the finger much. At least it wasn't on his right hand, the important one in the operating room.

When they all returned to the base camp at Tanada Lake, his wife made the comment, "That's nothing new. He gets hurt in some way every time he goes hunting, but, thank goodness, it's never very serious." She had accompanied him to Alaska, but stayed at the lodge, while the men hunted. She added, "He's said he knows how his patients feel when he repairs their injuries. He shows them his own scars and says 'pain is one of those things that comes down to mind over matter. The secret is to relax in the pain and learn to live with it. I know. I have been there. I know that the only thing that you can do when suffering is to keep going'."

Bud Conkle had the same basic philosophy about pain as the doctor. He withstood intense pain and kept going. He survived two serious accidents on our homestead, either of which could have been fatal. He was a tough man in body and in spirit. He wasn't an accident-prone person, just impatient to get the job done without waiting for someone to help.

One day, he was doing some repair work under the Weasel (a tracked vehicle). He just couldn't wait for the friend who was coming to help him and bringing a special tool for the job. Bud was an unusually strong man, and was pulling with all of his strength to loosen a bolt, when the cheater-bar slipped and slammed into his forehead. The blood was running down his face when he walked in to the cabin.

"It must have knocked me out." He told me while I washed the blood away and bandaged the ragged cut open clear to the skull.

"We'd better get you to a doctor." I commented.

"Naw, it'll heal. I don't have time to go (80 miles) to the doctor" he answered. Two hours later, he crawled back under the Weasel and finished the job.

On a cold winter day, I was in the garage with Bud, while he was hand cranking our 7 kilowatt Witte light plant generator. I was to pull the compression handle 'on' when he gave me the nod. The generator hadn't been used for several days and was reluctant to start. The very heavy metal handle, used to turn the flywheel, slipped off the spindle, hitting him on the chest above his heart. It hit with such force that it knocked him backwards and to his knees on the cement floor. It knocked the breath out of him, and for a few minutes, he just stayed there. I could feel his heart beating faintly. When he got his breath back, I helped him down to the cabin 500 yards away. The handle had slipped at the peak of the turn while he was leaning back with it, or I'm sure the full force over the heart would have killed him. He sat still in a chair for more than an hour in the cabin.

"I'll crank that S.O.B. and it'll start, too." He wheezed. Another hour went by. He went back to the garage, cranked it up and got it running.

"Yeah, and Dad's always telling the rest of us to be careful and avoid accidents." Colin commented.

We've had clients, not many, who paid for their big game hunt and said they had a good time hunting, even if they didn't get the trophy they wanted. Bud had a hunter, one year, who had a large Dall ram in the crosshairs of his sights and didn't pull the trigger. This man said he'd always have the picture in his mind of that ram standing proudly on the high ledge in his peaceful surroundings. He just couldn't end its life and spoil the picture of that majestic ram. He felt privileged to be among a lucky few in the world who got that chance.

I had a 37 or 38-inch ram in the crosshairs of my .243 rifle and I didn't pull the trigger. I thought it looked bigger than the one Bud had mounted and about the same size as the one Colin took when he was 12. I didn't think it a good idea to take a bigger one. But I think it was partly because I knew I would have to help carry it back down off the mountain, sliding over the shale slide we had crossed climbing up.

Memorable Hunts
and Hunters

In the spring of 1967, Bud joined Cleo in Fairbanks where his airplane was being worked on. Leaving Fairbanks together, they flew to Bettles, dodging threatening snowstorms. They flew into really bad white out conditions, and by chance, or sheer luck, made it to Chandler Lake. They were fortunate to land on an ice covered lake just when they ran out of visibility. They made themselves a comfortable camp with their emergency gear. A light wind cleared the fog during the night and the temperature dropped from zero, when they landed, to a clear, cold -30° by morning. The men enjoyed the quiet night on the lake, with only sounds of crackling lake ice for company.

Bud's first letter of the season included:

"The only two pilot/guides hunting out of here right now are Bob Cooper and Leon Shellabarger. They have two hunters waiting to go out for a bear. The hotel isn't crowded and we luckily got rooms downstairs for ourselves and Nick Craw, who should arrive on the next Wein flight.

"Ralph Marshall, Bill Ellis and their hunters left this morning before we arrived. They have more hunters arriving later, so will be back. I think they went to Kotzebue."

Cleo and Bud had their Cubs fueled, warmed and ready to fly when they picked Nick up at the airport. They gave him only enough time to change into his warmer gear. They were anxious to take advantage of good flying weather. They flew 2 hours without picking up tracks. They did land near a small bear and tried to get movies but never got close enough, even with a telephoto lens.

A very pleasant 30 year-old man, Nicholas Wesson Craw came from Washington, D.C. He was of the Smith and Wesson families and was Director of Development over the Project, HOPE. Bud doubted he weighed 130 pounds, wringing wet.

"It has been hovering around -30° here for 2 days and a cold wind is blowing." Bud wrote. "We flew both days and Nick got several feet of movies while flying over bears. He took quite a bit of film of a big, old sow with a cute little cub that kept trying to climb her broad frame while she was running. We never found any place close where we could land to get movies from the ground. And we found no big tracks to follow."

Nick got his bear on the fourth day. It was -15° and the wind was blowing hard and cold. He surely didn't let weather conditions slow him down. He was wiry and tough, and could exit the plane and get right with the program, whether with a camera or rifle.

They followed bear tracks for some time. Cleo flew far off to the left and back a ways. Bud was busy looking for a smooth place on the ice floe where the tracks disappeared. They had almost missed seeing the bear. Nick poked Bud and pointed. The bear was standing in the shadow of a low ice hump. It looked like he was hiding on purpose. It sure looked like a keeper.

Bud doubted it would stay there long enough for both planes to land. If it spooked, it had the advantage of getting away over rough ice—too far away for a long shot.

Man with a rifle is the polar bear's only predator. They were curious about everything and few of them ever encountered airplanes or humans, so they weren't easily spooked. This one hung around. The men flew low and throttled back for a quiet landing into the wind.

Nick shot twice before the bear stayed down. Each shot added a fresh scope track to Nick's forehead over his right eye. Nick was shooting a Weatherby .300 Magnum with Redfield scope, 2x7 variable. The blood ran down his face. Cleo took movies of the action, and Nick's bloody face.

Bud explained using 220 grain Nostler bullets. "You want a bullet that will mushroom, but hold together." He had also advised Nick to have his cameras and guns degreased for the Arctic cold. Nick took the advice and it payed off. Bud confidently said the first shot would have killed the bear, but the second shot was insurance. The boar measured 8-foot 6-inches and was as pretty a hide as they had ever seen.

"I got all the action. All of it, but I'm not too sure how much of the film will be good, because the bear was so close and the action so fast." Cleo laughed. "I was trying to get pictures of you each time you shot, especially of your scope tracks including the blood running down your face. I hope it shows up." Nick laughed and took the camera. He took all the pictures he wanted. Cleo got out his skinning knife, and he and Bud got busy removing the hide. Nick kept the camera

Nick's bear was standing in the shadow of a low ice hump. It looked like he was hiding on purpose. It sure looked like a keeper. US Fish and Wildlife photo

running, just to get the guides' working, as part of the hunt.

"I have done very little scope shooting." Nick said in correspondence prior to his hunt. Then, in a letter we received after he returned home, he wrote, "Everything happened so fast, it wasn't even necessary to have a telephoto lens on the camera. The movies Cleo took turned out great. That bear was practically in our laps and each time I shot, my parka hood jumped. My bloody face with the unmistakable scope tracks shows up real well. The movie was perfect and certainly adds a great touch to my hunt. I had a great hunt and I'll fly with you and Cleo any day. I have your letters and I thank you for the kind remarks about my shooting. It made my day. I regret I didn't get to go wolf hunting with you two. I know I missed another great time by having to leave when I did."

Nick was a licensed pilot, too, and was intrigued by the wolf hunting stories. They offered to take him on a hunt but he had developed an ear infection, and flying seemed to aggravate it. He was very concerned and felt he should get back to his doctor for treatment. They would have enjoyed taking him on a wolf hunt.

"I am bringing my .38 Chief's Special as a sidearm." He wrote before the hunt. "It's my insurance policy."

Bud wrote back to him, "Let me talk you out of bringing the pistol. You won't need it. If a polar bear charges and the three of us can't stop him, you with your .300 Magnum, me with the .375 Winchester, and Cleo with his rifle, then the only defense will be prayers."

After his bear was down, Nick said, "I was wondering which one of you was praying when that bear whirled and faced us at such close range."

The day after Nick's hunt, word circulated that Wally Rochester was missing. Called Walk Away Wally because he walked away from a crash or two. He left 2 days before, from either Fairbanks or Clear, southwest of Fairbanks, flying a Super Cub on his way to Barrow. This wasn't the first time Rochester was over due and it wouldn't be the last time.

When the hunt for him began, bad weather South of the Brooks Range forced the Air Force search plane back. Weather was still bad the next day. Eskimos at Anaktuvuk said they never saw him, and weren't worried. "He's only over due two days." They said.

He made it into Barrow, on his own, without having to be rescued. He had just been "settin out" bad weather.

Wally got himself lost flying to Bettles from Fairbanks, once. He flew around first, then ran out of gas just as he was approaching the Bettles runway. Coming in dead-stick (with no power), he hit a snow berm at the end of the runway, but luckily didn't do any major damage to his plane. Bud was there that time, overnight, heading south.

When Bud talked to Wally, he had asked Bud about following Johns River, after leaving Bettles. Bud suggested he follow it to Anaktuvuk Pass, being sure to turn left at Hunt's Fork. Going that way, he'd most likely be able to use the village as a marker. Bud worried that Wally had less than adequate gear with him, and it was -30° at Umiat the day before when Bud left there. Wally said he was flying to Barrow to fly cover for one of the pilot/guides already there.

Bud and Cleo had their hunter tags filled, so they took a hunter out for one of the other guides. After he had his bear, Cleo flew cover for Pete Merry for 2 days. Ward Carroll had been his partner and all of the pilot/guides were helping Pete out as time and hunting allowed. Bud took Charley Edwardson, a Barrow Native, wolf hunting. Charley was a dead shot with his rifle. Someone told Bud that Charley went

76

out with one of the guides, one year, and shot three wolves from a running pack, with his .243 on the first pass over an open lake.

Jack Skaldagger, Peg Leg Jack as he was affectionately known, froze his leg in an incident and it had to be removed. This was no handicap for Jack, and he was a good pilot/guide. His hunters were successful, so he flew cover for Bud and Charley. Lance, the young fellow arriving with Bill Ellis, rode as gunner in Jack's plane. They flew as far as Wainwright and between the two planes and gunners, they got three wolves and a wolverine.

The last hunter for the year arrived on schedule, and, with lucky weather, and a cooperative bear, he took an 8-foot 6-inch bear 2 days later. Then, Pete Merry had Bud and Cleo take one of his hunters out and they found him a nice 9-foot polar bear.

When Pete's hunter was successful, Bud flew in Pete's plane, to take movies of what bears they could locate. Guides rarely got a chance to take movies of their own when they had hunters. They're usually taking movies with the hunter's camera or they're working as back up with a rifle as their priority.

After Bud took movies with his 16mm Bolex movie camera, they traded positions, and planes, and Pete took movies. They got excellent footage of a couple of sows with cubs ambling along. The flying plane finally spooked them and they took off in high gear on their way to somewhere else. Both of them got movies of white arctic fox. The fox never got a bit excited about the low flying plane. They just raised their heads to look and never changed their pace.

Cleo decided to stay and fly cover for Pete Merry, who had two more hunters coming. Wally Rochester, the pilot everyone thought was lost earlier, flew south with Bud as far as Fairbanks. He sprang the landing gear on his Cub the day before on the Colville River Delta while wolf hunting. Bud and Cleo had helped him put the new gear on before they left. Bud was glad Wally had the new gear and they had no delays. The weather was great for flying.

Different pilots reported seeing rather big wolf packs on the north side of the Brooks Range. They hunted there on the return trip. Bud and Cleo took plenty of aviation gas and flew in one Cub.

Bud flew in Wally's plane as gunner one day. The next day he was gunner in Bud's plane. They got into two different wolf packs and Bud collected six wolves as his share.

On April 6th, Bud and N8464D were home again at Eagle Trail Ranch on Cobb Lake. His face was deeply tanned from the sun reflecting off the ice and snow. He was glad to be home again—until the next year rolled around, that is!

Sometime after Cleo and Pete finished the hunts, Cleo got some fascinating movies of Beluga whales in an open 10-foot wide lead. The whales gracefully surfaced and dived, two and three abreast, sometimes in line with a lead whale. I don't recall how much footage he took, but later, when we saw those movies, it was quite lengthy. It was like watching a beautiful and graceful ballet.

We've had clients who come to hunt with a borrowed rifle, or a rifle he has never sighted-in or even shot. Bud checked each rifle before the hunters left base camp. A really personable farmer from Kansas arrived with some type of army surplus rifle and ammo. He had confidence in it and, later, Bud had to give him credit. He proved he could, and did get the caribou and moose trophies he booked. Our advertising literature said, "Bring a rifle you have confidence in." Franze had a good German-made rifle and he and Herta both could hit a bulls-eye.

Two German hunters showed up one year with their custom-made rifles and unattached scopes. They assured Bud the scopes would be accurate when attached and the rifles didn't need to be sighted in. Bud was more than dubious after the long flight from Germany, but they were right. Their rifles did a fine job on the game they shot.

Don Steven's Hunt with His Young

Buud and Cleo had perfect flying weather from Fairbanks to Bettles. They fueled the Super Cubs, ate lunch in the local cafe, then took off for the arctic slope. While flying over large herds of scattered caribou, they picked up conspicuous wolf signs. It was obvious that a large pack was working there. They skimmed low over a couple of fresh kills, but didn't linger, assuming the wolves were holed up sleeping somewhere. At Chandler Lake, they caught up with four big grays chasing a small band of caribou. The wolves weren't serious about the chase, whether they were doing it for practice, or just because the caribou were there.

The planes feathered down onto the open tundra and Bud climbed aboard Cleo's Cub. He dropped the big old lead wolf on the first pass. Cleo flew low over the one that had been following the leader. Bud brought it down, and the other two scattered. They stashed the pelts and were quickly on their way again.

It was dark and -40° at Umiat. By the time they got the oil drained, engine heaters installed under the cowlings, and wing covers and insulated engine covers in place, their fingers were freezing. These priority tasks had to be done without mitts or gloves. There was no one living at Umiat, so they settled themselves in the Quonset hut with an oil-stove full of fuel, but unlit. Bud overhauled the carburetor. The deep cold of an unheated metal building turns all metal into skin-burning surfaces and any bare skin is seared instantly. Under these conditions, all tasks are more complicated and difficult.

While Bud was working on the oil stove, Cleo brewed tea on his Coleman stove and built an edible supper from their canned rations. Throughout the night, they struggled from their warm sleeping bags to get the oil stove going again. At daylight, they took off in a light fog, and arrived in Barrow at noon, a day ahead of a bad snowstorm. The pilot/guides already there told them a blizzard had kept them down for 3 days and had let up just hours before their arrival.

Don Stevens, from Webster, New York, was booked to fly with his 12 year-old son, Donny, who was flying along as an observer. In 1967 he hunted with us in the Wrangells. Then, his wife and three young sons came with him and stayed with me at Tanada Lake Lodge.

Bud was very pleased to have Don book a polar bear hunt. It meant he had confidence in Bud. A returning client brings great satisfaction and adds to the memories of exciting and rewarding times.

Bud and Cleo arrived in Barrow in early March. Pilot/guides Bill Ellis, Ralph Marshall, and Windy Windell, were there ahead of them with their hunters, and grounded for the three days waiting on bad weather.

There were lots of bears and they were closer to land than usual. Some distance from Barrow there was an open lead nearly 30 miles wide. Too dangerous to cross that distance, they would have to fly the greater distance around.

Weather favored them after the Stevens' arrived, so they flew every day. They found good-sized tracks, but they didn't catch up with a bear of trophy size.

Three days later, the open lead closed to 10 miles in width and was safer to fly across. Two hours to the northwest, Bud found the tracks of a big bear. Both planes tracked it for an hour. When they found the bear, the ice was too rough and no smooth ice within miles. Don took a few pictures before heading back to Barrow. "It was one of those clear, calm days that makes flying over the endless white world a pleasure." Bud said.

Back in the hotel, they enjoyed telling stories or listening to others. Ellis' and Marshall's hunters scored that day and those two pilot/ guides never ran out of stories worth hearing. Depending of course on the audience and how many drinks guzzled, the stories became over embellished and hilarious.

The next day, a perfect sunny day, and shadows so necessary for tracking, were sharp and clear. Stevens, in the back seat and Bud, saw the bear at the same instant.

"73 Zulu, spotted a bear, and he's a keeper."

Cleo started circling farther away to give Bud a chance to land on the ice floe.

"73 Zulu," Bud called again. "The floe looks pretty small for two of us, but I'm gonna take a chance and land. How about you staying up and watching. The way this bear is covering ground, he may be too far away by the time we both land."

He circled to lose altitude and slipped sideways to the right, then to the left, deliberately spilling air from the wings. He wanted to touch down as close as he could to the end of the ice floe. He alerted Don to exit the minute the plane stopped sliding.

"Start shooting as soon as your feet are under you and you have a clean shot." He told him. Don was a big, agile man. He was out of the plane and got off his first shot, before the bear whirled out of range. It was a long shot, and only wounded it. It shifted into high gear and galloped over a low pressure ridge. The big white bear hesitated a minute, looking in their direction when the plane stopped, and that gave Don just the one shot. The bear wasn't wounded badly enough to slow it down, so they climbed back in the Cub.

Their skis cleared the ice ridge with less than a foot to spare. From the air, they trailed the bear several miles across rough ice. The red patch on its rump showed plainly against its yellow-white coat.

They found an ice pan large enough for both Cubs to land. There was still rough hiking, a mile or more. The bear was laying in the hollow of a pressure ridge still very much alive. The bear was unaware of Don and Bud as they crept within shooting distance. Don fired from a bit over a hundred yards, and killed it instantly.

Cleo and Donny came from where they had been waiting, and Cleo helped roll the big animal out of the hollow and onto level ground and they took pictures. The men skinned the bear with the precision of years of practice. The green hide stretched 9-feet 7-inches, and if the game warden had measured the five-inch flap of the tail, it would have been a 10-footer. It was the biggest bear taken at Barrow that season.

Smaller green hides were tough packing jobs, but dragging or carrying a big one was a rigorous undertaking. It took all of them to drag it the long distance over rough ice.

Donny, perched in the plane, saw the magnificent bear and watched as the drama unfolded. He heard the killing shot and watched as the bear's pelt was pulled and shoved over the ice. How many boys his age get such a chance? He will never get the chance to make a hunt like this, or even to fly out over the pack ice. This kind of hunting will be told about only in story books.

The father and son Stevens left for home the day after Don got his trophy. They were anxious to get home and share their stories and pictures with family and friends. Both were fascinated with all facets of life in Barrow and didn't murmur or complain about meals or living conditions in the hotel. They never mentioned not being able to sleep during wild parties with yelling and fighting going on most of the night.

Barrow Eskimo were hungry for meat this particular year and every time the pilot/guides returned from a day on the pack ice, Eskimo were at the lagoon to meet them, anxiously awaiting any meat Bud and Cleo might have brought back. They liked to help secure the planes for the night, carry avgas, or carry sleeping bags and whatever else was needed back to the hotel, regardless if the guides had meat for them or not. It was Bud and Cleo's policy to bring back the polar bear meat that looked healthy, if there was room in the planes.

Cleo booked a client one year who liked the look of bear meat and wanted to try some. An Eskimo friend said his wife was a good cook and always cooked polar bear meat well done. She cooked a roast for him. He was impressed and convinced Bud and Cleo to try it. Bud wasn't enthusiastic about eating polar bear meat, or any kind of bear meat for that matter, and expressed concern about trichinosis, suspected to be in bear meat as well as pork. He did admit the meat did look very healthy, which wasn't true of all polar bears he had skinned. They brought in both hindquarters from the hunter's big bear and their Eskimo friend was waiting when they landed. With a big smile on his round, dusky face, he invited them to dinner at his home the following evening.

The client was enthusiastic about being invited into an Eskimo home. He showed an interest in everything going on in Barrow, including Eskimo history. Their methods of survival in the deep arctic cold and during long, dark winters held a special interest. He enjoyed the little Eskimo children in their colorful parkas and took many pictures, and they loved the candy he handed out so generously.

Bud and Cleo took him on an unsuccessful wolf hunt that day. He saw a lot of primal white vastness, willow-lined rivers, and ice covered rivers. Close to the narrow confines of the Colville River, they picked up the clearly etched wolf tracks in the fresh snow. They disappeared at the edge of a dense willow thicket and they couldn't flush him out.

After the tough day of hunting wolves, in blowing snow and hazardous landing conditions, Bud was apprehensive about dinner that evening. Their churning innards settled down by the time they sat to dinner and Bud was more than surprised to find the polar bear roast quite delicious. However, he never voluntarily ate any kind of bear meat again.

To escape the hunter, many polar bears would head for an open lead and gallop into the hazy distance of ice fog—commonly called sea smoke, the telltale sign of a large system of open leads on the pack ice. This phenomenon results when moisture rises from cracks in the sea ice and condenses as thick vapor. It hangs dark and uninviting, and rises high in the air across the distance of open water.   US Fish and Wildlife photo

The day after the polar bear dinner, the three of them walked out onto the ice pack to watch Native people fishing for tom cod through small round holes cut in the ice. They bid him a fond adieu the following day.

Bud wrote, "Chuck Gray and LeRoy Scheible's hunter, a major airline pilot, came in with a 9-foot bear. He killed it a good hundred miles out on the ice. He's the last hunter for this year and they will be leaving for Fairbanks soon. They will take this pilot back with them and do some wolf hunting on their way. I'm sure they'll have a great time. All wolves best beware. George Theil and Pete Merry have two hunters filled, but have two more coming in a few days. Our next hunter won't be arriving for two more days, so Cleo and I will take out a friend of the ANS (Alaska Native Services) doctor stationed here."

Bud and Cleo had already taken the ANS doctor and his wife on a sightseeing flight one afternoon. The couple was new in Barrow and expressed interest in seeing a live polar bear out on the ice; out where they belonged and were supposed to stay. The pilots showed them the tracks of a big bear, but never located it. They flew low over a handsome little white fox trotting along tending his own business. The doctor also told the guides of a friend, Colonel Kern, who was hoping someone would take him out for a bear. Bud and Cleo had free time right then, so the doctor telephoned his friend and he flew up the same day.

Colonel Kern was the Chief Surgeon at the hospital on Elmendorf Air Force Base near Anchorage. Talk about luck. Four hours after they left Barrow, the Colonel had an 8-foot 6-inch bear. He was on a large ice floe and they landed both planes side by side. The bear was a considerable distance from them and stood looking in their direction. Thinking the bear was sure to turn and gallop away, Colonel Kern, riding in Bud's plane, jumped from the plane and rammed a shell in the chamber of his rifle. Bud told him to use his own judgment as to the distance to make a killing shot.

They kept walking slowly toward the bear. It raised its head, then swung back and forth. In their white canvas-covered parkas, they presented no threat to the bear and it may have been just curious, waiting for them to get closer so he could tell if it was some of his buddies or something to eat.

Kern dropped to one knee, made a long shot and the bear dropped where it stood. The men ran forward and Kern took two more rapid shots. They waited a few minutes before Bud walked close enough to see if it was dead.

Anyway, after a couple of man-sized cocktails that evening at the ANS doctor's residence, Kern admitted he had been so airsick during the last half hour of the hunt he would have been willing to head back to Barrow. Just as he made up his mind to stick it out, regardless of how sick he got, Cleo's radio crackled with the message

"64 Delta—off to my right and he's a keeper."

The air was quite turbulent and Bud did a lot of maneuvering, concentrating on picking up the tracks where the bear crossed rough ice. Bud lost sight of them, then with one wing up, he made a tight turn, flying high enough just to clear the ice ridges. He was intent on handling the plane in rough air, as well as tracking, and hadn't given much thought to his passenger. Perhaps the sight of the bear made Kern forget his queasy innards, because the sick-sack remained empty.

Kern said, "I've flown many hours in rough air without getting sick. I'd have been mighty embarrassed to ask Bud to turn back."

Bud assured him he was redeemed by a clean, efficient kill. They didn't tell him they were glad he hadn't offered to help skin his bear. They had been down that route before!

The day ended with Colonel Kern taking all of them (the two pilot/guides, and the ANS doctor and his wife) to the cafe for T-bone steaks. They didn't have to wait in line at the cafe and the hotel wasn't crowded.

Talking about meals reminds me of the Air Force pilots who invited Bud and Cleo to dinner at the radar base on Point Barrow. Four Air Force pilots, stationed at Eielson Air Force Base near Fairbanks, flew two Family Cruisers to Barrow to hunt polar bear. They were staying on the Point at the Radar Station. They flew over the pack ice 3 days in a row without seeing an acceptable bear. They went out the fourth day and didn't return. No one seemed to know if they left for Fairbanks, or were stranded on the ice.

It started snowing. They didn't show up at the Radar Base or at Eielson that night, and word was they must be missing on the pack ice. None of the pilot/guides had any inkling of the direction they hunted and no one had radio contact with them. It was very likely they had radios and ELT's in both airplanes, but no one knew for sure. It was snowing too hard, with no visibility, for any search plane out of Barrow.

Two days later, when weather moderated and all of the pilots were readying for a search, the Air Force boys returned. They were exuberant young guys and the hotel lobby came alive with their spicy stories.

"We shot one bear late in the day," they said over drinks. "But bad weather swooped in on us and held us down. We just built an igloo, dug out our emergency gear and waited." Advance preparations and survival know-how serves all pilots well.

Later that day, the Air Force pilots invited Bud and Cleo out to the main DEW-Line Post on the Point. It was a unique experience. They flew over most of the DEW (Distant Early Warning) stations across Alaska.

The boys drove them out in a command car and introduced them to the commanding officer. They were treated like conquering heroes. After a generous supply of beer, when one bottle was set down empty, it was whisked away and replaced with a full one, they were all waving their arms around, doing wing overs, chandelles, s-turns, etc., and killing polar bears and wolves. All of the pilots told their latest story with embellishments and outlandish grandeur.

"The boys here sure have tough duty," Bud said. "Everything is housed in one immense building, including all of the instrumentation for the station. The personnel doesn't have to go outdoors for anything." They liked their duty station, but Bud said they were a pale next to the men who spent a month or two on the ice, in the sun, wind and snow.

Bud was impressed with the chow on the base. "They feed their personnel like royalty, to make up for the isolation, I suppose. For dinner, when they eventually got around to it, they get a choice of steak or fried chicken, potatoes cooked two different ways, several varieties of fresh vegetables and salad. Tea, coffee and even fresh milk (unheard of in the bush), and a variety of pies and cakes are always available." They were driven back to the hotel at 2 AM. It was a blessing they did not have to fly later that morning.

Bud wrote, "Two days ago, I was fire-potting the engine for an early morning flight. I was talking with a hunter waiting while his pilot/guide was fighting a high wind as he pulled the wing covers off. I turned my back to the wind and to his cussing a blue streak. I let the shock cord (a rubberized spring, larger than a bungee cord on the Super Cub's landing gear) get too hot and it parted company with the ski. I feel very fortunate it didn't let go when we were a hundred miles out on the ice. It would have been simple to replace, if I'd had an extra, but no one here had one to borrow, so I ordered two new ones from Fairbanks.

"A guy flew over from Kotzebue with his hunter and lent me his spare cord. I put it on my plane and will replace the other one when the new ones arrive. Luckily, it's been snowing and blowing for most of these 2 days and we didn't have a hunter getting antsy while waiting for the plane to be repaired."

Bud and Cleo had time before their next hunter arrived, so they each took out a hunter for Ellis and Marshall. Both were resident hunters. With new snow for easy tracking, one man got his bear the first day and the second day they had a bear for the other hunter. There was no shortage of 6-foot 6-inch bears and 8-foot bears were roaming around out as far out as they went.

Paul Schuelke, a 23-year-old man from Glencoe, Minnesota was their next hunter. Paul faithfully sent us a $75 check every month for two years until he paid the $1,800 down payment. When he came for his hunt, he brought a check for the balance. He wrote many letters during those two years and we got to know him pretty well. He was a big guy and wore a size 12 shoe. Bud wrote to him that we could lend him all of the outer clothing he needed for the hunt and not to invest in that extra expense. Most clients preferred their own gear.

Paul told us he shot a .340 Weatherby, using 225 Hornaday bullets and that he could hit an oil can at 100 yards. "Do you think I can hit a polar bear at that distance?"

"I'd say, that's about right." Bud replied.

The planes were ready to fly as the morning sun nudged the horizon. With this eager, young fellow in Bud's plane, they flew north from Barrow on a perfect morning for tracking. Paul was excited, poking Bud and commenting when he pointed to a polar bear and her three cubs lumbering across the pack ice ahead of them. Their bodies cast long, dark shadows that appeared running with them. The cubs were nearly as big as the mama and two of them outdistanced her when they were spooked by the approaching planes. Bud made two passes over them for Paul to get pictures.

Farther on, he lowered the side door to give Paul a better view of a lone bear ambling along. The droning engines startled him from his day dreaming, and he went into action, tumbled over, went into reverse and headed in a high lope the other direction. Paul was thrilled.

Flying northeast another 50 miles they came across a 'red bear' with two arctic foxes tearing into the carcass. It looked like a fresh kill, and most likely left by two pilot/guides and their hunter who had flown out ahead of them.

From radio conversations, Bud believed one pilot/guide found a keeper and was going down for a look. Bud told Paul, "Yeah, we'll hear all about it tonight at the hotel."

They flew toward the east without seeing any more bear. Back in Barrow, Bud and Cleo fueled up the hungry tanks on the planes, filled their empty stomachs and enjoyed the tales of the day's adventures.

They flew two more days before Paul collected his bear. His shot was twice the distance of his oil can practice shot. They were 80 miles north and east of Barrow when Bud called to alert Cleo he had spotted this bear.

"73 Zulu, I see a keeper in the distance, at 2 o'clock. He's going over that pressure ridge. Let's go look!" Cleo was flying so far to Bud's left that he could see only the red trim of his plane. He called Bud a couple of times, whenever he saw a bear, but on investigation, they weren't trophy size.

A patch of smooth ice, just long enough to accommodate Bud's Cub, and a quarter mile from their prize, was separated by a pressure ridge. With luck, the bear was still there and Cleo could land unnoticed on the other side of the pressure ridge.

Bud landed, knowing he would have to take off alone, with only the freshly skinned bear hide as cargo. Bud would need all of the lift he could get from the cold breeze to clear the pressure ridge in front of him. Paul would have to hike across the rough ice over a mile to the other side of the ridge where both planes could land and regroup.

This kid was good. He made a clean kill after getting from the plane—quietly climbing the ridge and peeking over the icy top to locate the bear. The bear was about 200 yards from the base of the ridge but turning to come back over the pressure ridge where Paul crouched.

Paul's Weatherby spoke, the sound ricochetted along the ridge and thunked into the bear. Skinning the bear was next. That green hide, with the head and paws left in, was about all Bud could pack, especially up and over that 8-foot slippery ice ridge. He was happy to load it aboard the waiting Cub. So ended this good day.

It's always a good day when our hunters are satisfied with their hunt. Bud personally felt Paul deserved and had earned the achievement. His bear hide, green, was 8-foot 10-inches with a skull measurement of 24 7/16 inches. It was a decent bear for an enjoyable client.

Bud had a less-than-subtle way of letting it be known that he didn't approve of dudes who overindulged and then expected to climb mountains the next morning. Most of them got his message and waited to do their serious drinking until after the hunt was over. Bud had a few experiences that really got to him, though. He flew out to the highway, late one evening, to find his two clients drinking heavily while they waited for him. They had a large bonfire burning and they were sitting close . . . on the full five-gallon avgas cans! Using the full five-gallon cans of avgas for chairs! I don't know what Bud said to them when he saw how close to the fire those cans were, but they looked very meek on their arrival at camp.

Many Wolves,
Many Memories

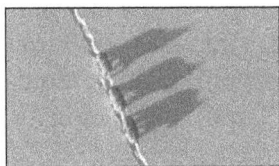

In most areas of the Lower 48, the mention of Alaska immediately conjures images of wolves, northern lights, big game hunting, ice, snow, and igloos where Eskimos live. The mystic of wolves in the primeval forests of Alaska holds us spellbound.

It could be enriching and thrilling for those whose fairy tale notion of Red Riding Hood's grandmother being eaten by a wolf, to venture into a country of big mountains, big lakes, open tundra, and dark, mysterious forests where wolves run free.

Our own preconceived ideas of wolves changed when we were no longer cheechakos. We lived in pristine wilderness where they roamed at will, hunting in packs for moose and caribou—taking the old and the young.

We learned about wolves from our own observations, and vicariously from our friends. The wolf is a magnificent and cunning animal, beautiful and admirable in many respects. Wolves running in large packs are an organized killing machine. It's killing tactics are fierce, often eating the intestines of an animal before it is dead.

Today, in Alaska's history, the wolf is a very controversial subject. The men, whose outdoor lifestyle gives them first hand facts of wolves and their prey, know them well. Too many so-called environmentalists, Friends of Animals members, and other 'anti' groups, have never seen a wolf, other than the ones pacing their zoo cages.

I have seen them singly, in pairs, and packs in their wild habitat. I have been entertained with their sleeping and playing on our lakes. I have flown over them and thrilled to their graceful, long stride as they stretched out, tails flowing, running full-tilt for the cover of nearby trees.

I have sympathy for those city dwellers who have never had the God-given privilege of living out in the wilds. They have never heard the spine tingling, eerie howl of wolves gathering for the hunt. Nor have they ever sat, unobserved, watching wolf pups romping and playing with clean bones from a kill. I will ever be grateful that I have heard a variety of howls, calls, and immature pup-yelps in the pristine wilderness at our isolated Wolf Lake camp.

I was the main cook in our Wolf Lake hunting camp, located in the Nutzotin Range, east of Tok. One year, for several successive nights, soon after deep dark, a wolf howled on a hill close to camp. The long, wailing howl came from where I had put out meat scraps and bones from trophies and kitchen trimmings. I put the scraps out for the ravens and camp robbers. They were always gone by morning. Did the complaining wolf eat them? Was it asserting its domain, telling us we were trespassing? After 30 minutes of silence, I'd hear the same howl from a greater distance, fading into the night. It was just letting us know it would be back.

I decided sleeping was a waste of time, when I could be getting a real wolf howl on tape. It was rare to hear a wolf howling so loudly and so close to camp. I oiled the squeaky hinges of my kitchen door. I set up my cassette tape recorder on the porch. When the wolf started serenading the camp around midnight, I was sitting by the fire in the kitchen, dosing. I carefully let myself out.

Sitting on the porch in the black night, I started my recorder and waited for the next howls to start. The hairs raised on the back of my neck. I knew the wolf was there. I felt its close presence. I only heard a small dry twig break under a light step. As quiet as I had been, did it hear me? Or did the wolf come to investigate the whirring of the battery operated tape recorder? There wasn't the slightest breeze. I don't think it could detect that I was there, by smell, but what about my loudly beating heart, could he hear it? He might have been just curious but I had lost my curiosity and quickly took me and my recorder into the cabin. I made plans for a different setup the next night, but those plans didn't materialize. The wolf didn't howl the following several nights, although the meat scraps were always gone in the morning.

As the nights got colder and the snow crept down the mountains, we packed up for the season. On our last night, that wolf left two big paw prints in the mud, not far from the porch. The memory of the wolf, and his visits hasn't dimmed over the years. I can truthfully say I don't know whether I was scared or not. I just know that I had a mysterious and eerie experience and a haunting memory like those I had reading Jack London's stories of wolves.

There was another time, another year, when I found myself quite close to seven wolves, a sight I like to call my Christmas present, because it happened the morning before Christmas. I was alone with my black cat, Mama-Kitty, in our cabin at Eagle Trail Ranch. It was a foggy December morning with a temperature of -20°. Mama-Kitty followed me, like a dog does, and was sitting by the open door of the outhouse. I stood up and started pulling up my jeans to quickly cover my exposed parts. The door doesn't need to be closed when occupied because it faces a little-used trail lined with willows and bushes and tall trees. Out of the fog, a large gray animal crossed the trail from the low bushes on one side. As silently as it appeared, it disappeared into the willows and trees on the other side. I stood motionless, wondering what I had seen. Before I had time to figure it out, six smaller versions of the first crossed the path in single file. Then I realized it was a family of wolves, with the big male in the lead, five medium sized pups and a bitch, just a bit larger than her pups. I hardly moved an eyelash. When I felt sure there were no more, I eased out, and without turning around, I reached up behind me to latch the door shut. To my utter amazement, the big dog wolf came back and stood 50 feet from me, sniffing the trail, never looking in my direction. When he was gone, I paced off the distance between us. Fifty feet. He apparently had other things on his mind, because ravens and camp robbers were soon flying over a caribou kill at the edge of the lake.

Where was my cat? I hadn't missed her, until I started back to the cabin. When I arrived, she was peeking at me from under the porch, growling. I went in, got the movie camera, and pussy footed down to the lake, and caught the pups romping, tossing bones, and chasing after each other.

"Wow, what a movie this will make!" I thought. Although they didn't see me crouching behind willows, the unfamiliar sound of the whirring of the camera alerted them. Papa Wolf emitted a sharp growl, and darted for timber, looking back over his shoulder, as the pups followed. A straggler didn't get the word, or didn't want to leave, and Mama Wolf ran back and forth near the shore, whining. When Papa came back out in the open, it streaked for cover, too. The whole family was a silvery gray color.

Mama-Kitty didn't emerge from her safe place under the porch until I returned and let her into the cabin, where she remained the rest of the day.

Another very memorable time, watching, unsuspecting wild animals took place on Cobb Lake. Our cabin sat just 20 yards from the shore. Bud and I had a ringside view for 5 days of a family of five wolves who spent the afternoons romping then sleeping on the lake ice.

We didn't accomplish much during those days. We took turns watching the wolves, as they lay, stretched out for their afternoon snoozes. No matter how pressing the chores, we'd keep our vigil until they woke up and left for places beyond our view. We worked like mad, doing neglected chores, until they returned the next afternoon.

The family consisted of the dog wolf, a smaller wolf bitch, two medium sized pups, and a smaller coal black female. We knew she was a female because she squatted to urinate. The other four were shades of gray. They had a caribou kill in the trees close to the Copper River, and we could hear them howling at night. It was easy to distinguish the pup's high pitched, yippee howls from adult howls. When they returned to the lake, each brought bones for snacks. They'd gnaw a bit, then, with a paw over the bone, they'd stretch out and snooze. Ravens wanted the bones too and kept them from sleeping too soundly. They'd grab a bone, then dart back out of range of the wolves menacing jaws. The ravens didn't often succeed in getting the bones, but they never gave up trying. Sometimes the pups romped and played with their bones, tossing them in the air and running after them, until they tired and snoozed again.

On the fifth day, we watched as they lay down to snooze. They snoozed a couple of hours in the afternoon sunshine. We didn't see the little black female leave. But a long, mournful howl made us drop whatever had taken us from our viewing and we ran for the open shore with our binoculars in hand. Papa wolf sat on his haunches with his nose pointed skyward and, at 1 minute interval, howled.

Mama sat up, looked around, then went to the two pups, sniffed them, then sat with her nose in the air and howled a long, singing wail of her own. Both pups sat up, put their noses in the air, and let loose with yelping, immature howls. This went on for a good 10 minutes.

Then the missing female came trotting out from the woods, dragging a caribou leg bone. She could have been gone for a week for the greeting she received! They sniffed her all over, rubbed noses with hers, and licked her mouth, while their tails went 'round and 'round.

An opportunist raven had most likely carried her bone away and she had gone back to the kill for another. She neglected telling the family where she was going. After their greeting, they promptly settled back down to finish their naps. She amused herself chasing ravens. She would leave the big leg bone a very short distance, stretch out and, when a feathered robber hopped close enough to snatch a bit of meat from the bone, she'd leap into the air after it. The raven would squawk and fly up, then land out of reach and wait for her to lie back down. I think it was a game both enjoyed.

We learned about wolves from our own observations, and vicariously from our friends. The wolf is a magnificent and cunning animal, beautiful and admirable in many respects. Wolves running in large packs are an organized killing machine. It's killing tactics are fierce, often eating the intestines of an animal before it is dead.   US Fish and Wildlife photo

Another winter month at The Ranch, we went to bed listening to wolves howling. The cabin at The Ranch was just a half mile from the Copper River. It was a natural place for wolves because of snowshoe rabbits thriving there.

A light snow covered the land early that morning. Then, reading the wolf tracks in the snow, an interesting story unfolded. Bud said it was like reading a printed page. Wolf pups had chewed the long tiedown ropes loose from the wings of the Super Cub where it was parked on its skis. Luckily there was no wind. Tracks indicated there were four of the playful rascals. They romped the length of the 900-foot runway dragging the ropes, probably in a tug-of-war game. They had the snow trampled the entire length and width of the airfield. Ropes were left in the jumbled snow when they departed. Mama and Papa had lain in one place long enough for their bodies to melt the snow and indulgently watched while the pups played. Most likely it wasn't the same family we had watched on the lake the previous winter, but their passage was a memorable sight in the fresh snow.

When a bear enters a cabin or tent, it generally exits from another opening, leaving a trail of havoc in its path. The mess a grizzly bear left when he broke into the cabin a Wolf Lake.

We had many grizzly bears, with different personalities, in our yards in the various places we lived, or built camps; destructive bears tore up a cabin; bears ripped open meat caches; even a bear tore up a roll of roofing tar-paper and the dog sled; and other bears passed through without doing any damage.

But the wolves were the most entertaining and welcome. There was the time a female wolf tried to entice one of our most important sled dogs out to where the pack waited. Had Bud not interfered in time, they would have torn him to pieces. Our wise old dog team leader nearly lost his life falling for that age old trick.

Timber wolves serenaded the lonely winter nights during the years we lived at Tanada Lake, and their hauntingly beautiful, sing song wails echoed across the lake and valleys. All of our dogs acted strangely when the wolves howled. Old Jim was always the first to jump from his perch atop his house and hide in the corner. The dogs seemed to have a natural inborn fear of wolves and didn't quite know what to do about it. Hearing a low-key, throaty growl, and if harnessed to the sled, they would cringe close to the sled and each other, looking up at us. If tied to their dog houses, they stayed hidden inside.

Maybe I wouldn't have been so pleased to know there were wolves around if they had killed our horses. The horses were important and expensive, and very necessary to our outfitter business. Other outfitters lost horses to the wolves and they hated the critters. I remember one big-game outfitter's wife telling about six wolves killing their horses.

"I want revenge. I want every one of those vicious killers gutted while they're still alive the way they ate our horse. I don't agree with Farley Mowat's fan club of wolf-lovers." She said. "Our years of intimate knowledge of the murderous predators don't agree with their ideas."

We had nearly 20 horses when we had hunting camps at Wolf Lake, and I'll admit, we were always concerned about wolves killing them. We had a grazing lease there and turned the horses loose to graze where the grasses were best, from early June until just before the first hunts in August. We never lost a horse to the wild animals, but we had no way of knowing if they were chased by roaming packs. The horses had loud cow bells on straps around their necks and they stayed close together, which may have deterred hungry wolf packs.

With a plentiful supply of easier animals to bring down, the wolves may not have tried the horses. But I have heard many horse outfitters say that once wolves start eating horse flesh, there is no stopping them.

We lost a horse one year, and he wintered alone, but was in good shape when we finally located him in the spring. He had deep healed scars, on his rump and one side. He couldn't tell us whether a bear or a wolf had scarred him, but he was alive and well. His attacker may not have been, if the horse was fast enough with his hind leg kicks.

One winter night, we literally had a wolf at our door. It was while Bud was away polar bear hunting. Colin and I were at our cabin at The Ranch. A full moon was shining on the white snow. It was almost as light as day. Colin looked out the window, "Mom, come and look," he called. A big gray wolf had sauntered out onto the ice of the lake and sat on its haunches alongside an airplane parked on the snow. It wasn't 100 yards from the kitchen door. The smoke from our fire and signs of human habitation didn't deter it from coming in so close.

Then, while we watched, it serenaded us. Standing in a warm cabin with the lanterns off and watching a big Alaska timber wolf point his nose to the sky, with the orange moon close above the hills beyond him were both thrilling and beautiful. It was out of character, from all I have heard and read about wolves, to show up so close, then sit there and howl. I opened the door stealthily, hoping for enough light to snap a picture, but it streaked for the timber and was silent. We heard it howling from the hillside in the early dawn. For three successive nights, we heard its mournful wailing in the distance. We timed its song. Its wail lasted 10 minutes each time. If it came onto the lake again, we never saw it—only its tracks.

I was concerned about the two half-grown puppies in their doghouse. If the wolf was after them, would he have howled? I left a Coleman lantern burning near the doghouses for a few nights. The pups were still there each morning.

What did the wolves have on their minds when they urinated copiously, down the fittings and skis of the three Super Cubs parked on the ice? What motivated them to come that close? Were they marking a new territory? Our lake was active with snowmobiles and airplanes. We had never heard of them coming so close and being so vocal.

We never shot any animal that came around The Ranch, nor did Bud allow our guests to do so. When Bud hunted and trapped, he went into isolated areas, away from home. We enjoyed seeing the wild animals that frequented the areas where we lived and did business. But we also knew that nature was ruthless in many ways, animals are often more so than man ever is to the wolves.

"Okay, you four-legged creatures, Bud won't let us hunt you in his back yard, but we'll catch you before this day is over, wherever you are snoozing or hiding!" one of the Super Cub jockeys exclaimed.

"Wolves are not fragile. They would steal your airplane if they knew how to start it," was the sarcastic remark by a guy from Anchorage, flying as gunner in a friend's Super Cub.

Bud was flying his Cub in the hills above Copper Lake once, looking for a moose kill. He planned to set traps around it. He came back with this story;

"After landing on Copper Lake, I walked on snowshoes, about a half-mile from where I spotted the moose-kill. The weather was turning sour and it was late afternoon. I was anxious to get my traps set and be home before dark. I followed a bend of the willow-fringed creek and came face to face with a wolf. It was standing less than 30 yards away, not much more than a shadow in the haze against the willows. Stiff-legged, tail straight, its cold, glaring yellow eyes stared into mine. Wide chest and large paws, luxurious gray hide and thick ruff, he stood stalk-still, intense. I felt he was reading my mind. I stood, caught in that cold glare, trying to decide if he were challenging me or warning me to stay out of his territory. The big wolf stood for only a 5 or 6 seconds, then he disappeared as silently as a shadow.

"An overpowering and mystical silence surrounded me when it was gone. Reading the story in the snow, I stayed and meditated. Several wolves had pulled a cow moose down. She had fought off the pack for a long time, and her struggle in death redeemed me from any guilt of avenging her. I set my traps and left, but those yellow eyes stayed with me, while I tried to understand my feeling of deep mystery it left. Was it connected with wolf's haunting calls? The song of the forests and mountains is freedom. They were free to kill when hungry, free to roam wherever they chose, free to raise and train their young.

Bud told me about another time when he was flying and checking his traps. A huge black wolf was in one of his traps, and, as he walked toward it to get close enough to finish it off with his pistol, the wolf wagged its tail, wiggling low on the ground in a submissive gesture of friendship. He was a wily old boy, but looking friendly and docile didn't fool Bud. Had he gotten close enough to release a foot from the trap, the wolf would have torn him to pieces with its long yellow fangs.

Besides being the cook, and half-a-dozen other things, one of my jobs was to drive the pickup, or station wagon, to meet the clients arriving by scheduled flights at Gulkana Airfield. I also return them when their hunts were over, unless they rented a car in Anchorage and drove out to our pickup point at Grace Lake.

I was supposed to meet two hunters who hadn't given us much information on how to identify them when I met the plane. I did know they were bringing a photographer along to record their hunt. They planned to show their hunts to their clubs or on TV. I arrived early and joined the bunch of outfitters, or their wives, waiting for the plane's arrival. I almost drove away in dismay when three men staggered off the plane, demanding to know what the flight attendant had done with the case of whiskey he had taken from them and promised to return when they got off the plane. One man had cameras around his neck and a camera case in his hand, so they were probably my group. My mind was busy deciding if I should drop them off at a hotel and pick them up after they sobered up, or if I could just leave them at the airport.

I could hear Bud saying when I showed up with them in this condition, "LeNora, you know better. Take them right back to where you got them."

I hadn't noticed the other three who were really our dudes, until they walked up to me and introduced themselves. Oh, that was a relief! Before I drove away, though, another outfitter arrived to pick up his three very drunk clients. He took one look at them, and I could read his mind, but he helped them into his station wagon, loading their whiskey along with the luggage. I heard all about the flight out from Anchorage from our hunters. "Welcome to Alaska." The flight attendants had to handle many of those types. And so did other outfitters.

Some Clients Are Hard to Please

After a few years in the big game guiding business, we thought we had all types of men figured out. We found we still had more to learn when Dale hunted a brown bear with Bud and Cleo. They used Cordova as their headquarters for the mid-October hunt. Dale booked the hunt for himself and a hunting buddy. He hunted with our outfit the previous fall and was a good camper.

On the brown bear hunts, it's necessary to have two paying clients at once. Two justify the expenses of two airplanes. It works better, too, if the two hunters know each other. It works best if they have previously hunted together. Clients had the privilege of bringing a hunting buddy, instead of sharing a camp with someone they haven't met before. Although each hunter had his own guide and hunted from different spike camps, they shared the same base camp.

Before this hunt, Dale wrote he had a hunting partner and he sent deposits for both. Dale wrote that this friend (his name I have long since forgotten, so I'll call him John) was a pleasant person of middle age, but was a lousy shot and couldn't walk very far. Dale wanted us to be sure to alert Cleo that this man couldn't shoot worth a darn and the guide would probably have to help if he were to get a bear. Dale stressed in all three letters about his buddies needs.

They arrived in Cordova on a late fall afternoon, Cleo and John flew out to established camps. It took an hour and a half flying time to the shores of Prince William Sound, just a few miles beyond Katalla. The comfortable tent camp was on a beach noted for brownies.

Dale liked to spend time in the bar, soaking up local atmosphere, and generously buying drinks for anyone who listened to his hunting tales. Bud and Dale stayed in Cordova overnight, and flew to the camp the following morning. Naturally, they didn't get an early start, although Bud was ready to go shortly after daylight.

Cleo and John left the main camp early and set up a spike camp in a different location than did Bud and Dale. Dale was pleased with this arrangement. He said he liked John very much, but didn't want to share the same camp until their hunts were over.

The towering peaks of the Chugach Mountains, dark forests and miles of gigantic glaciers spilling down the mountains, valleys thick with willows and alders made it an alluring hunt. It's a tough country to hunt in, with hillsides above dense, wiry alder thickets where bears were often found.

They were fortunate and had good weather, good if they ignored the infrequent rain showers and gusty winds, a normal occurrence for coastal Alaska.

They climbed high ridges every day, walked the beach, and glassed many areas without locating a bear worth taking. Bud was certain they would locate a brownie, hopefully a trophy, for Dale. In good physical condition, Dale, in his early 40s easily climbed to the ridges. The endless walking the beach wasn't a hardship.

On the fourth day, Bud decided to move their spike camp to a different area. The new spike camp was on a river bar, back from the beach but more sheltered from the prevailing wind and lashing waves. Cleo and John were still in their spike camp, when Bud and Dale flew over, and gave a sign they hadn't had any luck.

The two men were booked for a 10-day hunt, and Dale still had 4 days left. This was back in the days when pilots were allowed to fly, land, and shoot on the same day.

On this day they were flying, but the wind was strong and gusty, tossing the light plane around considerably and Bud was ready to turn back and land, when they spotted a really good, trophy brown bear picking its way along a rocky, ridge. His chocolate brown fur and silver-tipped top hair were rippling in the wind. He was a beautiful sight, alert and dignified looking—a magnificent animal.

Bud flew at a distance while his very excited client looked him over. The plane was bouncing around too violently for photographs.

Bud wouldn't hazard flying any closer to the mountain, and there was no place to land within miles.

Much to his surprise, Dale started coaxing him to fly closer and let him shoot the bear from the airplane.

"You're crazy!" Bud yelled over his shoulder. "Even if I were stupid enough to let you shoot it from the plane, you might only wound it, then we'd never recover it."

Bud got irritated when Dale kept pleading, wanting to shoot the bear from the air. He turned the plane and they bumped through the gusty air back to the spike camp, where Bud made a two-bounce landing. His normally congenial client was pouty and wouldn't come out of his tent for supper.

When he did emerge, later, Bud approached him and said, "Dale, do you know what a Super Cub like mine costs? This one cost far more than the price you're paying for this hunt, and much less than what a new plane would cost today. You and I both know the penalty for shooting a bear, or any big game, from an airplane. There's usually a heavy fine, the guns and aircraft are confiscated, your nonresident hunting privileges are revoked, and my reputation is ruined as a fair chase guide. Yes, there are guides in Alaska who will get game for their clients, by any means possible, and suffer no qualms about doing it illegally, but I'm not one of them. We'll go out again tomorrow, and we'll go out every day until you get your bear, and I won't charge you extra if we go over the 10 days you've paid for."

They flew the next day, hoping to find the bear down on the beach rather than in the hills, but couldn't locate it again. On their way back, Bud spotted a big bear that had just walked onto the beach from a thick willow patch. It had a dark, chocolate brown, heavy coat and appeared nearly as big as the one they spotted on the hillside the day before. He told Dale it was trophy size and Dale said he wanted it.

The only place to land was a short sandy patch. "If you get this bear," Bud told Dale. "You'll have to walk quite a distance to a longer runway. I can't take off here with you and a wet bear hide." Dale readily agreed, eager to go after the bear. It was a 2-mile hike to the bear.

They found good concealment, the strong breeze was in their favor, and they got close enough for Dale's .300 magnum. Dale was a good shot and dropped the unsuspecting bruin with his first shot. It bellowed and thrashed around a bit, but a second shot put a stop to that and it was dead when they walked up to it. Dale was happy with his 9-foot brownie. Bud took photographs of Dale and his bear in a variety of poses.

It was late by the time the bear was minus his fur coat and they hiked back to the plane. It was too dark to fly back to camp. They were both tired, but felt good about the successful day. Bud had plenty of rations along, but only one sleeping bag he always carried in case of an emergency. There was no shortage of dry wood for a warm campfire, and after a dinner from cans warmed by the fire, they gathered a generous pile of wood. Bud let his tired hunter have the sleeping bag and Bud curled up by the fire. The wind had lain, and for mid-October, it wasn't terribly cold.

The next morning, they spent a few backbreaking hours clearing big rocks and a tough willow patch. They cleaned a runway long enough to take off with both the hunter and the green bear hide. It scared the hell out of Bud, though when he used every bit of runway and engine power as he just skinned the boulders too big to move. He wished he'd let Dale walk to that longer patch of beach! But he only had microseconds to think about it as he talked to his faithful air-chariot. "Come on, you can make it. Come on, just another inch or two."

Cleo and John were at the hotel in Cordova, when Bud and Dale arrived. John had collected a 10-foot brownie, by sheer luck, and being at the right place at the right time. The bear had been traveling and they spotted it before he saw them, so they just waited in a willow-filled draw for him to get within range. A light wind was blowing in their direction, so the bear never smelled them.

"Yes, John shot the bear without any help from me. He waited until I told him to shoot. It was a well-placed shot, and I'm sure that was all it needed, but I told him to give it another, just for insurance," Cleo said.

Bud and Cleo offered to take the two men fishing or sightseeing in the 2 days left of their 10-day hunt. Dale declined. He wanted to catch the plane out of Cordova the following day. John would have stayed, but was willing to leave since his buddy wanted to go. Dale wasn't his usual exuberant, wisecracking self, during the evening in the hotel bar. He wrote a check for the balance of the two hunts and they left on the plane the next day.

We were taken completely by surprise when our bank notified us that Dale's check bounced! Bud was so sure he would make it good, which he sent it back with a letter,

"Did your wife deplete the bank account on a shopping spree while you were away hunting? You can pin this one on the wall in your trophy room where your bear will hang, and send me a check I can cash. I need it!" We never did collect.

Two years later, Bud was in Wyoming on an exchange hunt for antelope, with an outfitter who hunted with us. He told Bud that Dale hunted on his ranch, the year after the brown bear hunt. Dale told about seeing a monstrous bear, one that would have scored high in the Boone and Crockett Book of Records. "Conkle wouldn't land anywhere within miles, the bear would be long gone by the time they walked back to it." He said. "I saw some areas that were close by, plenty long and smooth enough to land the Super Cub." The guys knew Dale wasn't a pilot and the bear he was describing sounded exaggerated, but he made an interesting story out of it. John, the man who made the hunt with Dale, told the outfitter, "Dale stopped payment on his check because of a damaged ego." Before they came with us to hunt the brown bear, some big-money bets were made on who would come back with the biggest bear.

This wasn't the only time we had a client stop payment on a check for the balance of his hunt. Bud had to shoot a wounded polar bear once, because the dude put two shots into it. It only colored its white rump with red blood and put it into high gear, heading for open water. As backup guide, it was Bud's duty to kill a wounded bear, and he didn't shoot until he saw the hunter fiddling with his rifle. Bud wasn't about to let that 9-footer swim the open lead and get some place where they couldn't get to it. The guy bragged about being a good marksman, killing all of his trophy game with only one shot, and at ridiculous distances. We did collect from this guy, after months of hassle and, finally, threats to sue him for the balance, and our expenses to recover it.

Bud often wondered how the client would have reacted had his polar bear sank before his guide rescued it. He and Cleo, on two different hunts, almost found out.

They had a young fellow, from a Midwestern state, on a polar bear hunt. I'll call him Larry. The ice, out of Barrow, was rough, and broken up for miles that year. There was no new snow and the days were overcast and hazy. Unless there is bright sunlight to make shadows, a bear is almost impossible to track. They saw average sized bears, 6 or 7 feet, but had to pass on landing for photos, because they couldn't locate any place smooth enough. Flying low and close often disturbed the bears from what they were doing at the time which would have made good movies.

With Larry in Bud's plane one day, they did a lot of circling, while Larry was taking movies, hopefully successful prints. They spotted a big sow asleep, close to a pressure ridge, on very rough ice. She was stretched out on her belly, with her head resting on one front paw and both hind legs splayed flat behind her. Sleeping against her was a cub with its head resting on the back of another cub. Both cubs were almost as large as Mama. On the first pass, without flying too low, Bud opened the side window, and Larry took pictures. One cub raised its head to look, but when Mama didn't stir, he settled back down. On the second pass, Bud dropped to near 100 feet. Mama raised her head, as they flew over, and on the third pass, she sat up and watched them. Both cubs were scratching their way up the snowy pressure ridge to get a better look. On the last flight over, all three were high tailing it to more peaceful places.

Later, while flying 100 miles north of Barrow, Cleo informed Bud he was landing on the smooth ice pan just ahead. "64 Delta. Larry is getting airsick. I'm going to land. We need to work out the P Factor. You know, the duration of the flight equals the capacity of the bladder!"

They had been following tracks for the past hour, losing them on rough ice, then picking them up again, but never deciding the bear's size. Bud circled far out and picked up the tracks again, obviously those of a big bear.

"73 Zulu," he called to Cleo. "Get in the air quick. Spotted a keeper. He's heading for a pressure ridge. There's an ice floe big enough for both planes not far beyond the ridge."

"64 Delta. Roger. We'll be right there."

After landing both planes, they had a half-mile to work their way across rough ice. The bear was out of sight, on the opposite side of the pressure ridge. Cleo peeked over, first, to locate the bear, then maneuvered Larry to the top of the slippery 10-foot-high jumble of ice and into shooting position. The big old boar was walking slowly along the edge of a narrow lead on rubbery ice. He was about 250 yards away and hadn't paid any attention to the landing planes. His head was down, looking away from the men and in the direction of the open water.

They watched for a minute, to see what the bear would do, since it was very close to the open water. When it turned and sauntered back off the rubbery ice, Cleo said, "Take him!"

Larry's first shot was a bit too low for a vital spot and red blood colored the front shoulder. The bear went around and around, biting at the spot. Larry carefully timed his second shot and caught the bear on its third circle. The bear lunged for the open water, either to dive in or jump across. Its heavy hindquarters fell through the thin ice on the far side. The ice kept breaking under its weight, so it turned and climbed out on their side. Larry shot again, and the bear died, sliding back toward the water as the ice started giving away under it.

Cleo slid down from the ice ridge and ran out to the bear on the thin, cracking ice. Larry and Bud could see the ice flexing, ready to break through at any minute under the combined weight of Cleo and the big bear. Cleo already had a safety rope tied around his waist. He crawled out to the bear dragging another rope. The grinding and crunching and the unsteady ice kept Cleo tensely ready to move back in a hurry.

Bud was taking movies of the action, initially, but handed Larry the movie camera when they slid to the foot of the pressure ridge. Bud grabbed the end of the safety rope tied to his partner and held it taut, until Cleo had the other rope secured to the bear's front paw. He eased backwards off the rubbery, noisy ice. Cleo was taking a big chance, crawling those 200 yards to rescue the bear. Bud didn't want to lose Cleo, the bear, or the movies. He especially didn't want to lose his partner and friend, then have to fly back to Barrow and explain.

With the three of them pulling, it was marginal whether the bear was going to slide back off the swaying ice. There's not much purchase on ice, and although their mukluks weren't slick, they had no place to brace for the pull. Two of them might have held the big trophy where he was, while one went to the planes to get a hatchet, to cut footholds, but if the ice gave way, they would lose it for sure. With brute strength, they kept gaining, inch by inch, until they had Cleo and the bear on solid ice. Skinning a wet bear takes longer than otherwise, but its not too bad a job without a chilling wind.

Larry was one happy hunter when he left for home, with stories to tell of his hunt and the 9-foot 3-inch polar bear hide ready to be made into a rug-mount.

Bud took movies on another hunt, a few years earlier, of Cleo creeping out on thin ice to put a rope on a bear while the ice crackled and popped. Moving cautiously, Bud would jump back and wait a bit to see what the ice was going to do, then ease forward again. Even the expression on his face was readable in the film. On that hunt, they saved the bear and got good action movies.

Cleo isn't noted for talking much, or embellishing stories, like some pilot/guides do when they have a gullible audience, but he has had as many experiences as any of the pilot/guides around here, and a lot more than some. He surely was talking the night they got back from the hunt on that rubbery ice. They gathered in the lobby with other pilot/guides telling of their day's happenings.

"I was scared and I stayed scared!" he said. "Even with a rope tied on me, and Conkle set to pull me out, if I went in that icy water, I was still scared." His listeners nodded their heads or raised their glasses. His story brought back memories of their own experiences. "I didn't want our boy to go back home without a bear, and blame us for his loss."

We had a client at Wolf Lake get his hunt off to a shaky start. Colin met him at Grace Lake where he and a hunting buddy were waiting. The air was turbulent with gusty winds, but Colin assured the men it was nothing to worry about. Harry said he would go first.

"I want the flight over with." He said. "I've never flown in such a small airplane. And I do have a frail stomach."

Sudden gusts were lifting and dropping the Cub at frequent intervals and Colin said, "I could feel him hanging onto the back of my seat for dear life. I know he had his teeth clinched the whole way." Colin was too busy to explain his landing techniques on Wolf Lake. He was concentrating on judging the distance to the ground below the plane and the distance between the trees on both sides of the long wingspan. He crabbed the plane low across the cleared hill and aimed for the shortest distance possible to set the floats near shoreline. A shaken passenger was happy to exit and put both feet on the shore. A generous slug of brandy and the rest of the day in camp settled his nerves.

"I trust you as a pilot, Colin, but I think I'll wait for a calm day to fly back out of here. Or I'll let Jim take the car back to Anchorage and I'll ride out with the boys when they take the horses out after the hunts are over." He was serious.

Those two were on the last hunts of the season at Wolf Lake. They had their game, the weather was calm, it was a beautiful day to fly, and Bud was the pilot.

Graduation Present

Few young men are lucky enough to be given an Alaska big-game hunt as a high school graduation present. How many big game hunters are lucky enough to collect three trophy-class animals on a 10-day hunt and still pass on a fourth trophy, choosing to go fishing instead? Rusty Baker, from Louisiana, was just that lucky!

Colin was the chosen assistant guide for Rusty, and, as expected, these two young men had a great time. They enjoyed the beauty of the mountains and balmy weather, the full 10 days of their hunt.

Rusty collected excellent trophies of Dall sheep, moose, and caribou. He managed to get all three animals quite handily, in spite of a foggy rifle scope. On his first big game hunt, Rusty was the only hunter in any of our camps (excluding polar bear hunters) who went home with photographs of his trophies alive during the action and after.

Colin and Rusty ate an early breakfast, left their first spike camp, and climbed into the Nutzotin Range above Wolf Lake. They stopped to glass the peaks looking for big rams. The sheep seem to know when it was hunting season. They moved to the high meadows where they weren't likely to be seen from below. Normally, there are smaller rams stationed in key positions as look outs. Wild sheep are noted for keen eye sight (said to compare to a 9-power binocular).

Late in the afternoon, they spotted two rams laying close together, contentedly chewing cud. Not alerted by a smaller ram at a lower level, they were facing away from both hunters. Colin whispered to Rusty as he pointed out the larger of the two trophy-size rams. "Be ready to shoot. Let's get closer." Rusty managed to snap a couple of photos while they observed the sheep. They were downwind of the rams. At any minute, either of the rams could be alerted to their presence by a random wind gust and bolt for higher ground. The big ram just decided to get up, and suddenly it was on its feet.

"Take him," Colin said. The rifle spoke, and the ram pitched for-

Rusty Baker with his trophy Dall ram.

ward. It didn't stay down and followed the other two rams already disappearing. When the ram started to get up, Colin waited, expecting Rusty to shoot again. When he turned from the binoculars to look at Rusty, the boy was frantically wiping both ends of his scope. It had fogged on the inside the lens. He couldn't see the moving ram. Colin saw the ram's front leg was badly broken, and he was scrambling on the other three. Colin threw down his binoculars and ran uphill to head it off. The ram, seeing Colin, ran back downhill. Colin changed direction and remained in hot pursuit. The ram was beginning to outdistance him and Colin yelled, "Bring the rifle, Rusty." Rusty said later. It looked like Colin had the show under control, so I just sat there watching."

Colin chased the ram down the mountain and after a time, started gaining. It quickly climbed a ridge and hid in some willows. Colin didn't see it come out the other side, so he sat waiting for the ram to stiffen. Colin kept looking for Rusty with the backup rifle. Meanwhile, Rusty was thinking Colin would chase the ram back out into the open, so he sat, ready to shoot with Colin's rifle.

The ram finally started from the willow thicket. It bolted out of sight again when it saw Colin. This time it got tangled in some thick brush. Colin went in after it. He grabbed it by the horns and they had quite a wrestling match, thrashing about in the willows. The ram, weak from the loss of blood and the shock of injury, eventually lost. Colin kept yelling, "Rusty, help. Bring the rifle. Bring the pistol from

Colin and Rusty Baker with his moose where it fell.

my pack. Do something." When he finally put it down, he stood and panted and wiped the sweat from his face. "All the time I had hold of its horns I tried to hold his head at a disadvantage. I was talking to it explaining how I admired its fight to stay alive."

Colin, laughed at Rusty's reaction when he saw him holding that wild ram by its horns. He laughed again when he told us the whole story. "Not exactly the smartest way to collect a wild sheep, but it worked," Bud commented through guffaws.

Bud sparred with a story about being a young hunter in New Mexico. "I grabbed hold of the antlers of a deer that I thought was dead. It suddenly came to life and fought frantically. I wrestled that trophy sized buck until we fell into a ravine. It's a wonder I came out alive. I didn't get the trophy either 'cause it came out alive too."

Colin took a turn and told about George Benson and his first hunt of the season. "I was George's guide. We spotted a big ram and eased up a talus slope, across a rough ridge and finally got within shooting range. The ram didn't know we were that near and was soaking up the warm sunshine. We didn't see any other rams. George took careful aim and squeezed off a shot.

"We heard the bullet hit with a whack. But the ram just stood there, like it hadn't felt a thing. 'Shoot him again George,' I said, 'I don't see any blood. Bust him again or he'll be long gone.' George just stood there, confident the ram wasn't going anywhere.

"I couldn't believe my eyes. The ram just continued to stand there. Then all at once, he just toppled over. It never made another move, dead as a door nail. George shot it in the heart and was just waiting for it to fall down."

Rusty Baker and guide with Rusty's three trophies.

"I always shoot my game in the heart," he calmly told Colin. Everyone laughed wildly. "When we butchered it," Colin finished. "We found the bullet lodged in the heart."

Rusty was a very happy young man in camp that evening, and gladly told the whole story again.

Rusty's scope was brand new and shouldn't have misted up. This was the first (and only) hunt it was taken on. The company that sold it to him, replaced it after he got home. He used Bud's .243 Browning on his moose hunt. Two well-placed shots with the lighter rifle brought it down, but not to stay. They agreed, beforehand, that, rather than let this trophy bull get away wounded in the thick willows Colin would shoot. The bull jumped to its feet and went crashing through the willows, heading for a safer place. Colin used the .375 Winchester and dropped him for the final count.

On the next hunt, the two young men were dropped onto a small lake, set camp, and hunted the next day. The lake is at the 5,000-foot level of a long, open valley. Low rolling hills of the Nutzotin Range surround it on all sides. It's located several miles on the Alaska side of the Alaska/Canada border, along the eastern slopes.

While they ate a leisurely lunch of moose tongue sandwiches, they glassed the wilderness valley radiating under clear, blue skies and clean, crisp air. Colin turned and saw a big bull caribou. Its white chest ruff glistened as it shook its head. It had just emerged from beyond a low hill and was trotting along in the funny side gait peculiar to caribou. That side gait can cover long distances on the muskeg and uneven tundra. The bull was heading directly alongside the men

Guide Colin and Rusty Baker glassing for caribou.

sitting in the sun. It was 600 feet below them.

Rusty took his time in getting the shooting range right. Until the decisive moment, both had cameras clicking and whirring. Colin continued taking pictures while Rusty settled himself in a comfortable shooting position. At just the right moment, the bull slowed his stride to nibble on lichen. Perfect cooperation—timed just like in the movies! Colin took pictures and Rusty dropped the trophy bull caribou with a bullet through the heart. It never knew what hit him. He was collected clean and died with dignity.

Later, Rusty told Colin, "No. I don't want to get a grizzly on this hunt. I'm more than satisfied with the trophies I have already. Besides, I need an excuse to come back another year to hunt. Let's just go fishing!" Colin was just finishing the fleshing and salting of the caribou cape back in base camp. He suggested flying Rusty out to the highway to purchase a bear tag. They still had 2 days left on the hunt and Rusty could have stayed a day or two longer if they needed the time to get a bear. But, going fishing suited Colin just fine! Rusty kept him plenty busy carrying meat out of the field, and fleshing three capes, salting and preparing them for shipment to a taxidermist. Relaxing with a fishing pole sounded wonderful!

When Rusty paid the balance for his hunt, he took out $3,000 in $100 and $500 bills. He had carried his wallet and all that cash with him during his entire hunt. Bud expressed surprise that he hadn't carefully stowed it in his tent at base camp, or left it at The Ranch. We were more than thankful he hadn't lost the wallet.

Hal Dixson, of San Luis Obispo, California, was another 18-year-old who was given an Alaska Dall sheep hunt for high school graduation. His father and mother, Harlan and Doris Dixson, had booked a hunt for Dall rams at the same time. The Dixsons had hunted with us in August 1970, two years prior to Rusty Baker's hunt.

Hal, and his mother, Doris, hunted from different spike camps with different guides. They came back to base camp on the same day and both had scored rams with identically-sized horns, 38-1/4 inches! Then it was Harlan's turn to hunt. Bud was Harlan's guide, as he had been for Doris. They were a good-natured, fun family. They hunted as a three-some often, with Doris and Hal unfailingly collecting larger trophies than Harlan's, no matter which species they hunted! There was a lot of good-natured teasing between them about superior hunting skills.

Harlan calmly passed on a 40-inch ram their first day on the mountain. Bud had a hard time figuring that one out. "You'll not likely get a chance at a bigger one, Harlan. This one is bigger than both Doris and Hal collected. They'll never quit razzing you, if you bring in a smaller one." Bud told him.

"Oh, that's okay. They'll tease me about something, anyway. I just don't want to shoot a sheep the first day of my hunt. It would cool the high level of anticipation built up inside me ever since we decided on this hunt. I'm willing to take the chance." Harlan grinned. "I want the excitement of looking over more rams. I'm used to their sporting.

Four days later, the men climbed a high peak to glass a distant meadow. Bud saw a clearly trophy-size ram, quite a distance below them. He couldn't figure out where that ram had been while they had made the all-day climb directly through his area. It rapidly became Harlan's "Low-Level" ram, as Bud called it, and the nearly symmetrical horns measured a whopping 42 inches!

"Something gives me a distinct feeling that my dad is more than happy to share my sheep hunt," Hal said when his father proudly displayed the set of horns.

Maybe we can call Danny's Alaska hunt a graduation present, when Danny's uncle, Wilbur Conway (not their real names) took his nephew on a 21-day hunt. At the time, our guide service was at Tanada Lake Lodge, on the north side of the Wrangell Mountains. He graduated from high school that spring and was heading for college near the end of September. We adjusted our schedules to fit his. He wanted to hunt moose and grizzly, after getting a Dall sheep. The guides, assistant guides, outfitter, and outfitter's wife were all very grateful that Danny was the congenial person he was. But we all agreed that Uncle Wilbur was a real "pain in the backside." After 3 days into the hunt, we were glad his hunt was 21 days instead of the scheduled 30-day hunt. Most of the time we wished he hadn't come at all.

Conway had booked the 21-day mixed-bag hunt for himself and Danny, a year in advance. His correspondence contained change after change in the length and specifics of the hunt. Finally, after many concessions, he was satisfied. We were aware that Conway had retired from an extremely lucrative business. He was wealthy. He generally made two big game hunts a year, and had made two shikari in India and four safaris in Africa. This was to be his first hunt in Alaska. We were a struggling big game outfitter, trying to keep the bills paid, airplanes repaired, and buy new operating equipment. This man sounded like an ideal client. We would do our very best to accommodate him, and, hopefully, he'd be pleased with our services, and become what all outfitters look forward to, a return client who recommended our services to others.

"Oh, I knew I had a tiger by the tail," Bud whispered as we watched an overdressed, gray-haired man descend from the twice-weekly Anchorage bus. Immediately, and before introducing himself and his nephew to us, he started counting his expensive pieces of luggage with the point of his elaborately-carved cane. He made it very plain, during introductions that he was to be called Mr. Conway. (We all called him Uncle Wilbur behind his stiff back. There were other names frequently muttered under our breath that won't be repeated here.) Bud was in a hurry to put their luggage (two trunks, two large suitcases, four gun-cases and assorted smaller bags) loaded into the station wagon and get underway. It was a long drive from the bus stop to Long Lake on the Nabesna Road. The Super Cub on floats was tethered there, ready to fly to Tanada Lake.

Conway stated, in the written correspondence, that under absolutely no circumstances would he fly in a small airplane. The Super Cub was our only means of transportation to our hunting headquarters. We arranged with another guide/outfitter, Don DeHart, with his home-base at Slana, to transport Conway from Long Lake to Tanada Lake on horseback. When they arrived at the Hart D Ranch, Conway realized that Danny and most of their luggage would be flown in, while he rode horseback. "How long does it take to fly in?" He asked.

"Half hour," Bud replied.

"How long does it take to ride in on horseback?"

"Well, Loading and unloading horses from trucks, and riding up there, should take us 8 to 10 hours."

"My luggage goes with me. I never let it out of my sight." Uncle Wilbur screamed in tones we were used to. "If my luggage flies to Tanada Lake, then so do I!"

Bud looked at DeHart apologetically. Elaborate arrangements, along with adjusting two different outfitters schedules, had been made. DeHart just shrugged his shoulders and grinned as if to say "He's all yours!"

Bud convinced Uncle Wilbur to leave the two steamer trunks at the Hart D, because it was impossible to put them into the Cub. Then they drove on to Long Lake. Bud flew Danny in first, then flew back and picked up Uncle Wilbur. "Once Uncle Wilbur was in the plane and airborne, he seemed to enjoy the whole trip." Bud told me later.

We met them at the dock. Uncle Wilbur made a very undignified exit from the Cub. When he looked up and spotted Danny snapping pictures as fast as he could, he said, shaking his fist, "Danny, no pictures. You'll just have to remember this hunt, I am 65 and have traveled all over the world many times. "And I DO NOT FLY."

By early evening, we had Uncle Wilbur and Danny settled into the roomy guest cabin. Shortly, he marched into the kitchen and politely asked for the location of the bathroom. I pointed to the little outhouse up the trail a way. He marched off but was soon back barking at me, "Where is the bathroom." It was all I could do to keep from laughing when I thought of all the traveling he said he had done.

"Oh, we don't have modern bathroom facilities here. This is a remote Alaska hunting lodge," I explained.

"I believe I was told this lodge was modern. Well, I can endure if you will furnish me with adequate washing facilities."

" A bucket of water, tea kettle, wash basin, soap, and towel has already been supplied with the cabin." I told him. "But after dinner, I will put a large kettle of water on the wood range to heat."

At the supper table, Uncle Wilbur seemed to enjoy, but he disdained to join the easygoing conversation. When he was finished eating, he said, "Come now, Danny" and made a stately exit to the cabin. I put water in a large, white enamel tub and put it on the stove to heat.

"Now just how am I going to carry this tub of hot water to the cabin?" I laughed. "I suppose I should explain how to take a sponge bath too." The entire crew (guides, packers, and another hunter—Fred Packer) laughed hilariously when the door opened and Uncle Wilbur, the target of our merriment, stepped in and coldly requested a tea kettle of hot water! I immediately lost my courage for the ordeal ahead, and Fred volunteered to take Uncle Wilbur his bath water. He was soon back in the lodge and said, I informed him it shouldn't take a college education to know how to take a bath in a wash basin. "We all watched the guest cabin closely. Every minute or so, the door opened and a bit of water was tossed into the yard. This went on until apparently all of the water was gone. Just how did Uncle Wilbur take his bath?

A registered guide and assistant guide set up a very comfortable spike camp the day before Danny and Uncle Wilbur arrived. Jim stayed at the camp, 8 miles up Goat Creek, a long valley with sheep hills on both sides. Johnny, the assistant guide to Danny, brought the Weasel (a tracked vehicle, slow and cumbersome) back to the base camp at Tanada Lake Lodge. They left for the spike camp after breakfast the next morning.

Johnny wasn't much older than Danny and the two boys decided they would prefer to hike to the camp, rather than ride on the slow-moving Weasel. Halfway up the valley, the Weasel broke down. Bud walked back to the lodge for tools and repair parts. After starting repairs, he discovered he would have to fly all the way to our homestead to get another carburetor. He was concerned Uncle Wilbur would be upset over the delay.

"I have a book to read." He pointed out nonchalantly. "I will sit right here in the sun until you return."

Two frantic hours later, Bud was back at the Weasel. He found Uncle Wilbur contentedly reading The Tigers of Africa, a book lent to him that morning. After repairing the Weasel and well on their way, an exceptional bull moose ran across the trail ahead of them.

"Look at the horns on that old boy," Bud called to his passenger who was still reading as they lumbered along.

"Oh, yes, horns. How very nice. Well, a bull moose should have horns," and Uncle Wilbur went back to reading the book after just a quick glance. He never did appear to take an interest in the wonderful, wild scenery that surrounded him.

The two boys had climbed a mountain to hunt for sheep after they had arrived at the spike camp. It seemed like the normal thing for them to do, since that was why they were there. Uncle Wilbur was upset, though, when he got there.

"Why didn't they wait for my arrival?" He whined. "After all, I am the experienced hunter. I am here to teach Danny to hunt." Bud had to do a lot of talking to convince Uncle Wilbur that Danny would be completely safe with Johnny and might even return with a trophy ram that very evening. Then Bud returned to the lodge, leaving Jim, the registered guide, in charge, comfortable that he could handle any crisis.

The next day, Johnny hiked in to the lodge, a very dejected assistant guide. " He fired me." Johnny complained. "And to add to the insult, he sent a note with me asking you for a more competent guide—immediately." He threw his hat to the ground.

"It was almost dark that first night when they got back to the spike camp. Uncle Wilbur said he paced, called, and whistled for hours. He just knew we were lost. He had brought a whistle along, a relic of his safaris, blew it every 20 minutes 'to guide the lost boys home.' He also insisted Jim keep a bonfire blazing." He shook his head. "We couldn't convince him that firewood was precious that far above the tree line. I kept telling him, sometimes a sheep is shot late in the afternoon, and by the time its caped and packed off a mountain, it could be very late when the boys returned. We made plans to hunt a different area the next morning, but then he fired me.

"Jim told me, as I was leaving camp, 'You're lucky Johnny, wish he'd fire me, too.'"

Danny said how embarrassed he was and sorry because they had been having a great time. Later, Jim said, "Those boys were having fun together, laughing and teasing. It irritated me the old man was so bad. I think he was jealous Danny wasn't spending all his time with him."

Tensions eased after Herb was sent to guide in Johnny's place. Herb was older, quiet-mannered and extremely efficient. He knew, somehow, how to handle Uncle Wilbur. And Uncle Wilbur didn't blow the whistle even once with Herb in camp. It's a good thing, too. Herb said he may have calmly shoved it down his throat. Bud had other ideas of where it would fit if it was whistled at him!

The rest of the time in sheep camp was uneventful. Herb stayed faithfully within sight and call of his client, and Jim became Danny's guide. The mystery of the bath continued, even in the spike camps. The ritual was the same; a bucket of hot water, and a bucket of cold water, was carried to his tent, after a minute or two, the tent flap opened and a bit of water was tossed out until all of the water was used.

Fred Packer's hunt was soon over and we were all sorry to see him go. He was not only a pleasant person to have around a camp-fire, or the lodge, but had been a real help in keeping Uncle Wilbur out of our hair by taking him fishing and such. All of Fred's luggage and trophies were loaded in the plane when one of the boys hiked in from Uncle Wilbur's spike camp with an urgent note. Bud saw him coming, so he waited, expecting some kind of trouble.

The note, written in Uncle Wilbur's neat hand, had a precise list of groceries he wanted sent to the spike camp and included a demand for us to provide him with a bath towel "just like the one Fred Packer lent me." Every order from spike camp, and they were frequent, had requested a bath towel. And I had included a different towel in each shipment, until our supply was embarrassingly depleted. Now we understood.

"Fred, come to our rescue, please!" I pleaded. "Give me the bath towel that you lent to Uncle Wilbur when he was here. I'll send it back to you when the hunt is over."

Fred grinned and said he wasn't sure in which bag the towel was packed. Bud unpacked the whole Cub as Fred checked each bag. It was in the last bag, of course! He dug it out and sheepishly admitted that he would have left it for the lodge, except it was printed with the name of a hotel. He didn't want us thinking he made a regular practice of stealing hotel towels! And, he surely didn't want it sent back to him! A simple, hotel-style, thick terry-cloth bath-mat was all that Uncle Wilbur wanted!

That bath mat and Uncle Wilbur's note are put away in a drawer in our trophy room as souvenirs. It reminds us of another crisis smoothed over, and it reminds us of Fred's embarrassment at being caught with a mat with a hotel name stamped on it! How does that old adage go? "Your sins will find you out." Fred's virtues were many, his faults few!

When the Goat Creek spike camp returned to Tanada Lake Lodge, Danny had a nearly perfect trophy ram and Conway had a trophy ram which Herb had carefully skinned for a life-size mount.

It was our policy, when moving the camps from one area to another, to bring the clients back to the lodge at Tanada Lake for fishing or relaxing, while Bud flew the guides and camp supplies to the next spike camp. The length of time the hunters spent at the main lodge depended on the distance of the camps from the lake, and the game to be hunted.

Uncle Wilbur told us that he had already collected many trophies for himself and that he wanted Danny to get most of the trophies on this hunt. He would hunt only when Danny already had his. Bud was hoping Uncle Wilbur would stay behind at our comfortable lodge while he took Danny on a moose hunt, but Uncle Wilbur wasn't about to be left behind. He insisted that he and Herb go along to supervise. He wanted to make sure that Danny collected a good trophy moose, one with very large horns! And to assure Danny of collecting a "specimen" as he termed it, he gave absolute orders about which rifles were to be used (he was obviously used to giving orders, and having them immediately obeyed.) Bud and Herb were not used to taking them. Uncle Wilbur insisted that Danny use one of the larger rifles for the moose hunt.

So be it. Herb and Uncle Wilbur went along. But since Bud could only fly one passenger at a time in the Cub, and Uncle Wilbur had approved the suggestion that Danny hunt with Bud, Herb took him across the tundra to a hill where they could glass the surrounding area for moose. If the opportunity presented itself, he could collect a "specimen" while Bud was busy flying.

During his flights to and from the spike camp, Bud saw a good sized moose near a small lake. The lake was too small for Bud to take off with a load. When it came time to fly back to camp, Danny volunteered to hike to a larger lake a mile away where they landed with no difficulty and tied the plane to a tree. Then they spent most of the day stalking the big bull. He finally got comfortably settled for an afternoon nap at the edge of the timber. He was on a ridge facing a direction that made the easiest approach for the hunters.

By the time they were viewing the rack with binoculars and rifle sights, Bud and Danny felt they had earned this trophy in a fair chase. "Aim for the heart and hold steady." Bud whispered. Danny held his breath, aimed carefully, and squeezed the trigger. Nothing happened. He tried again then checked the safety lock. It was ready to go. Three times he tried, with no fire. Slowly, he eased the rifle back for Bud's inspection who couldn't find anything wrong either.

Then the gentle breeze changed and the drowsy bull caught their scent. He was suddenly standing, momentarily exposing himself as a perfect target. He turned and faded into the timbered background and was gone.

Danny wasn't disappointed in his unsuccessful moose hunt. He just said, "I sure wish I'd used my own judgment and carried my 30.06. I'm used to it and it's never failed me."

Bud thought, "Whew. I sure got out of a lot of hard work. Once that moose went down, the fun would have been all over."

Back at the little pothole lake, the wind had changed and wasn't good for even an empty take off. Bud said, "Hold onto that handle, Danny and give me a good start. When I signal, let go." Danny misunderstood the instructions. He was a husky lad and had wrestled in the top bracket of his high school team. He held on until the Cub pulled him into the water and was on the step, then he turned it loose and swam back to shore. Bud, not realizing why the plane was so sluggish, poured the coals to it and literally shot into the air.

Bud flew right over to the larger lake, to wait for Danny, sure he would head in that direction. After waiting for quite a while, he took off to have a look. Danny was nowhere in sight. The country had low hills between the two lakes but was sparsely timbered. Bud realized Danny couldn't be traveling in the right direction. He swung the Cub in a wide circle, looking farther and farther afield, and finally spotted Danny going the wrong direction. The boy was swinging something white, around and round over his head. It didn't appear to be a signal, so Bud thought it was meant to fend off mosquitos.

Bud buzzed Danny a couple of times, until Danny understood that he was to walk in the direction Bud was flying. When they were both back in camp, Bud and Danny laughed about his swim in the pot hole lake.

Bud shook his head in amazement, "Danny, all I can say is I'm darn sure glad you can swim."

"Me too. But let's not even mention it to Uncle Wilbur."

Nothing upset Bud more than to see rifles neglected. He found corrosion and rust in Danny's rifle. The sensitive trigger parts were worthless and unsafe. When they'd first arrived at the lodge, Uncle Wilbur stated in no uncertain terms that his white hunter always sighted in his rifles for him. We believed a hunter sights in his own rifle to suit his style of shooting. There was plenty of ammunition, so Bud and the boys had a field day playing at shooting elephants! After they sighted in the rifles, and carefully cleaned and oiled them, Uncle Wilbur ignored Bud's advice to leave them hanging on the wall rack. He stowed them back in their sheepskin-lined gun cases. The resident moisture, unable to escape the gun cases, formed rust on all of the rifles!

The next morning, Bud, still quite cranky, informed the camp that there was no point in staying to hunt moose or caribou with rifles that wouldn't fire, so he might as well move them all back to base camp. Uncle Wilbur very formally informed Bud that he should fly to the lodge and bring back Danny's 30.06. Uncle Wilbur didn't care about himself getting any "specimens," but he wanted Danny to collect at least a caribou and bear, if not a moose. Bud felt kind of sorry for the boy and agreed. He retrieved the other rifles and the cleaning equipment and Danny collected a really nice grizzly trophy after all.

Back at Tanada Lake when Danny and Uncle Wilbur were getting ready to leave the next morning, Uncle Wilbur gave the usual order, "Come Danny, we must go to our cabin now." Danny lingered, preferring to stay with the congenial group around the lodge's large table, telling hunting stories.

He said he wanted to apologize for his uncle's behavior. "I was elated to come to Alaska for a big game hunt and I enjoyed myself in spite of everything. After all, he did pay for everything."

We readily understood and told him not to feel bad on our account. He had done the best he could under the circumstances and had made himself well liked by all.

Danny's mother was Conway's only sister; he had never married nor had children of his own, so he was terribly over protective. He reminded us of an old mother hen with just one chick. He appeared to want to be a hero to his favorite nephew. We were all willing to make bets that Danny never went on another hunt with Uncle Wilbur, even if the offer was for a safari in Africa.

It was a trying 3 weeks, but we all survived; living to laugh about it and tell the tale many times again, especially every time we run across Fred's hotel bath mat!

These men had more to fear from the Sierra Club, the Friends of Animals Club, and similar environmentalist groups, than from all of Alaska's bears, wolves, or natural elements.

Are We Having Fun?

Time has dimmed my memory of the name of a resident hunter Bud had taken out on a polar bear hunt. The bear, I remember quite well. Bud had the hunter in his plane, and he and his wing mate had cruised above the ice pack most of the day. They were heading back to Barrow when they spotted a sow and her cubs sleeping on an open ice pan. They were the first bears they had seen all day. The sun was perfect for good movies and Bud circled low.

Mama was stretched out on her belly, with both of her hind legs spread flat behind her. The three cubs were snuggled so close to her that it looked like there were only two cubs. Only two black noses could be seen, since they had their heads laying on Mama's back. They were big cubs, almost as big as the sow. The third cub suddenly appeared in the middle of the cuddled family. All three sat up to look around and shake their heads, but when Mama went on sleeping, apparently unconcerned, one cub lay back down to finish his nap. The other two sat on their haunches, and studied the sky. They seemed a bit bewildered by the buzzing of our planes. They looked at Mama, then back skyward. Watching them from above, the men wondered if the cubs had any way to tell Mama about the intruders. Bud circled them twice, then left.

They had flown for only 10 minutes beyond those bears, when Cleo called on the radio, "64 Delta, a bear just came from behind the pressure ridge to the right of us. Let's go take a look. It looks like a good one from here."

They flew a bit closer, but stayed far enough away so as not to alert the bear, probably a 7-footer. The pilot/guides followed their usual procedure, landing on an ideal and handy ice pan. It was large enough for both Super Cubs and far enough from the bear to not disturb it. By the time they got out of the planes, the bear had sauntered about 20 feet from the base of the pressure ridge, then lay down. An erratic, wandering wind favored the guides and hunter, but the March sun was low on the horizon. They knew, if they didn't hurry, they'd be flying back to Barrow in the dark.

The bear, alerted to their presence got to his feet and stood broadside to the men. The .375 slug hit with a whoomp. The bear circled to bite at the spot where red blood colored her white coat, then fell without moving again. What startled the three men was when a second bear, about the same size as the first, came tearing out from under an overhang at the back of the pressure ridge. It had apparently been sleeping under there, out of sight in the shadows. Instead of fleeing the scene, this bear ran directly to the downed bear. It started licking the first bear, pawing it almost frantically. The men thought it was trying to get the dead bear to stand up. It would smell the blood and start licking it, walk a short distance away, bark, then run back.

They sure didn't want to collect two bears, but were faced with a situation that had to be settled soon, or they would be spending the night on the pack ice. They had to convince the second bear to leave, so they could get the dead one skinned and be on their way. Bud shot over the bear, trying to chase it away, but it held its ground and bellowed. The men stood up, yelling and waving their arms. The bear would make a brief charge in their direction, then go back to try to rouse the one down.

This little drama went on for nearly half an hour. Bud and Cleo were becoming desperate to get started on the skinning job in the little daylight that was left, hopefully without having to kill the second bear. Finally, with two high-powered rifles giving him cover, Bud walked slowly toward the bears. He was talking in a soothing tone of voice, and it appeared that the bear was calming down a bit and trying to decide if it should leave. It walked away from Bud, then stopped and looked back.

Bud moved forward slowly and it would go a little farther away. It finally stayed far enough away for the three men to feel comfortable. The pilot/guides got busy with the skinning, while the hunter, with a ready rifle, stood watching the second bear. The bear watched them, for a time, shook thoroughly, then ambled off into the evening. It swung its head side to side and let out a bellow then a bark until it was out of sight. The downed bear was a dry sow and the second one was probably a boar.

Bud said that was the fastest skinning job he had ever been involved in. When they were airborne again, they could see the second bear, off in the distance, loping away to new destinies.

Lights of Barrow looked especially inviting in the deepening twilight, and they glided, without difficulty, into their tie downs in the semidarkness. "After all," Bud bragged, "Our planes have landed in this place so often, they could find their own way in the dark to their tie-downs."

The welcoming committee of pilot/guides, were on the verge of searching for them, come daylight, and all the drinking done. Bud and Cleo alternately called on their radios to anyone listening that they would be in late or would be camping on the ice—no one heard.

Everyone has a different reaction of the following bear attack that happened in one of Bill Etchells' camps on a fall hunt.

Bill built a good log cabin for the cook house, and included a partitioned room for the cook. He hired the wife of one of his guides that year to cook for the hunters and crew. This young lady wasn't noted for bravery out in the wilderness, especially in grizzly country. But since she would have a snug cabin to live in while 'way out there,' she consented to work for the season.

Bill brought a hunter back to base camp one night and in the morning took the horses back out to a spike camp to bring in the meat and trophies of another hunter. That morning, the hunter heard the cook up and about, and saw smoke from the chimney drifting skyward. He waited just long enough for the coffee to start perking, then left his tent and headed toward the cook house. He was within just a few yards of the cabin when a snarling grizzly came from behind a tent and rushed him. It knocked him to the ground and ripped his coat.

"Get a gun." He yelled at the cook. He tried to protect his head with his arms. She opened the door to see what all the noise was about then slammed it shut and locked it, screaming at the top of her lungs!

"A half-grown, roly-poly cub came bouncing past the bear wrestling with me," he told Bill, "and galloped into the woods. The sow grizzly gave me one more bite to remember her by, then went bounding off into the woods after her youngster."

The cabin door was securely locked. He pounded on the door and finally convinced the hysterical cook the bear really was gone. "I need clean towels and bandages." He said.

She opened the door just wide enough to throw him some first aid items, then promptly slammed and locked the door again. She kept it locked until the rest of the men returned that afternoon. There was still enough daylight left for Bill to fly the terrified cook out to civilization. She was in far worse shape than the man who was chewed on by the bear. If she ever went into grizzly country again, I sure never heard about it.

"I gave up," he told me, "trying to convince the cook to help me so I went back to my tent to clean and dress my wounds. I was closer to my gun, too. I'm damn lucky my injuries weren't worse." He escaped with two long shallow gashes, and three bites on one leg. His heavy down-jacket was ripped. Feathers fluttered everywhere, but it had saved his hide. He was grateful the attack by the angry grizzly bear had terminated when it did. And he was able to chuckle about the cook's inconceivable behavior.

He was flown out, the next morning, to have a doctor take care of his wounds. He wrote to us and said he convinced the doctor to certify his hide so tough that a grizzly's teeth couldn't tear it up. This joker said he would always wear the scars to prove he had been closer to an angry grizzly than any of his hunting buddies ever wanted to be!

Herb and his brother, Carl, drove from Wyoming to help with our outfit's fall sheep hunts. They had been regulars for several years in a row. They were dedicated hunters and well known in Wyoming for their ability to guide their clients to a decent trophy. Herb, especially, could spot rams behind rocks on distant peaks with just his eyes, before the client or guide located them with a spotting scope.

They were typical Western cowboys—the kind you see in the movies. Both were exceptionally good horse wranglers, and capable, willing help for any camp chore. Naturally, they were always welcome in our camps. They were with us during most of our sheep hunting season. All they wanted for pay was a ram. When a cowboy is used to riding a horse and willing to backpack and hike long distances into the sheep hills, you know he loves to hunt!

On this hunt, they were in a fly-in camp. Bud had set them out with the Super Cub on a lake 5 miles away. The lake was above timber line in the Wrangells. It was a beautiful camp site at the base of steep, rugged sheep hills. Generally, only the most physically-fit hunters were sent to this rugged camp. It was Herb's favorite place to help the guides with nonresident clients. This year, the clients had filled their sheep tags and had gone on to other camps for other game.

Herb and Carl, along with an assistant guide named Herald, left their spike camp at daylight to hunt two Dall rams they had watched through the spotting scope the previous afternoon. After a long and arduous climb, and after stalking the two rams into the late afternoon, each brother collected their trophy. The daylight hours were fast slipping away by the time both rams were caped, butchered for packing, and strapped to three packboards. And of course many photos had to be taken.

They decided to save time and daylight hours and took a quicker

More the rule than the exception, when a sheep is killed, because of the rough country it calls home, it dies very close or on the edge of a cliff.

route down a ravine. They tangled with heavy willow brush and lost their footing more than once. The chosen route ended above a steep, high, waterfall. Slippery rocks lining both sides of the narrow confines of the waterfall made it too dangerous to climb down. They were obliged to retrace their route back to the top of the mountain where they spent the night.

They all agreed, however, it was a good idea to roll the packs with the sheep meat, down the side of the waterfall. They could retrieve it from below the following morning. By the time they made the climb back up the ravine, and found a suitable place to camp, it was totally dark.

Herb leaned against his pack board and dropped off to sleep. Later, apparently forgetting the heavy pack board was still strapped onto him, he leaned forward. Over the edge of the cliff he tumbled, falling a good 10 feet before landing on the narrow ledge. There he sat, shivering, until daylight.

"Where are you, Herb?" Carl called.

"I'm okay, now," Herb answered, from somewhere in the darkness below Carl.

"What are you doing down there? Wouldn't you be more comfortable up here?" Carl asked.

"Yes, I would. But I'm on a very narrow ledge down here, and I'd keep on falling farther down the mountain if I moved. I'll have to wait until daylight to climb back up there, "Herb answered pathetically.

"Are we having fun, yet?" Carl called to Herb frequently, keeping the banter going until daylight arrived. Herb rubbed the life back into his legs as he got his bearing in the early dawn and climbed back to the boys.

They had descended off the mountain and located the base of the waterfall, all they found of packs of sheep meat were the bones. Clean, white bones. The quarters had bounced off the slimy rocks during the fall and landed directly under the waterfall. The force of the falling water had torn the meat clean from the bones.

"Well, we won't have to pack all that meat back to Windy Lake and I sure ain't packin' bones," Carl muttered.

"We'll sure catch hell from Bud, though, for losing good meat," Harold remarked, "and I don't know exactly how to avoid his lectures.

"We've still got a front quarter, and the tongue and heart that Colin always asks us to bring back, so at least he'll be happy with us!" Herb added.

"Oh, yeah, and I know Bud will be happy to know we brought Herb back in one piece, instead of the 170 pounds of mush he'd be if he'd fallen off that mountain," Harold added.

That wasn't the only time Herb spent a cold night on an Alaska mountain side. It happened again a year later, when Herb had gone along to do some backpacking and help with camp chores. He was with the 'Honey-Bee' man from Alabama, Joe Berry. Joe's business was raising bees and selling their honey. Joe was just as skinny as Herb, but taller. Jim was the guide Bud sent out with Joe and Herb. All three men were about the same age and they had a great time on this hunt. Joe collected a 39 and 1/4-inch ram the fourth day of the hunt. It was a beauty, with heavy bases measuring 14 and 1/2-inches.

Big rams had been seen on the mountain, west of Grizzly Lake in the pass above Tanada Lake. Bud set them out on the lake with a fly camp they would pack closer to the base of the mountain. He made three trips with the Super Cub to get them and the camp gear they needed for a 7-day hunt. "I'll fly back in 3 or 4 days to see if you're ready to fly back out." Bud told them.

As a rule, in this area, most hunters get rams in 2 to 4 days. So, he was a little worried when he flew over their camp, 4 days later, and found no one in camp. He flew back up the next day, after an early snowstorm. He was sure the men would

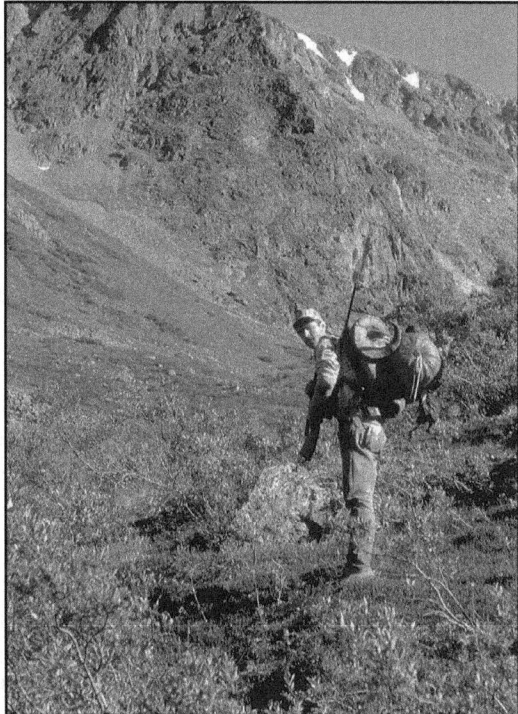

Jim Doran, a Nebraska hunter, packing his 42 inch trophy ram off the mountain. Packing out a trophy from high sheep country is always hard work, but, different from moose and caribou, the pack is generally down hill.

be ready to come back to the main lodge where it was warm and dry. But there was still no one in camp and the snow had obliterated any evidence of them having returned the day before. He became very concerned and spent the rest of the day imagining all kinds of disasters. He slept very little that night, and was ready to fly as soon as it was light. "If they aren't at their camp this time, I'll fly the rest of our guides and wranglers up this afternoon and start searching for them." he said. Much to Bud's relief, they were at the lake, ready to fly out.

127

When they were finally back at the lodge on Tanada Lake, Jim told us about the long night spent on the top of the mountain in the snowstorm.

"It was beautiful, 2,000 feet above the valley floor, with rolling green hills to the north. We could see for miles. Joe was fascinated with the scenery, the mountains, and the clean, clear air. All three of us were in good physical condition, just enjoying being there. We were in no big hurry to collect a sheep and leave.

We hunted the first mountain, then on the second day, we climbed higher. When we caught up with the rams we had glassed from below, they weren't as big as we'd expected. Joe passed on them, saying he'd hunt another day. Joe finally took a ram after crossing a wide valley and climbing a series of hills. We thought we could take a short cut back to our camp, by traveling in the valley, then pop over some low hills. We thought we'd come out in the valley that leads to the lake. But, after climbing up to where we had a view of the terrain, we found the route would lead us into a different drainage. So we had to retrace our course and take the long way back.

"What we thought was going to be just a passing snow shower became a blizzard. We climbed back up to where we just made out the outline of Grizzly Lake in the snowy distance, and found we weren't anywhere near a place where we could get off the mountain. It would be foolhardy to try."

"Gee, but I'd like to have taken a movie of those two. Neither one of them has an extra ounce of fat on their frames, and they were doing all kinds of acrobatics, trying to keep warm.

"I kept warm just scrounging what brush and willows I could find, green or dry, to feed a reluctant fire. None of us slept much, and, when it was daylight, we slipped and slid our way down to the lake camp."

At this time, none of us knew about the dangers of hypothermia, or we would have rushed them from Tanada Lake to a hospital. As it was, I encouraged them to get out of their cold, damp clothes, and sit close to the wood stove, while I plied them with warm drinks, homemade bread, and stew. It apparently worked, because after a long sleep in warm beds, they were full of action the next day.

And there was the time he flew Billy out, and we could hear his total vocabulary of swear words above the noise of the taxi-ing airplane engine on his return. A can of chewing tobacco spit had turned over and spilled in the plane. Bud didn't realize Billy carried it aboard. He would have made sure it was taken out.

Polar Bear Hunts with Wing-Mate Bill Etchells

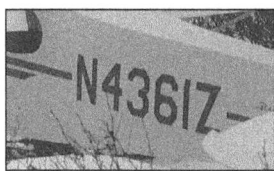

Bill Etchells, a young pilot/guide, 32 years old, tall, lean, sandy haired, and quiet, was Bud's wing-mate for 1969 and 1970 as they hunted the arctic pack ice. He was alert, serious, even tempered, and stable with a droll sense of humor. He was a sharp pilot, considering the few hours he had logged after learning to fly and getting a commercial license.

He came to work for us a few years earlier, shortly after being discharged from the U.S. Army. He proved to be a dedicated and willing worker. Horses were used on the farm where he grew up so he had never owned or driven an automobile.

Two years after coming to live year round as part of our family, he flew back to his home in Connecticut. His father taught him to drive and he bought a pickup and drove back to Alaska. Later, he bought some homestead land near Kenny Lake, a farming community in the southern Copper River Basin. After registering as a guide, he learned to fly and bought a Super Cub. He added a few more horses to his remuda and started booking hunts. Bud was pleased to have him as his wing-mate, not only during the polar bear hunts, but also during the fall Brown bear hunts on the Alaska Peninsula.

The experiences Bud and Cleo McMahan had shared, during the 8 years they were partners for the polar bear hunts, were no comparison to how poor Bill was initiated. Bud and Bill went on to have 2 lucrative years on the polar bear hunts.

Two days before, a snow storm dumped four inches of snow on the runway. Bill landed expertly. Both Super Cubs were heavily-loaded with gear and fuel. With the new snow, and ice on the bottom of the skis caused by the friction of sliding to a stop, they began a trip of difficulties. Colin, and Bob Nelson, a year-round employee, and I were recruited to dig snow and push aircraft.

In wet snow conditions, skis will stick to the snow, rather than slide over it. The four of us, including Bud, pushed on the lift-struts, the only safe place to push on a fabric-covered aircraft. As Bill's plane moved down the runway, we were immediately smothered in a shower of snow from the prop wash. Then, three of us pushed Bud's Cub into Bill's ski-tracks and he was soon airborne. We stood and watched Bud rendezvous in the air with Bill, and disappear into the north. They were several hours later getting away than planned. A two-and-half hour flight in good weather, they landed at Phillips Field in Fairbanks.

Only on the ground long enough to let Bud get the Cub's tube-type VHF radio repaired, then they winged their way to Bettles where they planned to stay overnight. The radio went dead again, just an hour out of Fairbanks. Radio contact between the aircraft was very important. They needed each other as they flew across the frozen tundra, unnamed rivers, and lakes. In canyons, over mountains, in valleys unpeopled, each wing mate kept the other on track.

Soon after leaving Fairbanks, they flew into blowing snow conditions and 30-knot headwinds. Each man kept the bright Piper-red and Daytona-white Cubs in sight. They arrived at Bettles at the edge of darkness. They had seen moose and caribou but no wolves along the way. They didn't really look, though. The lousy weather gave them plenty to do.

Bud had talked Bill into going polar bear hunting. He made wolf hunting sound alluring and told him again about the extra money he expected them to make. Bill thought it was a good idea and had been looking forward to it.

"We'll have better luck soon," Bud told him, after landing in Bettles. Bill remembered that statement several times over the next couple days.

While in Bettles, Bud removed the faulty radio from the cockpit and sent it back the next morning to Fairbanks with an airline pilot. Repaired, it was waiting in Barrow when they arrived.

The Brooks Range, via Anaktuvuk Pass and on to Umiat, reported poor visibility with whiteout conditions, so Bud and Bill decided to stay another night at the comfortable, but expensive, Bettles Lodge. The weather around Bettles was good, so they flew both Cubs west, almost to the headwaters of the Kobuk River looking for wolves. Strong winds and blowing snow forced them back and empty handed. They flew over scattered caribou, a wolverine driving through the snow in its peculiar hump-along gait, and a red fox busily digging for mice. They spotted moose, but no wolves. They tracked a lone wolf for several miles, but lost sight of its huge tracks when it traveled on crusted snow. Evidently, it was an educated old dog. They buzzed the willows and brush at the edge of a small lake but could not scare it out. Collecting enough wolf pelts to pay for the two comfortable nights and meals at the lodge was a dream and they should have been camping in a snow bank. They took enough necessary gear. Spotting a few caribou carcass and bands of caribou, convinced them the wolves were around, but, smarter than they—this time.

Weather was marginal when they left Bettles, and because they were unable to maintain radio contact, Bud told Bill, "We'll be following the John River and then to Anaktuvuk Village. Stay on course, if we get separated."

Bud marked it clearly on Bill's aviation chart and was sure Bill wouldn't get lost. If he did, they would find each other in the open country soon after passing over the village. Snow and river ice blended into featureless white. A dark line of stunted, ground-hugging trees and willows on either side of the river marked its course. Dark outlines of the hills and mountain peaks kept each pilot alert and watchful.

Remembering his own first flight through this pass in 1960, Bud wished they had radio contact. He would have enjoyed hearing Bill's comments. Now and then, Bud turned his plane a bit to the right or left, and saw Bill's plane behind him. Bud knew he was enjoying his first trip through the pass because Bill dipped his wings this way and that to get a better view.

Bud flew low and waggled the wings of his plane as he flew over the village. A plane, flying over the village, was a big event in this isolated Nunamiut Eskimo village. If it landed, everyone in the village ran out to watch. Bud had flown over many times, and landed a few times, and villagers recognized the airplane. But, this trip there was no time to land and visit. Time was essential and they flew on.

They encountered severe headwinds on the other side of the village and the engines guzzled gas. Umiat, looked very inviting when the lights twinkled in the distance, and was registering -35° when they landed. Bud was getting -20° readings on the strut thermometer and he wasn't surprised to find it colder on the ground. The oil temperature gauge on his instrument panel read dangerously low, so when they landed, he got the engine fire-pot going under the covered engine. The new insulated engine cover, with Velcro fasteners, was much easier to put on, especially in chilling wind.

We spent $85 for the bright orange engine cover but never regretted it. Until then, Bud had used an old homemade cover, closed with zipper fasteners. Those zippers were downright obstinate to bare fingers during -30° weather. But even that cover was better than the old draped canvas we used to cover the engine of our first plane, the old Piper J-3. It draped to the ground on all sides and a plumber's fire-pot was set under it. It was a terrible fire hazard if not watched closely, especially in a wind.

Bud re-taped every tear and hole in the cowling just as soon as he had been inside the cabin long enough to get his hands, feet, and face warm. As warm as Bud was, dressed in all his winter clothing, the wind seemed to find every hole and opening and chilled him to the bone. Bill's Cub performed really well in all the deep cold they encountered.

While in Umiat, Bud and Bill stayed with a man who worked for the State Department of Transportation. He took care of the airfield, among other jobs. "He's really likable," Bud said. Although he doesn't have much room for himself, he let us stay in his small cabin with him."

He was the lone inhabitant in Umiat while Bill and Bud were there. No one ever stayed there for very long. The loneliness and severe weather tended to wear down even the strongest constitution. That night, it dropped to -40° and they were weathered in for 2 more days. It was 2 days of welcome company for the man in this lonely outpost, but 2 days of irritation for Bud and Bill. Neither was good at sitting still with nothing to do but read or play cards.

They had tried to leave for Barrow the second day, but encountered headwinds gusting to 40 miles an hour with blowing snow, and they couldn't see a hundred feet when they finally turned back. The aviation gas was still at Umiat where Bud left it the previous year, but the gas cache near the headwaters of the Itkillik River was gone. So they were able to fly around in that vicinity just the 1 day.

The third day, soon after leaving Umiat, they ran across a pack of 16 wolves in open, flat country. Bud was in the lead, so he waggled his wings and turned away from the caribou who were milling around, obviously alert to the wolves who apparently had been chasing them. Bill's plane slid to an easy stop on the crusted snow, alongside Bud's 64 Delta. Bud unloaded gear from the tandem seat, so Bill could climb in to serve as gunner. Both sized-up the situation and landed with the caribou between them and the wolves, but far enough away that neither group would spook at the planes. Then Bud had ample time to get airborne again.

Bill had flown with him before and was an excellent gunner, the type of person who stayed cool even when circumstances were mer-

Bill Etchell's Super Cub and Bud's on Cobb Lake readying to leave for polar bear hunting out of Barrow.

ciless. Bud always said he appreciated not having to worry about Bill getting uncontrollable when flying over wolves that were scattering in all directions. Bud could concentrate on the flying in tight turns as well as staying alert to altitude and relationship to the ground.

The flying planes hadn't disturbed the caribou but on the first low pass, they panicked and scattered. The men were on the wolves before they realized why their meals were in such a tizzy. They were concentrating on the caribou, apparently trying to decide which ones would be the easiest to bring down. To be flying above such a drama in pristine wilderness country, gave everlasting memories.

They dropped two wolves from the pack, before the rest became aware of the danger and rapidly streaked into the forest. They lost no time skinning the two, full grown, male pups in prime condition. After poking the rolled hides into the already loaded planes, they headed for Barrow.

"Any time I come across a wolf pack of good size, I knew they were a related family." Bud used to say. "The chances were I'd get the grown pups easier than the older ones. I don't think the pups had been educated to planes yet."

For the aerial wolf hunters, it seemed far less cruel for an airplane to fly over with a gunner to drop a wolf, killing it instantly, than to see the guts torn from a live moose or caribou by a wolf, and observe the bloodied distance the animal had dragged itself before death came.

Of course, there were a few times, when a wolf was only wounded, and, if not too bad, managed to elude its pursuers, but they were easily tracked, from the air. The pilot and his gunner spent time tracking down the wolf, not only because they didn't want to leave a wounded animal, but because they wanted the pelt. Selling it helped pay expenses.

On one of their later wolf-hunting forays, Bud and Bill got wolves in the Chandalar River area. Bill was gunner in Bud's plane and they had dropped three wolves. A big, old, dark gray, dog lay some distance from the other two wolves. Bud started skinning the two big pups, while Bill went after the old one. When he got within sight of it, the wolf raised its head, watching Bill. When he got closer, it got up and started running downhill. Bill had his High Standard double-barrel .22, an easier gun to carry than his rifle or the shotgun. Bill started running, trying to get within the little pistol's range. He shot as he ran.

Bill and the wolf ran quite a distance before he made the killing shot. He carried that 150-pound critter back up the hill to the airplane. No easy task in deep snow. He was sweating heavily from all of the exertion, then he started chilling in the cold. The daylight was dwindling. There was only scattered green willow for a fire, so Bud loaded Bill into the plane with that critter in his lap. The warmth of the dead wolf probably prevented hypothermia, as they call it today. Bud skinned it in Barrow after Bill got to the hotel and started warming up.

Now to add a bit more adventure, for novice, Bill Etchells, the Gulkana FAA Flight Service Specialist gave Bill the wrong ADF (automatic direction finder) radio frequency. Instead of giving him the frequency for Barrow, he gave him the one for Point Hope. Bill's plane was equipped with a newer model ADF. Bud was following him, thinking 64 Delta's older ADF was showing the wrong reading. The East-West snowdrifts and the location of the sun didn't seem quite right to Bud and he had an uneasy feeling they were heading in the wrong direction. Bud didn't know for sure until he recognized a point where the frozen Chukchi Sea joined the land, north of the village of Wainwright. Instruments can fail, and often do, especially in the harsh arctic conditions, and some pilots have had serious "oh shit" experiences when their instruments failed. This time it was human error, not instrumentation.

The men landed their airplanes, still without radios, and talked. "I know where we are. Barrow is only a hundred miles up the coast. We will head in that direction."

They flew north for half an hour, but had to turn back, due to ice fog coming off the Chukchi Sea. The whiteout conditions made it too dangerous to land on the frozen lagoon near Wainwright. Without the ability to request permission, they landed on the U.S. Army field 5 miles out of town. A cocky, young Army Lieutenant dashed onto the field in a Jeep. They were told, "you haven't received prior permission to land. You'll have to leave immediately."

Bud informed the lieutenant, and in front of other GI's gathering around the planes, "This was an emergency landing, as you can see, that is if you're not blind. These two airplanes are staying right here

Bill Etchell's Super Cup weathering a fierce wind and blowing snow.

until the fog lifts and it's safe to fly." The matter was settled right there.

Bud was a ranking officer in the US Marines during World War II and spoke the language the cocky young man understood. He apparently didn't report them nor was he in sight when Bud and Bill took off 2 days later when the ice fog lifted.

Bill drained the oil from his Cub and said, "I met a lot of cocky, little bastards in my 4 years in the Army, but I didn't expect to meet any of them here. He should've left that stateside attitude behind when they sent him here. So I'm willing to make a bet that he is just fresh up here and hasn't come up against too many old boys like you!

He'll change that inhospitable attitude if he's ever caught in a bind away from this safe little base."

Bill proved he could handle it on the long, cold walk into the village of Wainwright. It was -40° with a wind chill. The ice fog created eerie, darkness. Their sleeping bags were slung over their shoulders and they carried their cans of drained engine oil. Both looked like spooks covered in ice fog.

The pure Alaska hospitality of the Wainwright school teacher and his wife, who took them in out of the cold night was a blessing. The couple were very hospitable to Bud and Bill. It allowed Bill time to get over resentment of not being allowed to stay on the base with the planes. A pilot really worries about leaving his plane on a strange field under adverse circumstances.

On their arrival in Barrow, more than 6 days later than they had planned, all of the downstairs rooms in the hotel were full, so they bunked upstairs in the dormitory rooms. Bud gathered from various conversations, and seeing a few walking mavericks in the hallways and lobby, there was no shortage of parties.

"It sure doesn't look like we'll be getting a quiet night sleep." Bud whispered to Bill. Bud sensed that a few of the hunters were getting bored and restless waiting for flying weather. The same weather that had Bud and Bill grounded in Wainwright kept the planes in Barrow for 4 days.

This same year, Ellis' and Marshall's Maule was lost, found, repaired, then flown to Kotzebue. Ellis was a noted aircraft mechanic, but this time he didn't think he'd have an airplane to repair. They flew their Cessna 180 until it started throwing oil. Windy Windell flew cover for them with his Super Cub. The days used locating the Maule, repairing it, and the 180, put Ellis and Marshall way behind schedule. Their clients became impatient, because their own allotted time was fading away. The solution was to farm them out to other pilot/guides who had free time. Two of their hunters arrived on the daily plane, and expected Ellis or Marshall. They didn't know nor particularly cared, why their guides were delayed.

Another pilot/guide's plane was down with a finicky engine and he was grounded until Ellis could take time from his own planes and hunters to get it flying again.

The flying weather was good. Bud and Bill still had half a day of light, and their own scheduled hunters were not due for 2 more days. They took a hunter of Ellis/Marshall out for bear. The other hunter went with another guide.

"I had a great time," Bud reported, "Flying in good weather over endless miles of barren ice. There wasn't one bear anywhere, not even a white fox so I just flew. He was a lucky guy, though, and got his trophy bear the following day."

McMahan and Merry's hunter scored, and he told the interesting story that evening. Two other pilot/guides had taken their hunters wolf hunting, but only scared the hell out of small pack of wolves. "It kinda sounded like all of the flying maneuvers, low altitude flying, tight turns, and sudden grabbing for altitude scared the hell out of the guy in the back seat more than the wolves we chased." Bud said. Bud and Bill added their own wolf hunting stories to those being circulated. They happily told their story about their welcome at Wainwright. And of course, Bud always seized the opportunity, with each new audience, to tell about the time he shot himself down years before while aerial wolf hunting.

In one of his regular letters home, Bud wrote: "Dr. Malcolm Reuben, from Pennsylvania, has been here and gone back home. We had a good hunt and he now has a good bear trophy. He was a very likable man. It's a real pleasure to hunt with clients who have been on other hunts with me for Alaska's big game." (Reuben, a slim, wiry man in his late 40's, had made a fall hunt with us the previous September. He collected a Dall ram and moose). "He obviously wasn't at ease in the hotel, but didn't complain. It was just too noisy and rowdy for him. Bill and I managed to talk another hunter out of his room so the Doc could have a downstairs room by himself, but he wouldn't have made it an issue had he been upstairs in the dorm with us.

"Doc shot his bear, a 9-foot old boar, 2 days after his arrival. The bear was sleeping on a smooth ice pan. It had plenty of room for both Cubs to land. Doc got with the program and was out of my plane, rifle in hand, as soon as we landed. The bear stood up, sniffed the air in our direction, more than likely trying to decide what those strange birds were that made so much noise. It still surprises me that most polar bears have never encountered humans or airplanes. They are curious. With a nod from me, Doc let loose with two shots in rapid succession and that was all it took. The trophy polar bear was his.

"We flew 75 miles northwest of Barrow in a perfect day for pictures. There was plenty of day left after Bill and I skinned the bear, so we flew Doc out over the Will Rogers and Wiley Post Memorial monument. In 1935, they crashed their plane a few miles south of Barrow and the Arctic Ocean.) We were airborne again for only a minute when we spotted two white arctic foxes not far from where we had skinned the bear. We figured they came to feed on the carcass. I'm convinced arctic fox know when they hear gun shots there is a free feast.

"We caught up with a small sow with one small cub, moseying leisurely on an ice pack. I lifted the top half of the door, flew low and to the left of her, and Doc took movies as she smacked the cub's rear end to get it running faster. I made a wide turn and flew back over and she made a tumbling reverse, still running in the opposite direction. The cub wasn't quite as fast as his mama and we could see her turn her head and encourage her baby to keep up. The little fellow was at her side when we flew on."

Bill Etchells didn't drink, other than a beer once in a while to be friendly. Bud was through with drinking once he was out of the Marines. It wasn't against his morals to have a couple of sociable whiskeys, but his system could no longer tolerate any more. He had no patience with slobbering drunks.

"I was glad Dr. Reuben left for home before a rowdy party a couple of nights later," Bud wrote. "I threw a drunk Eskimo down the stairs. I'm sure Doc would have felt compelled to use his medical skills to revive him."

Bud stayed in the lobby with his hunter, an affable fellow they had taken out that day. He was freely buying drinks, celebrating his trophy. "I was tired after a day of hard work. Bill had gone to bed and I was ready. Two other hunters had scored and the party was well under way by the time I left."

"My buddy kept insisting I stay for just one more. He was swaying like a wind-rocked tree and talking to a local gal. She was drunk too and leaning against the door jam like a wet dish rag. One old disheveled barfly with an irritating sandpaper voice was trying to talk someone into buying her another drink. Some of these gals have the morals of an ally cat when they were drinking."

On his way upstairs, feeling a bit woozy himself, Bud had to stand aside to let an overstuffed, middle-aged dude, holding onto the railings, stumble down the stairs. A young woman staggered behind him.

No one got any sleep that night. A bunch of locals, men and women, came into the hotel around midnight. All noisy, and very drunk, the women were louder than the men. " I was upstairs with the rest of the pilot/guides, who had to fly the next morning, trying to sleep. We periodically yelled to pipe down or leave, but it did no good." Bud and Bill finally dropped off when a fight broke out and woke them again.

"There are no locks on the dormitory doors and a drunk Eskimo staggered in and insisted I join the party." Bud was flaming mad and told him in a colorful language that could be understood by any one. 'Get the hell out a here. It better be fast or I'll throw you out.' I got settled down again but I was still mad. In he came again, staggered over and breathed his sour, whiskey breath right in my face. He had a cigarette dangling from his mouth and the long ash dropped onto my face. That was it."

Bud ground his teeth and jumped out of bed. He grabbed the guy by the seat of his pants and the nape of his neck, and marched him all the way down the long hallway to the top of the stairs. He slammed his head against the wall and threw him down the stairs.

"After he landed, he didn't move. The drunk was out cold. I was scared and thought maybe I killed him. I went back to bed, thinking I should get some sleep, in case there was a big investigation with a lot of questions in the morning."

Bill had gotten up and came down the hall, so when he looked

One of the local attractions of Point Barrow, Alaska is the Will Rogers and Wiley Post memorial marker. It occupies the spot where they crashed and died on the beach 13 miles from town. Nearly all bear hunters wanted to see the marker.

down the stairs at the limp figure, he turned to Bud and said, "Gee, maybe you should go ahead and buy the guy a drink. I think he's going to need one."

Bud didn't laugh.

The Eskimo's tumble down the stairs broke up the party and it got real quiet in the hotel and stayed that way the rest of the night. In the morning, some guys were still awake and said four locals showed up and dragged the limp guy out of the hotel. We never heard about the incident, so he must have survived. Drunks usually do.

The next morning, during breakfast, Bill had everyone laughing when he described Bud's baggy, underwear, flapping in the breeze while he marched that drunk guy down the hall. For the rest of the time Bud was in Barrow, he was known as "The Hilton Bouncer."

Dr. Reuben's wife, Ruth, and I made plans to fly to Barrow with her husband. Between hunts, Bud and Bill were going to fly us over the Arctic Ocean to show us a polar bear or two and, hopefully, some arctic fox. We were interested in seeing the Wiley Post and Will Rogers Memorial, too.

Ruth often accompanied her husband and both of us were excited about flying all the way to Barrow, and seeing sights I had always heard about. I had been to Barrow as a tourist one July and had dipped my fingers in the Arctic Ocean, but I hadn't seen the ice pack or polar bears.

Luckily, for us, we had to cancel our plans due to an emergency that forced Ruth to return home. The hotel was always full of a disorderly crowd. Now and then, someone's wife or girlfriend would come for a short stay, but it was generally when they had rented a house. Livable housing at any price, was hard to find. There were times when the girlfriend left on a plane just ahead of the wife's arrival.

One year, a man from Pennsylvania arrived with his secretary and they shared a room at the hotel. He met another hunter who knew him, as well as his wife. The two men were business competitors and not exactly the best of friends. Bud thought the one with his secretary in tow may have had a lot of explaining to do when he got home. He knew he was in a tight spot, but with his glib tongue, I'm sure he convinced his wife it was not him. I surely would have enjoyed listening to his explanation when his wife found out.

The camaraderie among the pilot/guides was real and strong and no one ever told all that went on during the parties in the hotel. Nor did they elaborate to their wives, what some of their clients or the other pilot/guides did while hunting at Barrow, Point Hope, and Kotzebue. Juicy gossip, gleanings heard or discussed in evening conversations were not repeated. They kept their mouths shut, believing that what happened during the hunts was the hunter's business.

Near the end of Bud's years up there, the 21-year-old son of one of a regular pilot/guide, flying out of Barrow, came up to try for a bear and to learn about bear hunting. He had his pilot's license and flew one of their Super Cubs. He was a good-looking young man, slim and graceful with appealing manners, and was quite a hit with the ladies of the far north country. Besides the experience he was getting with the flying, he was participating in all of the fun he could find and inventing some of his own. So it wasn't a bit surprising that he found the dances in Barrow.

Barrow's younger residents considered the dances off limits to outsiders unless they were invited. He managed to get himself invited. But he found himself in forbidden places due to roving eyes and hands, and it wasn't long before trouble started. It seems there was quite a fight in the dance hall, and someone notified the kid's dad. It looked like the entire Native male population of Barrow was ganging up on the lad. When his dad showed up, this lad slipped out a side door, leaving the angry crowd for his dad to handle. After all, his dad was a known womanizer (at home and abroad) and his son figured that his dad had more experience in handling this type of situation. In a short while, the father returned to the hotel lobby and nonchalantly remarked, "Piece of cake."

This lad never returned to Barrow to do any polar bear hunting and I never heard of him going to Kotzebue or Point Hope.

The pilot/guides never gave the slightest hint they heard an untruth or an exaggerated feat of bravery. When a fellow pilot/guide had the rapt attention of a roomful of unknowing hunters, they kept tight lipped. In the midst of a farfetched tale, the storyteller may have received a knowing grin or wink, but he was never contradicted or embarrassed. Sometimes, a listener, as he got up to leave, raised the leg of his trousers, ever so slightly, suggesting that things were getting really deep.

Peg-Leg-Jack (Foldagger) would come into the lobby, after a day on the ice, look over the faces, and, if he saw a new one, he would knock on his wooden leg with the handle of his skinning knife and exclaim loudly, "Gee, I must have stayed out on the ice too long while skinning that bear and froze my leg. I gotta git upstairs and thaw it out!" He thrived on their horrified expressions.

Jack had a lively sense of humor, a warm personality and enthusiasm for anything that seemed dangerous or a little exciting. It made him a welcome addition in any gathering. The stories the other pilot/guides told about him are legend now.

He was a character! "He was a capable and noteworthy guide and pilot." Bud said. "Having a wooden leg didn't handicap Jack."

One never knew when his ridiculous sense of humor was going to surface. One evening, while leaning his back to the bar, holding up a bottle of beer, he hit them with this question. "Did you ever think what a marvelous machine your body is, to change beer so damn quick into urine?"

On their return flight home, Bud and Bill had made big plans for hunting wolves, but lousy weather changed those plans, too. They decided to come home via the longer eastern route. While they were at Fort Yukon, they were called out of warm sleeping bags at midnight to fly to an isolated lake and rescue a family whose Cessna 185 had crashed.

The Hotel clerk nearly knocked their door down beating on it to waken them. "How lucky can we be. We're the only two pilots with planes here." Bill mumbled to Bud, as they hurried out to their parked Cubs.

It was a bright, moonlit night and they had no problem finding the lake, among hundreds, where the family was stranded. They brought the woman and two little kids back to Fort Yukon, leaving the pilot to camp out by his airplane. This story was told in my first book, Trail of the Eagle.

For the aerial wolf hunters, it seemed far less cruel for an airplane to fly over with a gunner to drop a wolf, killing it instantly, than to see the guts torn from a live moose or caribou by a wolf, and observe the bloodied distance the animal had dragged itself before death came.

Eskimo Whaling Camps

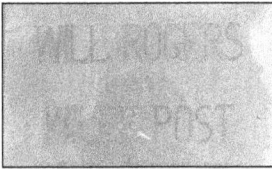

All Eskimo men in the village were busy checking their umiaks (open boats made of a wooden frame work covered with walrus hides) and sharpening their harpoons. Whaling skippers were rounding up their crews and getting ready for the whaling season starting late in polar bear season. The Eskimos used oogruk (seal) skins for floats and to carry water. They cased the hide when skinning the seal, tied the legs, head, and anus holes shut, then it would hold water or air. They smelled rank and I am told they drank the water from them while out in their umiaks. I don't understand how they can relish water with the taste it's bound to develop while in those hides. Bud wouldn't even try it, but I'll take their word for it that one eventually gets used to the taste.

Bud brought one home and I never understood why. It smelled and was unpleasant company in the airplane while flying home. I promptly relegated it to a shed far away from the house! I would have been happier with a small ivory carving or locally-sewn Eskimo mukluks—why couldn't he have brought me something like that back from Barrow?!

On opening day, sunny and pleasant, of the whaling season, Bud took Bill and their hunter out to Charley Edwardson's whaling camp, set up on the ice pack just off the Point. Paul, their hunter, already had his bear, so he had an extra day before leaving for home. They were out there all day, watching the action and hoping for a bowhead whale to surface. Action really starts when a whale is hit with a harpoon, called a strike. Bud took a lot of movie footage of the men launching their umiaks and placing their equipment. Charlie and his Eskimo crew were professionals at whaling. They had years of learning in their youth, and then doing it every year since. Subsistence hunting is still an important part of their heritage and lifestyle. One boat had made a strike just before the guides and hunter got out there, but the harpoon didn't hit well enough to hold the whale.

The harpooner stands in the umiak and the boat pulls close to a bowhead whale surfacing for air in the limited space of an open lead. Once the brass tip of the harpoon is embedded in the whale's blubber, hopefully in a vital place to hold it firmly, then the excitement really begins. A float is attached to the first harpoon by a long rope, which serves as both a locator and as a drag to keep the whale from diving. Other crew members throw their harpoons, the whale eventually dies and is towed back to the whale camp. Then everyone, men, women, and children, pull on the ropes and drag the whale onto solid ice. It is cut up and divided among the members of the crew, then among the villagers.

Bud hired an Eskimo boy, Justin, and his cousin to take them out with three dog teams. They had teams with six or seven well-fed, sturdy, and eager dogs. All of the village dogs were yapping and pulling against their chains, begging to go. The littler kids gathered around, watching the teams being hooked up. The dogs were jumping, straining, and yapping at the end of their harnesses and tug lines, complaining all the while. Sled dogs love working in harness.

The young hunter was fascinated. He read about the Eskimo lifestyle and now, he was seeing it for himself. He took pictures of everything and used an awful lot of movie film. The trail out to the whaling camp was rough. The rougher it was, the faster the dogs wanted to go. It took a good 2 hours to get there. While they watched, waiting for a whale to surface, Paul kept asking the boys questions about dog teams. Bud said he probably knew every dog's name before the day was over. He also enjoyed asking questions about schooling and home life.

On the return trip, Justin's cousin let Paul drive the dog team. It was a hilarious trip, but they made it with all of the dogs and sled intact. Anyone who has ever driven dogs knows that sled dogs are pretty smart (the leaders are, at least), and they recognize a cheechako as soon as he gets hold of the bar and hesitantly yells commands.

144

Watching Paul handle those dogs reminded Bud of our own lead dog, Jim. Bud had bought Jim from Gareth Wright, a champion sled dog racer. Jim was too old to run in Gareth's racing team but still had a lot of life left in him. Well, this old dog knew right away he had a greenhorn to train when Bud stepped up to the sled. It took him all of that first winter for Bud to realize that lead dog wasn't as dumb as he thought. It was Bud who was the dumb one!

The Eskimo boys were laughing and enjoying themselves and Bud had the impression the dogs were, too. If Paul yelled, "mush," the dogs stopped. If he hollered, "gee" or "haw," they went just the opposite direction of the command. They seemed to know exactly when there was a chance of tipping the sled over or yanking Paul off the sled runners. If the going was smooth and easy, the dogs trotted along, but when it got rough, they loped with joyous energy. If they got out of hand, their owner had only to yell a command and they promptly obeyed.

Paul was riding in the basket the once it was plainly obvious that the leader had swerved the team at just the right moment for the sled runners to go up a steep, sloping ridge. The sled naturally tipped over. A stern talking to by their owner kept them in line, but only for a short while. From then on, the Eskimo kids ran alongside the sled, instead of riding, and let Paul have the fun of driving the dogs. Driving an Eskimo dog team made a great finale to Paul's Arctic hunt, and a generous tip to the two Eskimo boys made a big impression.

"Jim Metheney had some bad luck yesterday." Bud wrote. "The engine of his Cub quit about 10 miles offshore, north of Barrow. He got the plane down on rough ice okay, but tore up the landing gear and bent the prop. His partner had the hunter in his plane, so flew on to Barrow and let him out, then went back and picked up Metheney. It wasn't a good place to leave the plane overnight but they had no choice. It was uncomfortably close to an open lead. When they flew back over the next day, the lead had widened and was only about 50 yards from the plane. Ellis came in early from his own flying/guiding, so he went with them later and put a new gear under it, installed a new prop and flew the plane back. It still needs major repairs, so will be setting awhile."

Wally Rochester was flying cover for Metheney and they were soon in more trouble. The Cub wasn't flying yet when the Cessna 180 started blowing oil really bad. They had two hunters waiting, getting impatient. They also had two more hunters coming in, and all of the pilot/guides were busy with their own hunters, so they couldn't help. Eventually, though, the problems were solved and the dudes got to hunt, and once they got their bears, everyone was happy again.

Bud and Bill took two Army officers out for a bear for Marshall and Ellis, while waiting for our hunter from New York to arrive. Colonel Brockwell got a 9-foot bear after they had flown just 6 hours, and the next day Major Baker got a 9-foot 1/4-inch bear. Colonel Brockwell was Wing Commander at Eielson Air Force Base for the Strategic Air Command. These guys flew jet bombers and Bud said they were interesting fellows to talk with. They swapped flying tales every evening while they were there; most were funny, but some were deadly serious.

A fellow flew his own Super Cub from New York to Barrow to hunt polar bear and wanted to hire Bud to fly cover for him. Bud backed away from the offer, because he wasn't enough of a gambler to be a cover pilot for a greenhorn, much less over pack ice. But he stayed interested to see which pilot/guide would take his offer, if anyone did.

All of the Super Cub jockeys, and the two other pilot/guides had their schedules full of hunters. Everyone was eager to get hunting over and head south while snow and ice conditions held. Bud said he heard the guy from New York went out by himself for a couple of days. He was still in Barrow when Bud and Bill left for the season. The next year, Bud remembered to ask if he had taken a polar bear and was told he had gone home without one.

They flew for 2 days with another hunter from New York, then were grounded 2 days due to high winds, blowing snow, and -20° temperatures. When they got good weather again, they took Pete, a 30-year-old fellow out and got him a bear. He was a likeable, big, clumsy guy. He tried hard to do everything just right, and he never ran out of questions. He rode in our Cub and Bud hoped our plane held together when he climbed in and flopped down on the seat, or when he clumsily got out. Bud stood by to make sure he didn't use the lift strut as a step.

The bear was sleeping, when they spotted it. Bud was sure it was going to wake up and be gone by the time Pete finally got out of the Cub and walked near enough to shoot. The Cub creaked and groaned when he hefted his weight and wiggled around. The bear must have thought it was the ice cracking and moving, so he paid no attention.

In another letter home, Bud wrote: "It's been staying -30° ever since Bill and I got here, with 20-knot winds, most days. Wind chill equaled -70°. My fingers are sore all the time from working on the plane at those temperatures. My ears are tender from being frozen so often while skinning bears out on the ice. The dorm rooms are as cold as igloos. Cleo and Windy solved that problem. They rented a house and moved out of the hotel before we got here."

Windy Windell was flying cover for Bill Ellis, because Marshall couldn't be there for some of the hunts. These guys usually hunted out of Kotzebue, but they made a couple hunts out of Barrow, too. Windell flew Ellis' Super Cub and Bill flew the Cessna 180. Bill Ellis and Windy flew together from Ellis' headquarters at Devil's Mountain Lodge on the Nabesna Road.

The year before, while Bud and Cleo stayed the night at Umiat, Windy landed there with the windshield so covered with oil that he had to open the side-window to land. Oil pressure was nil when he landed. He was lucky to have landed when he did. It was the usual -50° and he wasn't warmly dressed. He didn't have minimum emergency gear either. Windy was well known for being less prepared than he should have been. But he managed to survive. I am sure the rest worried more about him than he did about himself.

Windell was overdue in Barrow, when he got word to Ellis that he was in Umiat with problems. Ellis flew down the next day with the necessary parts and got the plane repaired. Then all four pilots and planes flew to Barrow together. They hit the flying weather just right and flew in during a lull in the weather. The day after they landed the weather turned sour again.

Bud felt Windell had come close, too close, to making the headlines on that flight. "He crowded his luck all the time." Bud said. "But he pushed his luck to the limit that time. I don't think Windy even noticed."

"Piece of cake," he said when Bud asked what good luck charm he carried.

There are pilots who go a bit beyond the safety limits, crowding the arctic, and nothing happens to them. But there are others who are cautious, who, for some reason, have a fatal accident.

In 1969 Bud had the toughest tracking and the coldest of any hunt out of Barrow. It was -30° in the air and much colder on the ice. When it's that cold, it doesn't snow. Without fresh snow, tracking was impossible. They needed sun to create shadows. On hazy days and unless the white bear was moving, it was almost impossible to see. Winds had blown the loose snow away, and what was left was hard, crusted, ice and even the biggest bears left no tracks. Often their black noses and yellowish white coloring were the only signs of their presence.

Dr. Wornock and Dick Edwards, both from Portland, Oregon, came to hunt the big bear. They lucked out, after a few days of hunting the open leads, Dr. Wornock had a 9-foot bear and Edwards an 8-foot 6-inch bear. Each day, both planes flew a littler farther away from Barrow, without seeing a bear. Now and then, they saw foxes but otherwise, the world of barren ice and bitter cold was a complete blank. They'd fly until it was time to fuel the hungry planes, and hungry hunters. Then, if there was at least 2 hours of daylight left, they'd fly out in a different direction.

They took both men wolf hunting for 2 days, but by the time the pilots had landed to let them shoot (hunters shot from the ground, not from the air), the wolves were long gone. One day, wolf hunting in the direction of the Meade River, they flew the men over and around the Will Rogers and Wiley Post Memorial. They were fans of both pilots and said if they didn't get to shoot any wolves, seeing where Post and Rogers had crashed was compensation enough. A wolf trophy, along with the polar bear hides, would have made an even better ending to a memorable hunt. The weather turned sour and there was no more wolf hunting in the immediate future, so the hunters turned their thoughts homeward and left the next afternoon.

John Cole, from Wisconsin, was the next hunter waiting to go out. A light snow had dusted the ice the day before. A bear's big tracks, crisscrossed by the delicate tracks of white foxes, led to the east, about 70 miles northeast of Barrow. Within minutes, they spotted the bear.

"39 Alpha, he's a Keeper!" Bud called to Bill. The bear ambled aimlessly, casting a long shadow. They continued to fly around a while, to give the bear time to decide his direction. It stayed on its original easterly course and went behind a pressure ridge. The pilots feathered their planes onto a short, smooth, ice pan. They preferred a longer one but it was the only one nearby. As it was, this one was a mile from where the bear had disappeared.

The bright, sunny day, cast welcome shadows and showed smooth ice. The ice pan had four-foot pressure ridges that they would have to clear on take off. They exited the planes, with rifles in hand, pockets bulging with ammo and cameras carefully tucked inside their warm parkas.

It took awhile to traverse the distance from the parked planes. They

148

were as quiet as possible as they slipped to the top of the pressure ridge. On reaching the top, they didn't know if the bear was anywhere close or had chosen to amble into the yonder. This one had stretched out for a snooze and never suspected the humans were about to make his hide into a rug. The bear's tracks assured it was trophy size, but the angle it presented to them made Bud want to be sure it was 8-foot or better. All polar bear guides were experienced enough to accurately gauge a trophy sized bear by looking at the size of the paw prints. But they always wanted to be sure it wasn't a little bear with unusually large feet.

"Be ready to shoot, John," Bud said. "But wait until I give the signal." The bear lay only a couple hundred feet away and gave John ample time to fire. Bud shot his .375 Winchester, lobbing a shell a bit in front of the snoozing bear. The startled bear jumped to its feet, then stood broadside to the men. It didn't know which direction the noise had come from. Bud signaled and John shot three times in rapid succession. Three well-placed shots dropped the bear where it stood and it stayed down.

John said this bear looked big enough for him. Bill recorded the action with John's movie camera. Photographs and movies were taken of the three of them, in various poses by the fallen bear. The skinning job was completed, leaving the carcass on the ice for the foxes, then the real work began. They each took turns packing the 8-foot 1/4 inch fresh hide back across the mile of rough ice to the planes.

All guides get a lot of backpacking experience, especially during the fall hunting seasons, packing heavy loads of moose and caribou meat over uneven tundra (commonly known as nigger heads in Alaska). It's tough work. The client is rarely obliged to carry anything but his own rifle and camera. Most younger men offer to help, and John insisted on taking turns with the guides. He was a tall, good-natured man, about 40 years old, and Bud guessed he weighed about 200 pounds. He was Bud's passenger so, while hiking back, Bud exercised his mind, and thought about the length of the ice pan. He wished they weighed a lot less. His own 160 pounds felt like it might even be too much.

They loaded everything from Bud's plane into Bill's, including rifles, cameras, and the heavy, wet hide. They estimated weight in both planes to be about even, so that gave Bud some confidence. Bill's plane cleared the lowest ridge with room to spare, then flew in circles off to the side, waiting for Bud to get into the air. Always, under marginal conditions, using the buddy system, one plane stayed in the air to watch what happened to the other plane. Then, if Bud didn't make it off, Bud and John would have a long, long hike to another ice pan large enough for Bill to land and pick them up. Bud was sure wishing for a wind to give him additional lift.

They pulled Bud's Cub as far back on the ice pan as possible. It sat without sliding back down the slope heading up to the pressure ridge. Still, Bud had to hold it, while John climbed in, so it wouldn't slide any further forward. "Lean as far forward as you can, John," Bud said. "Don't undo your safety belt. As soon as I rev the engine, your forward motion will shift some weight from the tail toward the skis." John leaned as far forward as possible, just as soon as Bud was aboard and gunned the engine. Then, fire-walling the throttle, sweet-talking and coaxing his air-chariot, ol' 64 Delta, the Cub lifted off the ice and cleared the ridge with just a whisper to spare. Bud whispered, "A miss is as good as a mile, but I prefer the mile," Bud told Bill over the radio. "I was scared there for a minute when we didn't grab altitude like I thought we should."

"Yeah," Bill replied. "I was holding my breath. Even from here, it didn't look like you had enough clearance to spare."

"A fat lot you two knew. John bantered. "I'll stay scared for a week, and have bad dreams. Besides, it's too late to say, let me out and I'll walk back."

Just before dark, while winging their way back to Barrow, they chanced across a big sow with a medium sized cub. It looked like they were playing together, or the cub was teasing his mama. The cub jumped up and grabbed his mama's nose. She turned away from the cub, so it ran around to the other side and jumped for her nose again. The cub bit a little too hard, because she swatted it with a front paw and sent it sprawling. She started running so the cub picked itself up and galloped after her. The men in the planes left them to their games and flew on to Barrow.

Bud said he was happy to be back in the village with his plane parked safely on the lagoon. He knew he had taken a risk that time, and, luckily for all of them, it paid off.

John was really happy with his bear and Bud was pleased he had enjoyed the hunt. John had worked hard and saved his nickels and dimes to make this hunt. Bud had been highly recommended by some of our former hunters.

Easter Sunday brought a 3-day storm with 60-knot winds. Six planes were tied down on the lagoon, and three or four times each day the pilots walked out to check tiedown ropes. Not knowing when the storm would end, they kept engines warmed. It was a hassle to refill the catalytic heaters, set them back inside the engine and fasten the cowling, all while trying to maintain balance in the strong, gusty winds. The engine covers had to be removed, held in some way to keep them from blowing away, then replaced and tied back on. Some language used would put a mule skinner to shame. I've heard some pilot/guides deliver, with unique finesse, some of the most colorful and original cuss words. One pilot/guide, in particular, could use the 'F' word as a noun, pronoun, adjective, and verb, all in one sentence.

Some guides and hunters went to Easter services in one or the other two churches in Barrow. Others played cards, slept, or told stories about other hunts.

Whenever weather held them on the ground, Bud, and sometimes others, would spend time with the older Eskimo men, listening to stories of their methods of hunting polar bears when they were younger. These wise, old men told stories of their fishing and whaling ways or how they hunted with blow guns and spears. Talk about ingenuity, they had it pretty well figured out. Bud admired their strength, stamina, and resourcefulness.

When any pilot/guides had a free day, they were invited out to the whaling camps on the Arctic Ocean ice pack. Eskimo camped and waited for surfacing bowhead. Their camps were situated near open leads and the older whaling captains seemed to have instinctive knowledge, besides years of experience, to know which open lead to watch. They seemed to feel where the whales migration path was and where to expect a surfacing whale.

Eskimo are a shy, but friendly people, and once you gain their confidence, you are a friend for life. They can tell you stories of their people and their way of life that is now gone. Stories about methods of survival and times of their people long past are passed on from one generation to the next generation.

This reminds me of a time when Bud and his hunter had walked up to a dead moose—at least they thought it was! Their rifles were leaning against a tree, out of reach, and Bud was taking his skinning knife off his belt while the client was getting his camera set. That bull moose had an impressive set of antlers. It looked very big when it jumped to its feet, red-eyed and snorting. It turned and ran for the timber. They would have been in deep trouble if it had charged, and Bud always wondered why it didn't. I'm sure it scared the hunters more than it was scared.

The Last Year Hunting Polar Bears

The last year Bud hunted the arctic pack ice for polar bear was 1970. Bill Etchells was his wing mate. They had just finished a hunt with a young client whose good luck was the only reason he had a good trophy white bear. The cost of his hunt was extreme.

Bud and Bill helped him carry his duffle bag of gear, and the salted bear hide he was taking to his taxidermist for mounting, to the airplane and said goodbye. They hadn't offered to take him wolf hunting because he was big and just too clumsy getting in and out of a Super Cub. Bud wasn't confident enough of his ability to shoot from the aircraft. He was a good-natured young man, but had a problem with airsickness and hadn't seemed to care if he went on an aerial wolf hunt.

What a contrast the next client was in comparison. The new dude, Albert, a 29-year-old from the east was pleasant enough in the hotel while waiting out the weather in Barrow the first 2 days. He listened to other hunters and pilot/guides relate their hunting stories and experiences. He didn't complain about the meals in the cafe. Bud and Bill got the clear idea he was used to better fare.

"I am not married and will likely never be," He told us, in one of his early letters. "I inherited a partnership in a very lucrative business and can easily afford to hunt with you." Albert had never hunted big game and had chosen the elite of America's big game animals, the monarch of the arctic ice, as his first hunt.

Bud and Bill worked in a world without most of the comforts of home. Albert was a spoiled rich kid and expected to be waited on hand and foot, no matter the cost or who suffered.

They flew for 3 days before locating a bear for him. He saw little white fox trotting along on endless expanses of white wilderness. They flew over a polar bear sow and her two little cubs romping and playing while she snoozed. Albert took movies of some half-grown cubs sliding down an ice ridge on their rumps. Bud told him of seeing grown bears do this on a snowy hillside, having fun, playing like kids do, climbing up and sliding down again. Bud and Bill put forth much time and effort so this client could take a variety of movies and photographs. Albert's money was just as good as the next guy and they did their best to locate a trophy bear for him.

Bud was starting to think maybe he and Bill had judged Albert too quickly, and were starting to like the guy. He seemed to take the whole thing in stride, knowing how completely he was out of his element.

Albert was riding in Bud's Cub on the third day out. They were about 100 miles north of Barrow when Bud sighted a big bear in the distance. "It's a keeper." He told Albert. "I'll land as close to the bear as I can, so get ready."

The nearest ice floe they could land on was a half-mile from the bear. The size of the pan was marginal for a safe take off, but the bear was definitely a trophy and they wanted it. There were larger ice pans another half-mile away and they would relay smaller loads to one of them, if necessary.

"39 Alpha," Bud called to Bill flying off to his right. "It's a keeper, but the ice floe looks a bit marginal, so how about you staying overhead until we get the bear, because it may be gone by the time we get over there."

"Roger," Bill replied.

Bud crabbed the plane onto the rough ice pan, sliding sideways on a glide into a cross wind, straightening the approach just before touching the ice, then stopping a bit close to a sharp-edged ice ridge. It scared the hell out of his passenger.

"How are we going to get back off from here?" Albert asked, as soon as his feet hit the ice.

"No problem at all," Bud answered, ironically. He eyed the length of the ice pan and took stock of the wind direction hoping it wouldn't change before they were ready to takeoff. Albert looked very concerned.

The two of them hotfooted it in the direction they had last seen the bear, staying out of sight behind low ridges of ice. It was close to where Bud had first seen it. When they climbed a low 5-foot ice ridge and peeked over, the bear was about 300 yards away, just standing there. "Get a good footing, Albert, "Bud whispered. "Stand up, take careful aim, then start shooting. I'll be ready to back you up."

The kid started firing at the standing bear. The first shot dropped it. Two more shots, in rapid succession, and the bear stayed down. He followed each of Bud's instructions precisely.

Bill looked the landing situation over carefully and landed after

Lost in the vastness of ice and snow, a lone polar bear on the arctic ice pack is almost impossible to see unless light conditions are just right. Even after a bear is spotted, a safe place to land must be located. Often the bear moves away to a safe place and cannot be seen.   US Fish and Wildlife photo

the bear was down, gliding to a stop just a bit closer to Bud's wingtip than either of them cared to try again—purposely or accidentally. Before Bill got halfway over to help skin the bear, he met Albert coming back, yelling and waving his hands in the very cold air. He had taken his mitts off and was almost crying because of the pain in them from the freezing air.

After Bud had taken all the pictures that he wanted of him with his bear, he started complaining of the cold. He had expensive down clothing, foot gear and mittens, but he kept taking his hands out of his mitts to do something or another, then told Bud his mitts weren't warm. Bud told him to put his hands in the mitts, then into his pockets. He suggested putting his bare hands under his clothes into his arm pits. Meanwhile, Bud started on the skinning job. When Bud got far enough into the job, Albert could put his cold hands between the hide and warm carcass.

"I don't want to stick my hands in all that mess, he whined. "I'm going back to meet Bill." Bud skinned the bear alone.

Bill went back to the airplanes with Albert and showed him how to get his hands warm. "I can't fly you back to Barrow, Albert. I am Bud's flying partner. In this cold he is in great danger without a wing mate," Bill explained. "Out here, the ice always moves. I'd never find him again."

"Are we lost? I don't want to be lost." Albert said.

"We are not lost. We'll be back in Barrow before dark."

Albert wasn't satisfied. He thought that since both planes had direction finders Bud could easily find his own way back to Barrow.

Bud hurried through the skinning job and carried, and drug, the heavy hide to the plane. He packed it into the plane as quickly as one man could so they could get to Barrow before daylight was gone. It was cold, -15° with a 20-knot wind, which equals a windchill of -60°. But they had survived much colder. Bud finished the skinning job and left the red carcass for the foxes. Albert was only concerned with getting back to the warm hotel.

The wind had picked up a bit and was blowing in the right direction for additional lift. Bill took the dude in his lighter Cub and cleared the ice ridge with plenty of room to spare. Bud saw the red wings of Bill's plane circling in the distance. He pulled his Cub back as far as he could get it to hold, then revved the engine and cleared the first sharp ridges by a comfortable margin, then 'hung on the prop' for an agonizing second before he cleared the second, higher ice-ridge. He had the heavy, raw bear hide and all of their emergency gear in his plane.

Bud told me later, "I wasn't sure I breathed until I had gained altitude and was heading toward Bill's plane. It was a calculated risk. I didn't want to spend a night on the ice pack, especially with Albert! In the hotel lobby that evening, Albert was full of himself again, and eager to let everyone know what a big, bad hunter he was. Bud and Bill were off to bed without waiting to hear much of it.

Albert would have left for home, happy with his trophy bear, if Bud hadn't told him about going wolf hunting after he got his bear if there was extra time. He wanted to go wolf hunting, so, they took him toward Wainwright and flew 4 hours without seeing any wolves. Before heading toward Barrow, they set their planes down on the smooth ice of an isolated, unnamed lake to eat their lunch and to refuel from the 5-gallon cans of avgas that they carried. The weather was deteriorating and they couldn't fly back in the direction they wanted.

While they discussed their return route, Albert said, I'm very disappointed we didn't see a wolf, or a caribou in all this boring white country."

"I love this country," Bud retaliated. "It is endless miles of beauty, of open space free of crowded cities, people, and pollution."

Albert just "harrumphed" and turned away.

They probably shouldn't have been flying in the -25° temperature and 25-knot wind the following day, but it didn't look too bad when they left Barrow. They flew southeast, skimming along at low levels, trying to pick up tracks until air turbulence was bouncing the planes around more than was comfortable, so they turned back. The deteriorating weather caught up with them and it started snowing heavily. If their ADF's hadn't been accurate, they would have had trouble getting back to Barrow. In their radio conversations, Bud and Bill debated setting down and waiting it out on the ground. At a time when a pilot is trying to make the right decision, it gets darn aggravating to have the guy in the passenger seat poking him in the back, or leaning over his shoulder, wanting to know how soon they would be back in Barrow. Bud could tell Albert was scared, especially in a couple of places where they couldn't see a quarter-mile ahead.

In the hotel, that night, waiting on weather and making plans to try another area the next day if flying weather allowed, their Dude informed them he had decided to go home. "I want my money refunded for the unsuccessful wolf hunt too." He said.

"We don't charge extra for wolf hunts and we don't make any guarantees on getting wolves. We are just dumb pilots who haven't figured out how to control or predict the weather, but we'll take you out again, when it's safe," Bud told him.

In an early letter, Bud had written it was almost a cinch to get wolves where they would try to take him, and it was our policy that the hunter keeps the wolf of his choice, if he were lucky enough to shoot more than one. He had also said that, since Albert was young and eager to hunt, he would surely enjoy the thrill of this wolf hunt, especially if they located a large pack. Even just flying over and seeing wolves scatter for cover was quite a sight for someone who had never seen a wolf. Later, Bud had written to him, before he came on the hunt, the Fish and Game had limited wolf-hunts in some areas north

157

of the Brooks Range where Bud normally hunted. They would have to hunt in different areas. Albert claimed that he never got that letter, because he had left home, on a trip somewhere else, long before he flew to Barrow.

Albert decided to go home. He raised quite a fuss in the hotel lobby, when he realized Bud wasn't going to refund some of his money. Bud was not patient under certain conditions and soon gave up arguing with him. When Albert made the remark that Bud had endangered his life, Bud blew his cool.

"You're acting like a child Albert. It would be best if you stayed in the company of children rather than pretending to be a man. I'll be glad to review all correspondence. I am sure I can verify what I have said about wolf hunts." Bud walked out of the lobby and went up to their room where Bill was already snoring loudly.

The following morning, Bud and Bill walked out to check their planes, then lingered awhile in the cafe with some hunters and pilot/guides. Bill went back to their room and picked up the correspondence file on the way to the cafe for breakfast. We always took along the clients' correspondence on all of our hunts, in the event there was a "difference of understanding" such as this. Albert never showed up for breakfast and when they got back to the hotel, he was gone. Someone had done them a big favor and helped carry his gear to the airport, so he was in the air and on his way to Fairbanks by the time Bud and Bill got to the hotel.

Their .375 Weatherby rifles were normally stored under the cots in their room. They found Bill's rifle laying on top of the cot. The bolt was missing. Under the circumstances, there was no doubt in their minds how the bolt got out of his rifle. Very likely, someone was looking for the correspondence relating to his hunt and not finding it, took the bolt out of a rifle he thought was Bud's. They couldn't understand why the person would have any reason to be upset with Bill. Bud was the one who booked the hunt. Bill is left-handed and had his rifle modified accordingly. "Maybe that 'someone' wasn't smart enough to notice that the bolt was on the wrong side of the gun for it to be Bud's," Bill said.

They looked in the garbage cans and had everyone else looking. They looked in snow banks all the way to the airport and paid the kids to look. They looked everywhere but never found the rifle bolt.

Naturally, Bill wasn't happy. Bud offered to lend him some favorite cuss words, but he declined and used some colorful ones of his own. It was more than an inconvenience for Bill. He lucked out when another left-handed pilot/guide lent him a spare rifle for the rest of the season.

Bud and I used some underrated, honest profanity, when Albert's check had a stop payment on it. That was taking his hurt feelings a step too far. We gladly paid an attorney the hunt price, to collect what was due. Bud wouldn't have objected too much if he'd taken it all, if Bud could have had his hands on that Dude for just 5 minutes.

That was the second time we had to pay an attorney to collect on a stop-payment check. Both hunters had collected trophy bears. The other hunter had taken a huge brown bear. Both times, attorneys wrote just one letter and the money was collected. Bud told Bill, "We're just in the wrong business."

All of the professional pilot/guides accumulated many hours of flying time and copious personal experiences when flying over the arctic pack ice while polar bear hunting. But, those experiences didn't prove as upsetting as were some clients they took on those hunts, and we were thankful those weren't the norms.

They enjoyed the good times and tolerated the difficulties, be it weather, aircraft repairs in the stinging cold, or a client's erratic personality. And wherever you find an assortment of people, there is invariably good and bad, easygoing, and difficult temperaments among them. And always, there's someone with a sense of humor that will alleviate the strain.

Bud was the object of jokes and witty remarks for the duration of his time. Especially among the pilot/guides, whose discussions were spiked with wit and strongly underlined by a penetrating sense of the ridiculous. They teased Bud about learning to read between the lines and make a better selection of clients. They teased him about thinking more about the money than the client. One of them even went as far as to suggest Bud take up big game hunting for a living, instead of being an air-taxi pilot and bear-hide-packer for rich Dudes.

"Yeah, I became a pilot and guide because I couldn't make an honest living doing anything else," Bud answered him.

"You're so right!" He relied.

One evening, the conversation turned to talk about some clients who complained and outfitters' ingenuity. A noted guide, who had a big outfit in good game country, chimed in, telling about a Dude on a fall hunt.

"This overfed, overdressed old duffer came complaining to me that his guide was a very poor cook in their spike camp. So I told the Dude, 'Well, did you come here to eat, or to hunt? That boy is an excellent sheep guide and I don't think you'll completely starve to death in his camp, but you are sure welcome to stay in our base camp, where we have a good cook, but no game to hunt.' That was the last I heard of his complaining. And it was the guide who had a legitimate gripe, after pushing and pulling that Dude up the mountain to get a Dall ram."

That brought to Bud's mind the question one of our young guides asked, just before he took a Brown bear client on a hunt. "Hey, Bud. This guy wants to know if we have toilet facilities out where we'll be hunting. He tells me that in all the years and places he has hunted, he has never been any place where they didn't have toilet facilities."

"Hold him under his armpits while he squats, then drop him at the precise moment," Bud told him.

They were 80 miles off the north-coast of Alaska. It's prime polar bear country. The world below them was pure white, with a light dusting of fresh snow, ice jumbled in various heights, black water in open leads here and there. There were no landmarks.

"Bear tracks at 4 o'clock," Bill called, "I'm going down for a closer look."

They followed the foot-long tracks of a big bear. It led them across the flat ice pans, over high ice ridges and across open water. They picked up the tracks on the far side of a wide lead. A few miles farther on, they caught up with the bear, and flew close enough for movies. It was a very big bear, with silky, yellowish fur rippling in the wind. Ambling along, it was agile with lumbering grace. The sense of beauty and effortless energy the bear displayed was overpowering. They turned landward and went on their way, thankful to have seen it.

They were on a picture-taking safari with a client who got his bear and had a few days left before he was due to fly home. "I'd prefer going back to the pack ice for photos. Could we do that instead of wolf hunting?" He took a lot of footage of fox fossicking for scraps near holes in the ice where a polar bear had killed a seal. He'd taken many scenery photos, but he really wanted to see a sow with cubs. They had perfect weather for flying and photography, lots of sun and shadows. On this day, the client was with Bill in his Cub.

They came across two young bears, probably three-year-olds. They were a curious pair. The men landed took pictures of them from atop a three-foot ice ridge. The bears would sit up to watch in the direction of the men. Then, curious, they would come a little closer. They became uncomfortable when they approached within 40 paces from the whirring cameras. When they finally picked up the men's scent, they decamped with comical backward glances.

Another time, with another hunter, the men had a perfect setup to land and get movies of a sow with two cubs snoozing. Bud was with the hunter as he was creeping a bit closer to get telephoto shots. Mama-bear was sleeping soundly and never moved until one cub, which had its head resting across the other cub's back, raised its head, then sat up, staring toward the men. Perhaps it let out a low rumble the men didn't hear, but Mama heard. She sat up, sleepily shaking her head, and yawned deeply, showing ivory-yellow teeth and her purple-black tongue. Then, apparently hearing the whirring of the movie camera, she stood up and, looking in the men's direction, let out a menacing growl. They immediately gathered up their camera gear and walked backward to the airplanes. She didn't appear over the ice ridge. They buzzed off and saw the two cubs standing atop the rise, looking skyward.

Cleo McMahan had finished with his hunts at the same time, and with the usual delays on weather, the three pilot/guides landed at their home bases the same day. This was also the last year Cleo hunted polar bear, and the rest of the pilot/guides stopped hunting them the following year. There is a subtle beauty and a magic in the land of the polar bear and Bud said, "I will always be grateful for having had the privilege of spending time in the arctic the past 11 years."

The Boone and Crockett Club—Records of North American Big Game—has removed the polar bear from its list of trophy species. The big game committee strongly questioned whether aerial pursuit of animals constituted fair chase.

Too little was known about the world's polar bear population and whether 10 years of locating and hunting the animals from aircraft had affected their numbers. Before and since the big game hunts, the Eskimo populations of Alaska, Canada, Siberia, and Greenland, harvested very small numbers of animals, using all of each animal for either food or clothing. Currently, Alaska game managers agree that the polar bear population is no longer dropping and has become stabilized.

Brown Bear,
Wrecked Airplane

lthough Bud and Bill Etchells couldn't hunt Polar bear, Bud convinced Bill the brown bear hunts on the Alaska Peninsula were just as profitable, not as lengthy—or as cold.

"We'll be gone less than a month." Bud told him. "The hunts will last less than 2 weeks, with 2 or 3 days preparation and flight time.

We booked 15-day hunts, beginning October 15. The clients flew commercial airline to Anchorage then to King Salmon. Bud and Bill would meet them and fly them, in the Super Cubs, to remote hunting camps. Clients were encouraged to arrive a day or two ahead of the opening date of the hunt because of unreliable weather. We booked two, and never more than four hunters a hunt. We wanted to make sure their hunt was unforgettable.

Bud's plan sounded very good. Bill went with Bud to King Salmon, shared expenses and profits. Bud hunted in that area for several years and the trophy brown bears were plentiful. But none of us foresaw the problems that lay ahead.

Bud's bear camp was located about 10 miles north of the McNeil River Sanctuary where many movies are taken of brownies fishing for salmon. From camp, the view of Mt. Augustine Volcano is magnificent.

They hunted an excellent area on the Alaska Peninsula, near Kamishak Bay. The Alaska Department of Fish and Game allotted this area in Unit 9, along with portions of two other Units as Bud's exclusive guiding areas. The allotments curbed other pilot/guides raiding small prime regions.

Bud did most of his hunting on the Peninsula in the spring, when weather was milder. He hunted in various locations with another pilot/outfitter. Our brown bear hunters came for a May hunt, and Bill booked three Texans for a fall hunt. One of Bill's clients hunted with Bill the previous year. This year he brought two buddies

In mid-September, we finished the last hunts at Wolf Lake, and, luckily, everyone had been flown out from that small lake. It was an unseasonably, early cold snap for Alaska. Bud and Colin had to break the ice away from the pontoons of the Super Cub before they could fly home. Ice was already a quarter of the way out from shore on Cobb Lake, but there was plenty of open water in the middle for landing. The sound of ice cubes being crushed in a blender, filled the autumn air. Shattering of ice under the aluminum pontoons sounded like it was ripping them open. They had to get the plane to shore. By holding just the right amount of throttle, Colin plowed a trail through the thickening ice. They unloaded the plane and began the cold, wet work of tying the airplane onto the wheeled-dolly. The plane was towed onto the shore with a bulldozer. We didn't dare leave it in the water another night.

Bud had to work hard and furious before leaving for the brown bear hunts. The hunters' trophies had to be crated for shipment to the various taxidermists, and meat stored for the winter. Hard winter would be at The Ranch by the time Bud was finished. We had to replace the Cub's floats with wheels, load tents and groceries for five men and the necessary camping equipment, tools and spare parts, extra gas cans, etc.

Most taildragger owners did all of their own minor repairs. Most could do their own fuselage recovering and engine overhauls. Licensed mechanics checked their work and wrote the certificates. The pilot/guides had to know every inch of their planes and keep them working. They were accustomed to the intense cold of the arctic or the nonexistent landing fields of the brown bear areas.

Bud hurried to finish the chores and made the changeover from floats to wheels. The Cub was loaded and parked in front of the garage, ready to leave when the snow stopped, probably the next day.

A grizzly tore up our Super Cub parked at home base the night before Bud was to meet Bill at the Palmer airport. They planned to fly through Lake Clark Pass, then stay overnight in King Salmon and then on to camp. Lake Clark Pass can be quite treacherous, with bad winds and poor visibility. There are several unretrievable wrecked aircraft on the slopes of the steep, rocky mountains in the pass. Bud wanted to fly with Bill because it was his first flight through the pass and he didn't want Bill's Super Cub added to the scenery.

Bud was up early, fidgeting, and wanting to get going. The snows finally stopped and a pink glow slipped over the mountains. He headed for the outhouse, before going up to sweep the snow off the airplane. There were fresh grizzly tracks around the cabin. We found its dirty, snowy prints on both of the kitchen windows where it had stood up and looked in without disturbing our sleep.

The night before Bud was to go brown bear hunting on the Alaska Peninsula, a grizzly bear got into the Super Cub and did extensive damage to the plane and gear. Bud said he'd like to get even with the bear, but maybe the bear was just getting even with Bud—in advance.

I wrote a short story about the bear's visit, titled Grizzly Raid and it was published in *Alaska Flying* magazine:

Bud let out a war whoop and turned and ran to the Cub. I ran out of the cabin to see what all the excitement was, and to my horror, saw the fresh grizzly tracks in the snow, heading straight to the airplane. Bud began yelling oaths that could be heard all over the 160-acre ranch. I understood his feelings, for I could have cried when I saw the scene of destruction; I'm sure Bud could have too, had he not been so busy working his way through his list of epithets!

The damage was extensive. Both sides of the fabric-covered fuselage were ripped to ribbons. The tail section had many bear bites and three-cornered tears. Cameras and gear were strewn all over the snow. The strap on the Pentax was chewed to shreds, but the case was intact. Emergency ration cans were chewed into but not eaten. (If a bear wouldn't eat them, no wonder Bud saved them for emergencies!) Bud's expensive Eddie Bauer sleeping bag was pulled out on the ground, but luckily, wasn't torn up.

Bill Etchells gassing up his Super Cub 4361Z getting ready to leave for brown bear hunting on Alaska Peninsula.

With apprehension, I looked for the new nylon wing covers I had recently stitched (in rare stolen moments of spare time). To my relief, they were undamaged. Bud was sure I wouldn't be able to finish them in time for the hunt, but I had, and secretly put them on after dark the night before. Bud's expensive .375 Winchester Magnum rifle was pulled out onto the ground with several bites on the stock and the strap was chewed and torn. Lucky for Mr. Grizzly, there hadn't been a shell in the chamber!

Bud's raincoat was completely shredded. There was dry moose blood on the coat from the last hunt. Surprising because Bud was meticulous about putting anything in his airplane with a smell that might attract a bear. We wondered if the bear smelled that little bit of dry blood, or if it was passing through and became curious and destructive?

Bud didn't have much time, so cursing a blue streak, he began pick-

166

ing up the scattered gear. Then, while I drove to Grizzly Lake Ranch 7 miles away to request help, he started taking bolts off the lift struts. Two neighbors, Benny Taylor and Jimmy Knighten, came immediately to help, and soon they had the wings off and the fuselage moved into the garage. They tightly closed the heavy doors, in case the bear came back for the canned rations it hadn't eaten.

Once the plane was tucked away, Bud telephoned Bill, who was waiting for him in Palmer. "I'll have to fly commercial and bring the gear with me to King Salmon. Damned bear. I'd love to make him pay for this."

Bill said he had met a pilot who was willing to be his wing to King Salmon. That was good, because Bill could fly on to the camp with his

Bill Etchells in brown bear country on the Alaska Peninsula. Both Bill and Bud found brown bear hunting warmer than polar bear hunting.

load, then come back to King Salmon to meet Bud.

All pilot/guides in the area at the time were busy with their own hunts and it was impossible to hire or charter an airplane to help with the flying. That left Bill to do all of the flying and there was enough involved with the hunters coming to keep three airplanes busy. He flew Bud out to set up camp while he ferried load after load of hunters, gear, groceries, and gas.

One dude was noticeably upset because there was only one airplane and let them know he had been told there would be two Supper Cubs. It didn't matter to him it was an unavoidable accident—and to have a bear tear up an airplane was a unique excuse. It has happened to other pilots in bear country and now it happened to us at our home base. These dudes felt they were being cheated because there was only the one Cub to do the flying, wasting 2 days of their hunting time. Bud assured the men they could stay over as many days as it took to get their bears, but even that promise didn't get this hunt off to a good start.

One man, Jim, hunted with Bill previously, so Bill guided him and Bud took turns guiding James and Brooke. Brooke had been a third on this hunt and he said he would share a guide.

Bud and Bill took these men out to hunt every day, despite the weather. When they murmured about going out in the rain or the wind, Bud or Bill convinced them the big bears would be around, regardless. Come evening, they were happy to be back in a warm tent with full bellies, listening to hunting stories.

The Alaska brown bear is the largest carnivore on land. Its top weight can be as much as 1,600 pounds. They are many on Admiralty, Kodiak, Afognak Islands, and the Alaska Peninsula. So, when one refers to a small brown bear, it can be as large an any grizzly, its cousin.

Jim was the first to get a bear. It was an old swaybacked boar, but he was viciously tough. Bill told us Jim was shooting a .300 Weatherby with loads that should have killed it and probably would have, given time. But after each shot, that bear would stagger to its feet and make a lunge for them. Bill said Jim must have put a dozen shots into it before it stayed down! That bear was on the fight and would have torn them to pieces if he could have reached them. His hide and fur were scarred from many fights.

It was James' turn to go out. There was a scarcity of bears close to the camp, so he and Bud hiked to a good lookout ridge, then sat and glassed the countryside. Bud said, "The wind tried to blow us off the mountain during our climb. I'd turn my back to catch my breath and it would try to rip my glasses off. If James opened his mouth to speak, the wind filled his cheeks and blew his windbreaker hood off his head."

"Are you sure the bears are out in this kind of weather?" Jim asked, when they were settled on the side of a ridge and sheltered from the wind.

Bud was busy glassing the open hillsides and trying to decide if he'd tell him the truth or not, then he said, "You'd better believe they are! Look to your left and up a bit, but don't move."

Out of the corner of his eye, Bud had seen movement and then a medium-sized bear stepped out from some heavy brush in a ravine. The old girl stopped, peered at them through her little, beady eyes. They saw a half-grown cub trailing her. She appeared to examine the men and the air was electric with tension as they watched her. The men sat frozen, hoping she decided they weren't a danger to her cub. She stood there a full 3 minutes. She turned, rumbled low in her throat, and with her cub close at her heels, she disappeared back into the brush. In just a short time, the men saw her and the cub galloping across the open hillside, putting distance between them—and that suited everyone just fine!

"Would you've shot her, if she came closer?" James asked.

A hunter and his big trophy Alaska Peninsula brown bear.

"Hell no! Without getting our scent, she wasn't sure of what she was seeing. She only wanted to be sure that we weren't a threat to her youngster," Bud answered. He didn't mention how thankful he was she hadn't made him eat his words! "I've heard many old-timers tell about meeting with grizzly and brown bears and not wanting to shoot them, so they just stood quietly. Once the bear had decided they were posing no threat to them, they went on their way."

Bud went on talking and looking for bear. "No matter how experienced you are in bear country, you know that you're only a guest. It's best to go carefully and respectfully. Do what you came to do and leave without harassing anything."

James got a decent brownie, not as large as Bud would've liked, but

169

under the circumstances, he was happy with the bear and the exciting hunting story. It was a very pretty chocolate-brown, well-furred hide. It had looked like a bigger bear when they came across it in a thick alder patch. Jim shot just as it emerged, it bellowed and crashed back into the alders with two shots in it. The sounds of growling and scuffling didn't last long. Bud gave it time to lie down and stiffen up or die, before going in after it. He had to trust his hunter to cover him, if he plowed out of the alders, with a mad bear behind him, screaming "Shoot! Shoot!" This one died, quietly, not far into the alder patch.

Brooke was a congenial man and pleasant company, but not in very good physical condition—he tired easily. He and Bill had been out all day and were back in camp ahead of Bud and James. He didn't have a bear hide to take home with him, but assured them it wasn't their fault. The guides had tried and he said he had an enjoyable time. The Mauser rifle he was shooting didn't have the necessary reaching power. He had opportunities for quick shots, but the bear elected to keep its hide a while longer. It got away, unwounded, on a bushy hillside and he never got a shot at another bear.

All three men were ready to leave the rainy and windy tent camp in brown bear country. Jim was the first man that Bill flew back to King Salmon and they were glad to get him on his way. His filthy, profane vocabulary was tiresome and unnecessary.

"We flew over two big bears digging in the sedge flats," Bill told them, after flying Brooke out. "I think it was a sow. Her cub was about the same size. I lost altitude in a wild turn. Brooke got to see those brownies break into a lumbering lope and disappear into the willows. He didn't get much movie footage, but he was excited about seeing them."

Another Year, Another Hunt

Ed Jocke, from Columbus, Ohio was a congenial man. We booked Ed for a hunt and Bill had a doctor and his wife booked for the same time. They would take turns hunting with Bill. Bill also brought along an assistant guide, Jeff, who helped him on other fall hunts.

The doctor and his wife hunted with Bill on a previous hunt for moose, caribou, and grizzly. She hadn't scored on a grizzly, and wanted to try for a brown bear. She and her husband had a bet going that her bear would be bigger than his—or at least bigger than his 7-foot grizzly.

Bud and Bill went to the Peninsula early to get the camps set up. They scouted the area before Jocke arrived. He would be settled in camp before the doctor and his wife got there. A lot of flying is involved in setting up outlying camps where everything used in the camp is flown in and either consumed or flown back out.

Jeff stayed in camp with Jocke, while they flew to King Salmon to meet the doctor and his wife. Their gear, and what groceries would fit in the leftover space, would travel with them.

To their surprise, this couple wasn't on the twice-weekly plane. There was an urgent message from Bill's wife to telephone home. The doctor telephoned of an unforeseen emergency and neither of them would be coming on the hunt. He asked Bill to refund their deposit. "Not at this late date." Bill told his wife, "No way can we refund their deposit."

Ed Jocke enjoyed his hunt with the total attention of two registered guides and one assistant. He wasn't the type of hunter who needed all of that attention and he offered to share the chores and even took a turn carrying his heavy bear hide back to camp.

When breakfast was over at daylight, Bill and Ed would hike out of camp. Carrying their lunches, they would settle themselves on a mountain side and glass the adjoining hills for bear. They spotted bears every day, often the same bears, but Ed was willing to keep looking for a bigger bear.

Finally they saw it moseying along the shore of a small lake, high

A brown bear family cruising a hillside on the Alaska Peninsula.

above Bruin Bay. They would have to cross a bushy ravine just to get within shooting range. But tall brush would hide their passage. The bear ambled leisurely in their direction. They lay down in the tall grass and waited. It was a rare, clear, sunny day. No wind. Ducks were splashing and quaking on the lake and the heat of the sun warmed their backs. Then they heard the bear splashing after fish.

Ed said. "I want that bear. He looks like a keeper."

"Wait until the bear is out of the water." Bill whispered.

When it finally came ashore, it was just far enough away that Ed wasn't confident of his rifle's power. Bill said, "I'll take a try, if you want. Watch the bear. We'll stand up if he turns opposite our direction."

When they stood up, the bear stood up too. Ed pumped the five shells in his .375 Winchester into the bear, hitting it three times. It kept running away. Suddenly it turned. "Looks like a charge! Get ready!" Bill yelled as he shot and broke its back. The bear roared. It was madly thrashing, bellowing, and tearing up the brush. It bit its front paw so hard the crunching bones were heard by the men. Ed quickly reloaded and put it down.

"It's amazing how much lead it takes to kill one of those monstrous bear," Ed said as he lowered his rifle. It was a fine specimen with a

Bud's Super Cub landed on the beach at Paule Bay on the Alaska Peninsula.

coat of luxurious chocolate brown.

Bill had the 9-foot green hide (with skull and feet still attached) on his pack and was staggering under the weight across the rocky, uneven hillside when they met Jeff coming to help. Jeff carried his Sako .338 Swedish-made rifle. "Looks like a perfect hide. Let me spell you off, Bill."

Bill was quick to take Jeff's offer and eased down in front of a boulder. He let his pack rest on the boulder and slipped out of the shoulder straps. Bill and Ed balanced the pack and Jeff slipped his arms through the straps. With a grunt and a lunge, he hefted the weight to his shoulders, picked up his rifle and led the way. As I had mentioned earlier, it's best not to weigh a pack before you put it on your back. You'd swear you couldn't lift it.

Unless it's really early in the day and camp can be reached before dark, the guide will leave the head and paws on the hide. The touchier job of carving the paws and head away from the hide can be done in camp.

The men were a good 5 miles from camp. It was late in the afternoon, and the head and paws were adding weight. "Now, this is what

Brown bears, Ursus arctos, include the largest of the North America's carnivores, Alaska brown bears and Kodiak bears, may reach a length of 10 feet and weigh up to 1,700 pounds. Their range is near the ocean where food is plentiful, which probably accounts for their size. Grizzly bears, whose name is derived from the white tips of their brown fur are also an Alaska brown bear, but they live a more austere life in the interior. They may be 9 feet long and weigh 900 pounds.   US Fish and Wildlife photo

an assistant guide does." Bill laughed. Jeff stumbled through tangled alders and climb up and down rocks. "Part of their training is to carry bear hides back to camp." Jeff huffed and coughed.

"Here, let me help, big fella," Bill said. And they traded off.

Bud met them the last mile from camp. "My turn," Bud offered. As he hefted the heavy pack, he grunted, "Damn, you should've taken two assistants and split this pack."

While Jeff was fleshing the bear hide and turning the ears and lips, Bud improved a net from fishing line and miscellany he found around the camp. He set it in the stream near camp and caught a 7-pound Dolly Varden.

"I'm impressed," Ed said. "Give me another helping, Bill."

Ed had taken a little-boys-delight in seeing salmon swimming upstream in a creek. He tried in vain several times to pounce and catch one with his hands, like the bears do.

Bud remembered 9-year-old Colin, catching a 20-pound salmon with his hands, in a narrow stream that ran by our Afognak Island camp. "I heard him yelling, 'Help, Dad, Help me!' I went over there and he had a big salmon out on the bank. The surprising thing was Colin was hanging onto the head and a fox was pulling on its tail. He was yelling for me to rescue his fish from that determined fox." The fox gave up when Bud got close. It went a few feet away and sat on its haunches with his red bushy tail curled around his feet. Colin and Bud cut off the big head and tossed it to the fox. It was all the fox could do to haul it away. It tugged the heavy, slippery fish, heading up the steep bank to the willows. It must have taken him 20 minutes, pulling backward up the 15-foot steep bank. The fox never turned loose of it once. At the time we hunted on Afognak Island, foxes were many and would come right into camp.

Ed's hunt was successful, as were the movies he took. One especially delighted him. A sow and her cub slid down the mountain on

Brown bears are heavyset with a massive, long-snouted head and a short stump of a tail. Short, thick muscular legs end in large, five-toed feet, and each toe is armed with a long, heavy claw. The powerful jaws are lined with wide, flat-topped molars for grinding food and four long canine, or eye, teeth. Most have loose skin and long, shaggy fur. They have an excellent sense of smell but poor vision and hearing.   US Fish and Wildlife photo

their rumps in the new snow. We have seen other brown, grizzly, and polar bears enjoying this activity.

The weather cooperated with Bud and he flew Jocke back to King Salmon to catch a flight home. The weather was kicking up and Bud considered staying overnight. He decided he could make it, and fighting gusty winds and squalls, he made it back to camp. By evening, the wind had picked up and tents had to be secured to the tundra with big rocks carried from the surrounding area. In these kinds of winds,

175

nailing the tents to the ground with 12-inch spikes, and several large rocks, was an absolute necessity. The airplanes were parked facing into the wind, one wheel half buried in the sand, wings and tail tied down to big rocks.

On another hunt, Bud and his hunter returned to camp to find the camp completely scattered by sudden winds. Even the stove pipe was blown right out of the tent. The tent was ripped and cooking utensils scattered so far away, they were never found.

Two days later, in calm weather, they flew back to King Salmon. With the two airplanes and Jeff to help, they had the camp dismantled and in just two trips each, left the land as clean and virgin as it was when they arrived. They left no trace of having been there. The only trace was the trampled grass where the three tents were tethered, and that would be gone shortly.

Bill stayed at Iliamna to pilot/guide for another outfitter who had

Bill Etchells by an abandoned cabin on the Peninsula near bear camp.

German hunters booked. Terrible weather kept the German hunters, and the outfitter, trapped in Iliamna and they were becoming impatient. It's tough on an outfitter, especially if he is the pilot also, to have more than a couple of hunters waiting to go on a hunt. The outfitter made a generous offer to Bill to finish the season with him.

Everything was going well and hunters were getting their game, new ones were going out, and they were well into the hunt, when the weather changed. The wind came up quite strong. Bill and Frank, the man with him, were flying some distance from their spike camp, southeast of the lower end of Iliamna Lake. Winds suddenly picked up and worsened with each gust. Bill spotted a smooth landing place and thought it best to set his plane down before the next powerful gust

176

blew it out of the air. The next gust was timed perfectly. The Super Cub flipped onto its back just as the wheels touched down. The men barely had enough time to escape.

"The wheels were still spinning when we were far enough away to feel safe," Bill told us. Working in the mighty winds, the two men worked fast and carried enough rocks and boulders to lie on the plane's underwings to hold it steady. There wasn't the remotest chance of getting the plane upright until the wind laid and they had help. The radio in the plane was useless because the antenna was broken. No one would be looking for them for a couple of days, expecting them to be in the spike camp.

Super Cub on tundra on Alaska Peninsula at Bud and Bill's bear camp.

They spent a miserable night huddled behind rocks, in the lee of the wind. It was too strong and gusty to set up a tent. They crawled into sleeping bags and survived on cold rations.

They were rescued by an Army helicopter 3 days later. Another plane, flying in the vicinity, had heard the ELT (Emergency Locator Transponder) from Bill's plane and called for a rescue aircraft. They were flown back to Iliamna. Two days later, when the winds abated, another pilot flew Bill and a mechanic out to retrieve his airplane.

The airplane was a mangled mess. Wind had beat the plane, loosened ropes, rubbed them thin until they broke. The wind bounced the plane on the rocks and stumps. Bill looked it over, then sold it for salvage where it lay. Bill never flew again. "I'll never find another Super Cub as super as that one. I can't settle for anything less."

Another time when Bill was with Bud on the Peninsula hunting and guiding, they had been grounded by an incredibly strong storm.

177

This time Bud was sure they were going to lose both of their Super Cubs. The wind came up quite fierce in the afternoon. Tents were up and secured. They dug holes in the ground and buried the wheels half way to the hubs of both planes. By night, the gusts had increased and pummeled the tents and banged against the planes. The planes were facing into the worst of it, and were riding it well. During the night, the wind changed directions. The popping and billowing of the canvas tent woke Bud and Bill from a fitful sleep.

"Bud," yawned Bill. "There won't be a chance of turning the planes in this. They gonna ride it out?"

"I'm awake, listening," Bud said. "I've been wondering what the planes will look like come morning. I'm afraid to look tonight."

Along toward morning, the wind died down, almost as suddenly as it had come up the afternoon before. When Bud peeked out the tent flaps at sunup, he turned to Bill, who was expecting the worst, "The tails of both planes are buried in snow. I can see just the tops. The tops of the wheels are covered in drifts. Every thing else looks intact. We just have a digging job ahead of us."

Bill Etchells guided and outfitted with his horses for fall hunts, very successfully for another couple of years, then gave it up entirely. He lost his plane, which wasn't insured (most aren't, even now). And then he had a big fuss later, with clients who insisted they have their deposits refunded on the canceled hunt. It soured him on rich hunters and outfitting for big game hunts. He turned to farming full time on his ranch at Kenny Lake, plowing and harvesting the crops with his horses. We bought hay from him for our own horses for many years.

Bad luck still plagued him. He had an accident while plowing. His leg was badly broken and he was laid up for much of the working season. A farm needs lots of attention. His neighbors helped and fed his livestock throughout his recovery. One neighbor, who came to feed the horses one morning, missed the big Percheron stallion. A couple of days later, it was found fallen through the ice on the small lake. It died trying to fight its way back out.

When hunting season rolled around the next year, Bud was still hunting in his exclusive guiding area in Unit 9, but only for the spring hunts. Colin was now his partner. Colin had many experienced hours and his own Cessna 180.

On their first trip together to the Peninsula, they got separated while trying to go through Lake Clark Pass. Just by chance, they found each other on a small airstrip. Colin had seen the strip as he flew over and when he encountered dense fog in the pass, turned back to the strip. The 180 is much faster than the Cub and Bud had gone on, skirting the edge of the fog, thinking Colin was ahead of him. They had lost radio contact and Bud decided he'd best turn back while he had room to do so.

"I thought you already landed some place, when you didn't answer my calls on the radio," Colin told his dad. "I saw some dead airplanes that didn't make it through the Pass, then I turned back. I was surrounded by a kind of ghostly silence. The engine was quiet and I was alone for a full 20 minutes on that tiny field. Then I heard the most welcome sound of a Super Cub's engine, muffled by fog, and soon you circled 64 Delta to land." Colin rekindled the fire Bud had extinguished while landing.

An Alaska Peninsula brown bear camp after a wind storm scattered camp gear in all directions.

There was still no clear dawn, but the day was awake in the thinning fog. They exited their pup tents and comfortable sleeping bags. In the distance, a gloomy, gray snowstorm threatened to hold them there. But it didn't appear and they were airborne at noon. Soon, Lake Clark Pass was behind them and they winged their way to King Salmon. They arrived in time to close their flight plan.

Colin was his father's partner for 2 years on brown bear hunts on the Peninsula. Then Colin went to work flying full time for a commercial air-taxi service out of Fairbanks. So Bud lost his partner again.

Johnny Morris and Tom Wolfe, from Montana, and Jim Doran, from Nebraska, were our three clients for the 1984 brown bear hunts. All three were young men, experienced big-game hunters. As great a trio as any outfitter could expect to take on a hunt. These men hunted with us on our Interior hunts, and they were the kind of guys who make you know all of your time and efforts in the outfitting business are worth it and you wouldn't want to be doing anything else. Morris

179

is a well-known rodeo champion and a top coyote hunter. He designed aircraft and built one and named it the Coyote. He and Tom Wolfe flew his Cessna 210 from Montana to our hunting camp on the Peninsula, and dodging all rocks and obstacles, landed like an old bush pilot.

These men hunted hard in all but the worst blizzard conditions and the weather didn't favor them too many days of their hunt. Tom collected a beautiful, big, dark brown bear, 8-foot 10-inches, his coat thick and shiny. It would make a handsome rug. Doran got a trophy. He worked hard for it and was happy with it. It was well earned.

Morris promised his wife he'd be back in time for a long-planned trip to the Hawaiian Islands. He shortened hunting time to take advantage of flying weather back to Anchorage.

Bud made several coyote hunts with Johnny on his ranch, as gunner in the Coyote. They agreed that Johnny would come back the following spring to get his brownie. He said he had a hunting buddy he would bring.

Bud wasn't around to make that hunt. Johnny never felt slighted just sad that his favorite big-game guide and gunner was gone.

There were accidents in our camps that could have been serious. All of our tents were equipped with airtight wood-burning stoves. More than once, a stove was filled with wood, the draft left wide open, and no one stayed to monitor the fire. The stove would get red-hot and would have burned the tent down, if not caught in time. Robin Wade and his buddy caught their tent on fire. They had been drinking heavily, celebrating their successful hunt. Next thing they knew, the whole camp was awake and out, scooping snow onto the blazing tent. They managed to get the fire out without too much damage. Wade's new chamois shirt was flaming, as he ran out of the tent, the fuzzy cloth merrily ablaze, shooting up his back. They nearly buried him with snow. He sat up and said he needed a bit of snow inside him, too, but he wasn't hurt.

Hunting at Wolf Lake with Horses

Titled this book *Hunting The Way It Was* because nonresident hunting will soon be an activity of the past in the Wrangell Mountains and the Nutzotin Range. We conducted our hunting business from Tanada Lake Lodge and from Wolf Lake. More than likely, subsistence hunting by residents will soon be eliminated from these areas, too. The U.S. National Park Service will eliminate all types of hunting when they can quietly phase out each type in the Wrangell/St. Elias National Park and Preserve.

We sold Tanada Lake Lodge and the 5 acres of land we had patent title to. We began outfitting, using horses, on the north slope of the Nutzotin Range, an extension to the north and east of the Wrangells. The Nutzotin Range was known as the Snag River country. We established a floatplane base on a lovely little lake, nestled at the foot of towering peaks where Dall sheep lived. It was virgin game country, impossible to get to except in small aircraft or on horse back. Bud enjoyed working with horses, and at one time, we had 20 riding and pack horses. He grew up with them. He worked on ranches in New Mexico. He rode in rodeos. He was a horse wrangler and guided for wild game living in his native state.

Wolf Lake is located in the heart of an area that a pack of wolves claimed as their territory. We didn't ask their permission to be there but willingly shared it with them. We named the lake for them, in gratitude for the many nights we were serenaded with their haunting calls.

Wolf Lake didn't have all of the water depth and width a Super Cub pilot preferred for take offs and landing, but it certainly kept the competition out. Skill and experience were needed to successfully operate from Wolf Lake. A pilot had to judge cross winds, no winds, and heavy loads. Often, when the water was at a low level, the pilot pulled the pontoons, floating on the water, as far back onto the shore as possible. He then firewalled the engine to get the loaded plane off the water in time to clear the narrow spit of land jutting into the middle of the lake.

LeNora, the camp cook, in a spike camp. Wives and companions of pilot/guides are very important partners in the big game and fish guiding business. They frequently handle most, or all, of the written correspondence throughout the year. They generally do all of the business-related accounting, advertising, and banking. When not in camp they stay home and maintain the home-fires, which includes the power generators and/or huge woodpiles. They keep the other aircraft free of snow and protected from moose, caribou, and horses. They transport hunters and trophies, tons of groceries and barrels of gas and supplies. They entertain non hunting spouses and companions. They feed the horses, water the dogs, sew the airplane covers, repair tents, repair saddles, sleeping bags and frequently, the men themselves.

The only supply of water for the Wolf Lake was the annual snow, and rainfall, and a couple of small springs that seeped into the lake year 'round. We always hoped for heavy winter snows and plenty of rain during the summer.

We wanted the rains to stop just before our arrival at the beginning of August and hoped the snows would hold off until we were gone at the end of September. Some years worked out that way, others left us wanting more water in the lake and less on us. Super Cub jockeys,

Entrance to Eagle Trail Ranch at Cobb Lake, Bud and LeNora's headquarters.

Bud and Colin, were quite adept at landings and takeoffs from other small lakes and they learned the secrets of this one in a hurry. Colin had his commercial license and was doing most of the flying, and quite a bit of the guiding for us during our last four or five hunting seasons.

Bud and his crew, guides, assistant guides, and horse wranglers, cut a swath of trees, little more than the width of the Super Cub's wings across a low knoll at the west end of the lake. The pilot could glide in low across the top, then sideslip in to land close to the shore. Both made hundreds of take offs and landings there and never had a serious incident. Sometimes, their flying caused the hunters to gasp and hold their breath, but I rarely paid much attention. Either they'd get off or they'd pull up before it was too late. I trusted their flight acumen implicitly.

We started with tents. But within a couple of years, Bud built a sturdy log cabin for the cook-house, with a small room at the back for the cook—usually me. In the later years Colin's wife, Cheri, or her friend, Liz, did much of the cooking. He also built a screened-in high cache. Mother Nature's Peaks, twin peaks on the northeast side resembling women's breasts, reflected in the quiet lake waters, with a perfect view from camp.Everyone photographed Mother Nature's Peaks, too. They were real conversation starters. Everyone immediately saw the similarity!

In the evenings, many mud ducks swam and dove along the shore, their little tails poked above the water while they fed on the bottom. trees lined the lake rim, deep in shadow, creating a scene admired and photographed by every client, guest, and helper who visited. Smoke

Orville Kuester and Val Zohner with their trophy moose and Dall sheep taken in the Nutzotin Range.

plumes rose from six stove pipes poking out of tents along the shore.

Super Cubs were our planes of choice. They were quick to respond, easy to fix, and hauled an impressive load. We flew them loaded; hunters and game meat on flights out to the highway, or hunters and groceries on flights in to camp. It was a half-hour flight each way. We just couldn't afford to fly it empty.

Wolf Lake was small. If there wasn't a wind to give the plane the necessary lift, the pilot had to make the flight with a lighter load, or none at all.

Grace Lake was just 3 miles west of the Alaska/Yukon, Canada border, and next to the highway. It had ample room for Super Cubs and larger planes. It had no trees for 'bookends' so it was easy to take off from with a heavy load. One year, a man waiting to fly in with Colin was a big fellow with plenty of luggage. He was used to flying in larger airplanes, but said nothing as he watched the load get packed behind the passenger seat, nor when he was seated and his long legs were doubled up almost to his chin. Then Colin loaded his duffel bag on his lap, leaving him room to see out only one side.

When this guy was unloaded at Wolf Lake, he said he would like to have Colin fly him back over the knoll and make the same short landing in the lake, when he could watch without an obstructed view.

"I could see some of the terrain we flew over and there were high mountains in the distance, then suddenly there were trees going by, with their tops above us. As Colin throttled back and glided onto the water, the plane rocked back and forth. Now that I'm standing on the ground where I wished to be when I thought the airplane was crashing. Now I'd like to see how he did that landing. It scared the

Guides and hunters riding out from Wolf Lake to go hunting. We used horses to get the men into the field, but we could not have successfully hunted without the ever present Super Cub.

hell out of me, but I looked at Colin and he had a calm look like there was no problem."

"You'll see that landing again, more than once, before you leave here," Colin answered.

This dude wasn't particularly fond of riding horses. It was the only method of getting to the spike camp to hunt the big ram. He decided to ride. Anyway, it was too far to walk.

Bud assigned him a horse named Baldy. Baldy was a gentle horse, but Bud forgot to mention Baldy had an aversion to walking through a bog, or stepping over a fallen log, if he could just jump over it. After Jack got dumped a second time, he stayed alert to the trail, instead of letting the reins lay loose on the horse's neck. I guess even the gentlest horse likes to surprise a 'sleeper.'

It's a 6-hour ride to what we called Cottonwood Camp. The trail skirted the foothills of the high mountains, followed older trails left by old sourdoughs of the late 1890s seeking gold. Most found only the true beauty of the land. The trails still show their ancient blaze marks.

Dall ewes and their frolicking lambs could be seen in high meadows. Occasional, at lunch, clients were encouraged to glass the high peaks. Everyone got excited, if rams were spotted. Our country never ceased to charm clients who hunted here. They carried a complete camp outfit on packhorses. There were plenty of ideal camping spots by singing creeks draining from the canyons. Twice, Bud talked Jack out of camping further on. Jack thought they had reached the most

Horses packed to take hunters out to a spike camp.

beautiful camp site. But, Jack did want to hunt the rams they spotted from the trail. Bud knew where the best chances were to find the 40-incher he had promised Jack.

Cottonwood Camp was nestled in the timber, a short distance from a wide gravel bar. It was right at the base of the foothills where the 6-foot-wide Cottonwood Creek flowed from a wide canyon. The canyon lead up between the tallest mountains of the range. It was an ideal camp with plenty of firewood and good water. During August and early September, delicious blueberries were huge, and abundant on the lower hillsides.

"After a long day's climb up talus slopes and shale slides, we got to a rock outcropping. I decided this was our destination. The two rams, we had glassed from below, were a short distance above us and within shooting range. The wind favored us, too. I told Jack to take his time and catch his breath while I eased up to peek around the rocks. Two rams were feeding where I had seen them, less than 250 yards above us. I looked them over carefully, then ducked back down to let Jack look.

"I musta been wrong," I told Jack. "I'll guess the bigger one is close to 38-inches but without a heavy base. The other ram will probably go 36-inches, or better. It has a heavy base that looks like it's 14-inches, plus. Let's let these go and find a bigger one tomorrow. I'd sure like to see you get one that will make-the-book."

"Hell, no!" Jack said sharply. "I'm not after a record-book ram. I just thought I'd take a really big one if it was convenient. I'd have been happy with a 40-incher. After that climb and seeing the height of the rest of the mountains in Alaska, I'll be happy with this guy. Let's get him."

"Okay. It's your hunt. They don't know we're here, so take your time and aim carefully," I whispered as he rested his rifle barrel across his arm braced on a rock at his side.

"At the loud crack of his .300 Magnum,

Joe Berry, an Alabama hunter, with his trophy moose and caribou antlers.

the ram buckled and went down, all four legs kicking as it rolled against a rock. Another quick shot, the ram was dead. I had my binoculars trained on it and he had made a killing shot the first time, but we couldn't take a chance on it kicking itself off the rocky shelf. I've seen them do that. The smaller ram bolted, then stopped, looked back like it couldn't figure out what had happened. We had moved within 50 yards before it noticed us. It left in a hurry, on its way over the top. We reached the dead ram and were shaking hands over his success, when Jack, looking past me, said, 'Look there, Bud!'

"I turned around and a ram was running up the steep slope from a slight draw, with another one running right behind it. Just before they topped out, they stopped and looked back at us. 'Hell, Jack! Those are the rams we saw from below when we were glassing. We probably couldn't see these two from the angle below. I'll bet that bugger would go 40-inches, plus. Sorry about that.'" I said, as he handed me his camera to take the pictures, before I started caping and butchering his 38-1/2-inch Dall.

"'Don't feel bad, Bud. I'm happy with this one. I'll come back and get the other, next year, if he's still around,' Jack answered."

Jack wasn't our first client who initially wrote about the big ram he wanted, but after the first, second or third day's climbing, most dudes are willing to settle for what they can see in their sights. It's tough climbing up there, even for the best of hunters.

Super Cub on small lake high in the sheep hills.

I had gone to Cottonwood Camp to cook on this hunt. Lee and an assistant guide and a horse wrangler had got the camp up and running earlier. Bud built a semipermanent high cache at this favorite camping area and we stored what we could leave there in sealed barrels, cooking pots, fry pans, and a variety of canned goods. It started snowing after we left the base camp at Wolf Lake, and continued snowing and blowing on the long ride to Cottonwood. Two hunters and their guides had returned from this camp the day before. "Leave the cook tent rolled up in its canvas," Bud told the guide in charge. "Bring the rest of the camp back on the horses."

Jake, the guide in charge knew we'd be setting up camp for another hunt, the following day. He felt he was doing us a favor by ignoring Bud's order and leaving the cook tent standing. It was a sunny day with no threat of snow when he left. He didn't bother leaving the sides rolled up, either, so a bear could easily go in without having to tear its way in. (A technique we found successful if we had to leave

188

a tent set up.) A grizzly had come in during the night and one whole side of the tent was a ripped mess. It was snowing heavy, wet, flakes on our arrival back at Cottonwood.

The grizzly had ripped through both sides the full length of the five-man tent. The zippered side was hanging loose. Oh great! Welcome to my home for the next 10 days. Bud's comments about his guide's judgment were not complimentary, nor printable here.

The horses were unpacked, grained and staked for the night. The hunters' tent was raised, and they got their cots and sleeping bags organized. We got a fire going to dry all of us. The assistant guide and horse wrangler were busy getting their own tent up, while Bud and I

Wolf Lake and surrounding as seen from the top of a nearby mountain.

were setting up housekeeping in the good part of the cook tent. My cot and sleeping bag had to be as far back as it would go. Bud quickly set up the Coleman stove. The chimney hole was too ragged to run a stove pipe through it without setting the tent on fire. I arranged the groceries to feed the crew the best I could. Bud moved in with Lee and Mike and left me to handle the grizzly if he decided to return and finish ripping the backside of the tent.

The two hunters each had a bear tag and they promised to shoot it if I hollered loud enough to wake them. I promised to scream loud enough to wake the dead if necessary!

Wade came to look over my tent and started helping me pull portions of the rips together. I held them in place, while he laced them with thin strips torn from the inner lining of the tent. I always had a few safety pins and needles and thread for minor repairs, but this was major. He systematically cut small slits on both sides of the rips and laced it just like lacing a shoe. No one dared take his shirt off, or it would have been torn into strips for tent repairs, as were my two dish towels! This was a really messy and uncomfortable task in the snowstorm. The tarp that we normally used as a floor under our cots was stretched over the tears that were too ragged to pull together. The zippered entrance just wasn't repairable. Wade's ingenious repairs to my cook tent deserved recognition. We called it the "Wade Hilton Hotel."

Al Clayton, Dr. Ortega, and Chuck Ennis with Dr. Ortega's trophies.

Denied experience—one often has to invent knowledge, so this type of ingenuity reflects the resourcefulness of making due with what you have and know and learning from it.

I used my ingenuity and experience to feed five hungry men, too. I crawled in and out of the tent by going under the flaps. I handed the large pot of stew, cooked at Wolf Lake, out the torn chimney hole. The plates and everything else to go with the dinner went out the same way. The food was heated on the Coleman stove, then Lee carried it to the hunters' roomier tent, some distance away, and the men ate there. Lee returned for more victuals and utensils, making many trips back and forth. My ratings as a cook reached 100% when I sent hot toddies to their tent, from my stash of Christian Brothers Brandy, while I prepared the dinner. I had thoughtfully packed the bottle in a wooden pannier, along with the Coleman lanterns. Events like these happened on hunts where good-natured clients really appreciated us, and we them.

When the snow let up, a gentle breeze rustled the spruce trees that rimmed our camp. Good conversations flowed around the blazing campfire. The men's return from their long day's hunt was always a time for relaxing, getting acquainted, and telling stories.

We had a good-natured doctor from South Carolina in camp one August. He came on a 10-day sheep hunt at the beginning of the season. An early snow blanketed the area and lasted 5 days. It began snowing right after he arrived. Bud brought the other two hunters

At base camp, horses are packed and riders are ready to leave for spike camp in the sheep hills to hunt Alaska the way it was and will never be again.

into camp the day before. I flew out to the highway with him on the first trip, and drove the pickup and transported hunters and groceries to/from the plane each trip. When all the hauling was done, I'd fly back into camp with Bud.

That was a memorable flight. A snowstorm caught us between the highway and Wolf Lake. Bud had to decide whether to turn back or go ahead. I couldn't help him make that decision so I tried to wait patiently. It looked marginal either way.

"I knew I had the option of landing on one of the lakes ahead of us. Going back, I didn't have that option," Bud said. "From many flights back and forth across this terrain, I could picture every hill and possible landing sight. There was a break in the thick snow and fog ahead, so I hopped from one cloud to the next until I could see the low hills in the distance. I headed straight for them knowing Wolf Lake was just beyond."

Sometimes pilots who flew without instruments, are caught in turbulent weather. They climb above it, if they can, then skim along the cloud looking for a hole to descend into to get their bearings. It is known to pilots as cloud hopping.

It was only a short distance between the hills and the lake, but it seemed like forever to me, when we were enveloped in the snow/fog. I was praying, Bud was sweating. He might have been

Jim Doran, a Nebraska hunter, packing his 42 inch trophy ram he had taken in the Wrangell Mountains.

praying, but I'm betting he was cussing under his breath. I breathed easy when he trimmed the controls and feathered the Cub onto the fog swirled Wolf Lake. Everyone in camp was standing on the shore, holding their collective breath. When they heard the Super Cub's 150 horse power Lycoming engine, they exhaled.

We were lucky that Bud and I weren't forced down on an isolated lake. We discovered someone had stolen the emergency gear out of the Cub. The Cub had been anchored at Grace Lake. Bud had driven the half mile to our trailer at Scotty Creek. We think that is when some happy hiker took our groceries. He had already flown in the new grocery supply that morning. We would have been stuck 5 days. Colin believed we were at our trailer. The folks at Scotty Creek Lodge assumed we were at Wolf Lake. I doubt we'd have starved. Bud had an uncanny way of making do. He would have caught a duck or a fish. He knew where to look for berries under the snow, too. It wouldn't have been very pleasant, but we'd have made it.

We were trapped in base camp 5 days with bad weather before we could leave for the spike camps. Card decks were worn thin and stories were being repeated, nerves were edgy. I had been camp cookie many times and knew the truth of the saying, "an army runs on its stomach." I worked hard, and creatively to keep everyone well fed. No one complained about not being able to hunt.

Heavy, wet snow continued and kept Bud and his helpers busy sweeping the snow off the tents so

A hunter high in the sheep hills of the Wrangell Mountains. No hunter will ever see the sights he was looking at. The National Park Service will not allow hunting in this area any longer.

they wouldn't collapse. They kept the wood cutting detail busy for all of the stoves. Bud frequently swept the snow from the plane wings. Five feet of snow fell in 5 days. It was only the second week of August.

Camp Cottonwood, nestled at the base of the towering Nutzo-tin mountains was beautifully breathtaking. A white, quiet world surrounded us. We even lowered our voices in reverence. A clear, crystal stream gurgled close to camp. Wolves howled in the night. In the morning wolf tracks covered the gravel bar. All three clients forgave Alaska for the delay to their hunt. The men spent the rest of the week working quite hard hunting. The snow drove the Dall rams lower to feed, and they seemed quite cooperative.

Mike Olson, an even-tempered young man had the patience of Job. Mike guided many of our clients and they enjoyed their time with us. They were very generous in their praise of his abilities. But, on a hunt with a doctor from Germany, Mike blew his cool. The doctor brought his girlfriend along and they laughed, talked, and drank in their tent half the night. Dr. Franze insisted Herta climb the mountain with him every day they hunted. Herta had a pleasant personality and was a good climber. Mike had no problem with her climbing with them for sheep. He just couldn't keep them from talking all the way up and back.

Mike glassed some big rams on their third day of hunting. Rams were feeding in a high bowl. The shale slides would make the climb a

Louisiana hunter, Rex Boyette, with his Dall ram taken in the Wrangell Mountains.

challenge to get within shooting range. The doctor and his girlfriend were willing to try. Fog kept drifting in and out where the rams were last seen. That would be to their advantage. They might be able to climb higher than the sheep before they spotted them. Mike kept motioning to them to be quiet. They would stop talking for a few minutes, then one would make a comment on the view or about the scary shale and rock slides. They encouraged each other to follow in Mike's footsteps. Talk, talk, talk. Each word got a little louder. Mike explained all of the sheep hunting tactics the very first day and again each night over supper. Apparently they hadn't listened. He had them quieted down, easing up to the rim of the bowl. He instructed Franz to get ready. "When the fog drifts away, I'll give the signal to shoot and at which one. Herta, you wait a few steps below."

When Mike and the hunter reached the position Mike had chosen, the good doctor, experienced big game hunter, stood up and exclaimed, in a voice you couldn't call even a loud whisper, "Whet-ooh. That was a climb."

"We might as well go back to camp," Mike said through his teeth. "Those rams will be on a far mountain long before we get down off this one." He didn't know where the sheep went, but they were no-where to be seen when the fog lifted a few seconds later.

In base camp that evening, the doctor was saying that Bud, his outfitter, must be afraid to climb the mountain. "We have been here 5 days and Bud hasn't climbed with us." Bud had been in a spike camp with the other hunter, who had come from Germany with Franze and Herta. When they arrived back in base camp later that evening, Mike explained why his dude hadn't got a ram. "He thinks your making excuses, because the first day, you were flying and didn't guide. He's made the remark that probably his outfitter was too old to keep up with him on the mountains." Bud was in his early 60s at the time. Maybe his white hair gave Franze the wrong impression. It usual-ly made the hunters wonder about their guide's abilities, until they started walking or climbing, then Bud walked their legs off and he never even lost his breath.

Bud brought his dude back in with a good, big ram, "Mike." Bud said. "Tell the doctor to be ready, early, in the morning. I'll take him sheep hunting." They came into the kitchen for an early breakfast while the boys saddled the horses.

Louisiana hunter, Rex Boyette, with his caribou.

Bud told Franz "I want it understood that only one of you will climb with me for a ram. Herta can go to Cottonwood camp with us, but only one of you will make the climb with me."

Herta agreed, and I went along to cook at their camp, leaving Mike to entertain the other hunter in base camp. Herta was a pleasant com-panion in camp. From the open gravel bar at spike camp, Herta, Bill, the horse-wrangler, and I saw a big ram, skylined high on a rugged peak with two 'sickle heads' standing guard.

All three of us spent the morning and into the afternoon watching with our binoculars. We knew Bud and Franze should be nearing the top after a climb up the back side of that peak. Late in the afternoon, we heard two rifle shots echo across the quiet hills, then two more, then one. When the sickle-heads dashed around an outcropping and disappeared, we were elated and believed that they got the big one. Herta and Bill grabbed their packboards and left to climb up from our side. They wanted to help pack the big ram off the mountain.

Sometime later I saw Bud returning to camp from a different direction and, since he wasn't leaning into a heavy pack, I read the message. His hunter and the two eager helpers were trailing some distance behind.

"We'll go back up there and get that ram tomorrow, after he's settled down. We gave him a real surprise. He knew something wasn't right, but I doubt that he knew we were there. The way he jumped into action and left without looking back makes me wonder if he'd been shot at before."

"We'll go back to Wolf Lake in the morning," The doctor said. "And you will fly us out to the highway."

On the ride back through the valley to base camp, Herta spotted rams at various times on the hillsides. Bud and Bill spotted them about the same time. Franze had his mind made up to fly out and refused Bud's offer to set up camp again and take him for another ram. Bud was sorry it had been Franze, instead of Herta, who got the shot at that ram, because he was sure she wouldn't have missed.

"Bud was too far ahead of me and wouldn't wait for me to catch up. I think he spooked the ram before I could catch my breath and get into position to shoot," he told the boys in camp, while they unpacked the horses.

"Win some. Lose some," Bud commented, shrugging his shoulders. The boys were teasing him about running up the mountain, leaving his hunter behind, then scaring the ram out of the country before the client could get a shot at it. "He was polite as he said goodbye, at Scotty Creek Lodge. But, let me tell you, that's not the way it really happened. The guy couldn't hit anything, not even a rock, the way he was breathing!"

What a guide dreads most is the disappearance of the game. He is well acquainted with the territory and knows the animal's habitat. He's convinced the hunter that is where they'll find it and assures him he had seen it there earlier. Some dudes get impatient and lose confidence in their guide, assuming the harder the hunt and the more miles traveled, the more game they will see. It doesn't happen like that. Every guide and outfitter has had an experience in which the client blamed him for the lack of game. But the guide knew he had done the best he could under the circumstances.

Jokers Wild

Two hunters rode the horses out with the boys one late September. Mickey Reilly and his friend, Bill Coleman, were both from Maryland. Coleman was a quiet-mannered, southern-gentleman type, but Reilly, was a former hunter and a totally unpredictable cutup. On his first day in camp, when the two horse-wranglers, both young boys, and an assistant guide were close, he emerged from his tent wearing a Daniel Boone coonskin cap. A huge cartridge belt hung on his hip, and he was shooting some type of popgun into the air.

"Oh, we're going to love this clown in camp." Bud whispered.

At sunup the next morning, the sound of a trumpet echoed across the still lake . . . Mickey was blowing reveille a sound never heard before in a wilderness setting as isolated as this lake. It will probably never be heard again. That evening, right at dusk, taps sounded across the lake, reverberating into the hills.

"Mickey, do you want to hunt game? There won't be a squirrel left to hunt with all that unfamiliar noise!" Bud laughed.

When Mickey was out of his tent, Bud found the trumpet and kept it until Reilly was back on the highway and leaving for home.

Mickey's eyesight was impaired from a birth defect, and growing worse. He still had peripheral vision, in his early 30s, but didn't think of it as a disadvantage. He wanted to do many things while his eyesight was fair. We called him our Blind Hunter and he wanted a

197

grizzly bear. "And a moose and a caribou, on the side," he told us. It was an interesting 20 days for all of us at Wolf Lake.

His first trophy, that year, was a camp robber I fed from my kitchen and it, was quite tame by this time, as were many other birds. I am convinced he took the blame to protect the guide, who was fleshing Coleman's moose cape in the morning sunshine. Mickey was playing a cassette of Spell of the Yukon recited by Stewart Hamblen. I started to the high cache, and saw the bird laying on a recorder, on it back, its feet in the air. "Who killed my bird?" I demanded.

Bud with mountain goat in Chugiak Range.

"Well, LeNora, it was like this. Cock Robin was sitting on the recorder listening. The Shooting of Dan McGrew came on. When the gun that killed Dan McGrew fired, it scared this bird so bad it just fell over dead," he said, all wide-eyed innocent.

"Am I supposed to buy that story?" I asked.

After dinner, Mike Olson came in to the kitchen and apologized for killing the bird. "I tossed a stick at it to chase it off the meat. I guess I hit it dead-center." Bud had told him to not let those eager birds feed on the choice loins. Then Mickey made up the story before Mike could confess.

A Pennsylvania hunter and his guides with an over 70 inch bull moose.

Reilly truly enjoyed being in the great outdoors, whether he got any trophies or not. He wanted Coleman to get a moose and was elated over his buddy's 60-inch trophy moose rack as if it was his own. He talked Coleman into coming on this hunt. They had hunted together, for deer and smaller game, since they were boys.

Bud was flying back from a trip out to the highway, and on the return, he had flown over a grizzly feeding on a moose kill. He instructed Al Clayton, "Leave the horses with Jerry at the foot of the hill. There is a small clearing there. Take Mickey, Coleman, and Mike with you. It's about a quarter-mile to the edge of the clearing. You'll see if the bear is

Guide Cliften Carrol caping a Dall ram.

still there. Don't take the horses that far or they will spook the bear. That bear is a real trophy and smart too. Other hunters have seen him and tried for him, but he's always disappeared just in time to save his choc-

olate-brown hide. Play it cool, Al. Get Mickey a grizzly bear hide to show off at his concession in the HUD building in Washington, D.C.. Then he can prove he really can shoot a grizzly. You know how he's been bragging to the employees and his clients."

Al got Mickey within 300 yards of the bear, but it blended into the dark background of thick tim-

In a spike camp with hunter's trophies.

ber and underbrush. It was still feeding but Mickey couldn't see it. It was only a dark blur to him. Mickey was carrying his .300 Magnum

199

rifle, with the recommended grain for grizzly. Although there were three heavy-caliber rifles there to back him up, he said "No, leave it for someone who can shoot it without backup help. I don't want to just wound it. Looking for a wounded bear in thick brush is dangerous. I would much do without the bear than without you guys." Mickey did get another grizzly, on an open river-bar.

Reilly's said "If there isn't any adventure, invent it and learn from the experience." He and Coleman rode the horses out to the highway after the hunts were finished at Wolf Lake. Theirs was the last hunt of the season. Both wanted some more adventure. Guides, Al and Mike, and two horse wranglers took them on horses the 70 miles to the highway.

Colin with Doctor Meeter and his Dall ram.

Mickey rode my horse, Tony, a really pretty palomino with a long tail and mane. Tony didn't like bull-moose, especially a bull in rut. Two close calls on the trails kept him very alert. One bull in particular harassed him while he was staked out.

Mickey heard the variety of stories about rubbing a stick against a dry tree trunk, or calling a bull in rut by grunting. The day he got his trophy bull, they were returning to camp, when, on a trail not a mile from camp, a very angry bull moose came charging down the trail and challenged the pack horses carrying the meat and moose rack. Al, Lee Hotell, and the two wranglers had their hands full controlling panicked horses and Mickey had his hands full trying to keep Tony from bolting. They managed to get away from the moose without having to shoot it.

When they got to camp and related the encounter, I admitted I was the culprit who got the bull stirred up. I heard the bull grunting and saw it emerge from the timber across a shallow bay from where I was standing. I had never tried calling a moose, but started grunting like I heard others do. It scared the hell out of me when it came charging across the water, snorting and shaking its massive rack. That was the first time I had tried the ladder behind the cook tent. Bud thoughtfully built a ladder from tree limbs. If a bear wanted in the cook tent I had no plans for defending its contents. I'd just climb the ladder.

The bull was mad enough to put me up that ladder and the two boys helping Bud, up a tree. The angry moose nearly tore the tree down with the two boys in it. It finally went on its way, snorting and hitting trees with his horns. It went down the same trail Al and Mickey were using to come back to camp.

On the evening of the second day, while setting up camp on an open gravel bar of the Chisana River, a bull moose came out of the nearby timber. Mickey thought it would be fun to try calling it, just to get its reaction. Like me, he got results he didn't expect!

"I didn't know how fast hobbled horses could travel. I got the chance that time," he said. Two picketed horses broke their stakes loose and left camp, snorting and galloping down the bar, dragging their 50-foot ropes. Loose horses scattered in all directions. The last ones were caught a day later.

Two elk hunters with their trophies and their guides on Afognak Island.

Al Clayton is one of the most efficient registered guides we have been fortunate to have with us in a hunting season. He sets up a comfortable camp in record time. Clients complimented him on his abilities. They enjoyed his affable companionship, too. He was very experienced, and capable with horses. But Al had an astonishing economy of words, especially for a man with the experiences he had from many years of guiding on big game hunts. When he was finally coaxed into telling one of his stories, men were impressed and knew he was telling it like it really happened, without embellishment.

Mickey's comment, later, about the incident was, "Al made the appropriate noises, then went about putting the camp back together."

"I was getting ready to start cooking over the campfire," Al said. "I didn't notice Reilly and Coleman walking along the river bar, away from where the boys were setting up our tents. Then I saw this bull come splashing across the river toward the horses. They started snorting and pulling at their stakes. The loose ones galloped away. The staked and hobbled ones were not far behind. There was no chance to catch any of them."

Mickey really liked Bud and didn't want to upset him. He was afraid Bud wouldn't let him come back for another hunt. He may have gotten by without Bud knowing about the incident, but there were no horses in camp when Bud flew over the next morning.

"Uh-oh . . . best I not be in sight when we get to the highway. I've heard Bud use about the worst profanity in the woods. If I'm not in sight, he may feel free to express his opinion of my ignorance. I would have been in big trouble, though, if one of his horses had been injured by that moose, next to his airplane, his horses take priority," Reilly said to Al. "When that bull headed for you and you abandoned your cooking fire, heading for your rifle, I wasn't sure how it was going to end."

"I wasn't too sure, either, but let's not call any more moose into camp, okay? You both have your moose. What we want now is a bear," was Al's unruffled reply.

The next day, Mickey shot his bear. She was a really pretty, gray-phased, barren grizzly. She sauntered onto the open bar near where Mickey was walking, leading Tony. Mike was close and spotted the bear at the same time, so he held the horses while Mickey pulled his rifle from the scabbard and shot the bear.

"Don't shoot anymore. It's a dead bear! It'll leak like a sieve with any more holes in it!" Al said, as he rode up, leading the pack horses.

"I didn't want it to get away and I wanted to do it without any backup help," Mickey answered.

Al estimated the bear was about six years old. There was no evidence she had been nursing a cub or had an older one with her. "This is a pretty hide and will make a really attractive rug."

"I'm going to have my bear mounted life-size—standing up!" Mickey replied. "I saw this little bear and I knew she was just the right size for me. I'll take her to my 13th floor apartment when she comes back from the taxidermist. Won't she be a conversation piece? The tenants in my building bet I'd never get the mounted caribou head into my apartment. You know, the one I got on my hunt with Bud last year? I'll probably have to get a bigger place, though. When my moose head comes back from the taxidermist, and with this bear, there won't be enough room where I live now. I am glad I didn't shoot that bigger bear."

Sometime later, Mickey sent us pictures of Suzie, as he called his bear. She was standing at a gun show where he displayed his collection of Winchester rifles. Another was at various antique shows. His bear definitely was a conversation piece.

Bud and I had a favorite tent. It was blue, 8-foot square, with an attached canvas floor, and screened windows and door. It was always pitched the farthest from the cook cabin. The five tents were pitched

Super Cub on tundra on Alaska Peninsula at bear camp.

between. I abandoned the tent around midnight, one moonlit night, when a snorting, rutting bull was standing in the lake, not far from our tent. Bud was snoring louder than the moose was grunting. I kept hearing it splashing closer and closer to the tent. Bud's snoring got louder and louder and the canvas walls were looking thinner and thinner. I poked Bud, he'd snort and gurgle and go back to snoring, starting on the note where he had left off. I was used to Bud handling difficult situations, so I left him to handle that one, too! And if that bull charged the tent with him in it, I was going to wait until morning to know the results. His snoring must not have been a deliberate challenge to the bull, because he never knew it was out there. Bud didn't know I had left to spend the rest of the night in the cook cabin, either!

It takes experience to keep groceries necessary to feed a bunch of working men in isolated camps and no grocery store nearby. I thought I was quite good at it, until two dentists from Denver used my entire supply of onions and sent someone back to base camp for more. "Are you fellows using onions for target practice?" I asked.

Al Clayton was the registered guide and Johnny Tremko was the assistant guide. Both clients were named John, so with three Johns in the same camp, we nicknamed one hunter Big John, the shorter one became Little John. Tremko was Walking John. He was the one who was sent walking back to base camp whenever they needed more supplies, especially onions. Their camp was 5 miles up a draw with an ideal lookout into the timber and moose trails. They weren't real serious hunters and in no hurry to leave camp. And they stayed longer than planned. They reminded me more of boys playing hooky from school, or maybe from demanding wives. They said they were hiding from demanding telephones.

These two were elaborate in their praise of Al as their guide. The variety Al carried in his backpack fascinated them. They were an hour out from camp when Big John suggested tea time. "If only I had told LeNora to put lots of tea and onions in our camp supplies," he moaned.

"I have tea," Al said quietly. He built a squaw-fire and brewed up a pot of tea, setting out four mugs and sugar from his backpack. From then on, every 2 or 3 miles was tea time. Their spike camp was already set up and Al suggested that I put extra onions and tea in their groceries. He liked to cook the camp favorite, fried potatoes with onions.

These men had tags for moose and bear and said they had a great time, even without seeing a bear.

"No, LeNora, we don't use onions for target practice, we eat them raw like apples, especially when they're the sweet kind you had in camp. In our work, we can't eat onions or garlic, so we catch up when we go hunting!" Big John said back in base camp.

Each to his own taste! Some people liked to have the brains from their animals cooked, some liked liver and heart. Eskimo in the far-north country like their fish raw and aged. Now I know there are some who like to eat raw onions the way I eat apples!

Alaska still has plenty of wolves. There are some areas where too many wolves are thriving and reproducing. The state is willing to share them with any takers from the Lower 48. There are those Outsiders who are making such a fuss about Alaska's wolf control measures. They want us to keep them all in Alaska, but don't kill any for any reason.

Epilogue

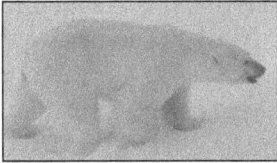

Polar bear hunting sometimes seems easy. A few hunts were, but, bush-flying over the frozen land beyond the Brooks Range, and on out over the frozen Arctic Ocean, especially under whiteout conditions, is unimaginable. Storms lasted for days. Pilots made life saving decisions whether to wait them out or fly through them. Polar bear pilot/guides flew before technical advancements we know today. They navigated this land of snow and ice with little, or no, landmarks, regularly dealing with treacherous landing conditions. Their sense of responsibility for their clients, and for the aircraft was phenomenal.

These pilots who flew and hunted the polar bears were a special type of man. Most were courageous for the most part, but sometimes foolhardy. They flew their mechanical birds across vast unmarked distances, through all kinds of weather and intense cold. Their aircraft had to be kept in top condition, and was solely their own responsibility. They had to understand their planes to recognize each noise change, each balance change and its capability.

What motivated these entrepreneurs, the professional pilot/guides who hunted the great white monarchs of the arctic ice? I suppose it was the adventure, and the money. I think Bud enjoyed the hero worship by those who could not go and those who were afraid to go. Camaraderie of their fellow pilot/guides and their clients who shared the adventure and came to know the real risks of such a hunt.

The excitement of the hunt, the challenge of man against the elements, machismo, and competition spirit had much to do with their attitudes and motives. All these pilot/guides whom I've known, personally impressed me with an aura of successful endurance. I would describe these men as persons with intense individualism, innovation, and audacity.

Whims of nature are frequently unforgivable, in the arctic vastness, or on top of a great mountain. Inventiveness is a tool of survival, and more than once, a pilot/guide has brought himself, his aircraft and his client safely back because he was capable of inventing the method. These men had more to fear from the Sierra Club, the Friends of Animals Club, and similar environmentalist groups, than from all of Alaska's bears, wolves, or natural elements.

The pilot/guides, and their clients, were grateful for experiences they shared in that fascinating land. The land, when they hunted there, was very similar to its appearance 100 years ago, before oil was discovered at Prudhoe Bay, and before the Trans-Alaska Pipeline was built from the Arctic Ocean to the Gulf of Alaska. The land and its people have changed.

Barrow has changed quite a bit in the many years since the hunts. There are modern office buildings and hotels and health clinics. They have water and sewer services. The new high school has a swimming pool. All of those little kids who used to follow the pilot/guides and hunters are middle-aged adults now, with children of their own. Instead of dog teams, there are snowmobiles and ATV's parked in each yard. Vast herds of caribou still roam across the northern slopes of the Brooks Range. The oil boom and the pipeline haven't affected their nomadic lifestyle at all. Modern jets fly daily to all points in the north. Polar bears roam through the villages and towns occasionally, and show no fear of mankind.

Many of these well-known pilot/guides are gone now. Hal Waugh and Harley King, highly-respected among their peers, are gone. Wally Rochester is gone. Jules Thibideau, known as the Walking Pilot, walked away from several crashes, but not from the last one. Jim Methaney died in a fiery airplane crash. Bob Cooper died in an aircraft accident. There are many others that I haven't mentioned.

"We just didn't know we couldn't do it," Cleo said to Colin once, when he'd asked about flying in small tail-draggers in the extreme conditions. Colin flies those same routes now, but he sits in the comfortable, warm cockpit of a twin-engine with a plethora of instruments and radios to help him navigate.

My late husband and I saw many major changes come to Alaska. We were pioneers in territorial Alaska, arriving in 1946 soon after World War II. Of course, we were just cheechakos when compared to the true pioneers of the late 1800s. Alaska we were first acquainted with had already been through dramatic changes, and it continued to change during our 40 years together. None of us were forced to like the changes, but we had to either reverse them or live with them.

I will always have my memories of those years at Wolf Lake when we were there in August and September for the fall hunts. I only hope the log cabin and cache will not be purposely destroyed, as many have been, in other places. National Park Rangers, after the last tenants were evicted, claimed the area to be within the boundaries of the Wrangell-St. Elias National Park and Preserve. Those isolated cabins saved many lives under various circumstances. I like to think of them still there.

I treasure the picture imprinted in my mind of a cow moose and her yearling calf, standing in a silver path of moonlight, the full moon hanging above Mother Nature Peaks, the lake calm and silent at midnight. All lights were out in the tents along the shore, the Super Cub riding at anchor in the sheltered cove, horses staked along the opposite shore. Wolves howling nearby and wolves answering from the far side.

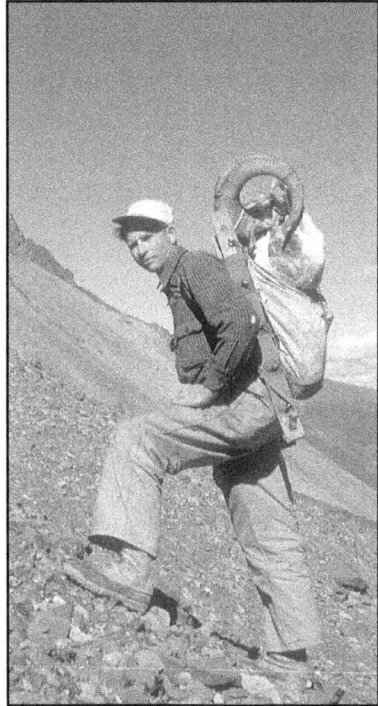

Bud backpacking a hunter's ram across a shale slide in Bud's hunting area in the Nutzotin Range. Unfortunately, the National Park Service's policies to steal the land from the honest hunter will survive both Bud and I, and hunting, especially the hunting areas in Wrangell/St Elias National Park, will never again be the way it was in our changing Alaska .

I remember cow moose coming in, late in an evening, to feed on the sedge growing underwater, lifting their heads to breathe again. Water from their long noses splashing back into the water. The clear picture stays in my mind, of the bull moose with impressive antlers that came to feed in the lake at dusk. He paid no attention to the activities in camp, leaving only when an airplane took off or landed. He seemed to delight in shaking his antlers at my horse Tony and watching him run at the end of his stake rope in desperation.

There are stormy nights to remember. Wind gusts tried to lift the long-winged Super Cub out of the water. The crew stood in the icy water, holding it down while Bud and/or Colin filled the floats with water to literally sink them. They then used a heavy weight set in the water, tied to the handle at the tip of the floats. I remember them worrying if all that would hold it. There was an AM radio in camp to receive messages, but no way to send a message out. I kept the coffee pot filled, while they were tending the airplane, and a warm fire going in the kitchen. A client from Texas carried his sleeping bag and moved in that night, going to sleep under the long table. He told me of an experience he had during a hunt in Africa where a tree blew down on his tent, across his cot. That night, he wasn't taking any chances in his tent among the thrashing trees. Winds of that severity happened twice before while we were there.

Late in the afternoons, the lake shoreline was too dark to cast a reflection. The water was dark and glassy. At that hour of the day, the pilot didn't have perspective to touch down. He needed the reflection of the trees in the water to give him perspective. That's when the pilot envies the cat that can see in the dark. Everyone in camp carried lighted lanterns to the lake, waved them or set them on the shore as guides. We'd shake our heads and heave a sigh of relief when he was down safely.

We had no major accidents in all the years we operated at Wolf Lake. We had a few narrow escapes, however. There was the time a guide, a friend, wanted to fly his Super Cub in to the lake to bring his own client. He told Bud he would help with the flying and the guiding. It sounded good, but after watching his first landing with the passenger aboard, Bud talked him into leaving the Cub parked, until he took off in it, alone.

About a week before he was due at Wolf Lake, he flipped a Super Cub onto its back in the Copper River, but managed to escape. He towed it to shore before it sank. He lost his glasses in the river accident but borrowed his girlfriend's glasses . . . and I think it was her Super Cub he was flying to come to our place, too. It was real luck that he managed to land without wrecking. It was lucky for his client, too. Jerry was noted for doing things like that and surviving. He literally lost his head, though, in a careless accident. He should have known better. He was on a beach somewhere near Cordova, taking movies of a Twin Otter. He stepped too close and too late to get out of its way. I'm thankful I wasn't there.

The Alaska Bud and I knew, is changing. It is changing for the generation of our son, Colin. Colin could not see a future in the hunting business with a growing family to support. The changes were too great and too confining. He didn't take over the business in which he had grown up. He became a commercial pilot for an established flight service in Fairbanks.

His daughter, Corrina, then 2 months old, spent a month in our hunting camp at Wolf Lake and again the next year, when she was an active toddler. Seeing a baby in an isolated hunting camp took our clients by surprise—pleasantly. Will Corrina and Wesley, her brother, ever be able to hunt and enjoy a life like their grandparents did? Probably not. I worry about them building worthwhile memories like mine when pleasures of camping and hunting in the wilds are taken from them.

We sold our horses and the cabins at Wolf Lake to Doc and Phoebe Taylor of Grizzly Lake Ranch, after Bud was awarded an exclusive guiding area in the Chugach Range. Wolf Lake is located within the Wrangell-St.Elias National Park and Preserve and Doc can't sell his investments where he now hunts, nor will his sons be able to take over the business and guide hunts there. As I understand it, Doc is limited to the number of horses he can put on the nonrenewable grazing lease we also turned over to him. There are a limited number of hunters he's allowed each hunting season. The insurance required to hunt in the Preserve is outrageously expensive. So, he is working for . . . what? His own pleasure? Well, he can do that on his own time, without the hard work involved in outfitting for big game hunts with horses and airplanes.

The National Park Service is well known for its underhanded ways of eliminating hunting in 'their' parks. They especially want all guides and outfitters out of Wrangell-St.Elias National Park.

Bud is gone now, as are many pilot/guides who hunted the pack ice for polar bear or hunted wolf from the air. The Super Cub—8464D— doesn't fly anymore. There is a saying I have heard and know to be true—"The only permanent thing is change."

Once Bud Conkle made up his mind about something, he never deviated. He could withstand physical hardships with stoical indifference. He was hand-cranking the D4 Caterpillar when the massive heart attack hit him. He had a definite opinion about hospitals and doctors. I thought he would say, "I am not dieing." But this time, he wasn't given a choice. A power greater than his made the decision. It's just as well. Bud would not, and likely could not have, conformed to all of the recent changes.

I have a radiotelephone at Eagle Trail Ranch now that replaces the CB radio for communication. My friends can proxy-hunt for me. I have a dependable 5kw Lyster generator with an electric start. It furnishes the electricity to run my modern house. Bud's wolf hide parka, the one the Eskimo lady in Barrow made for him, his sealskin mukluks and beaver fur mitts, hang on a mannequin in the trophy room. They're only a conversation starter now. His .30-06 Model 70 Winchester, with its patina of gun oil, hangs on the gun rack on the wall.

Often, with an old-timer friend, we toast the Alaska we knew. We know our Alaska is gone. Now we pass on our legacies to a new generation of Alaskans, who approve of the modern improvements and enjoy the luxuries the early pioneers did without. But won't they need to know how it all came to be? Won't they need to know our stories to lend continuity to their own? I think so.

Sitting alone in front of the warm fireplace, the only sound is the crackling of burning logs and the fragrant smell of wood-smoke. The memories rise with the smoke and bring back memories of many campfires shared. 〜M〜

The National Park Service is well known for its underhanded ways of eliminating hunting in 'their' parks. They especially want all guides and outfitters out of Wrangell-St.Elias National Park.

Editor's Notes

It has been an honor, and lots of fun, to help LeNora with the editing and publication of this, her third book. I've heard these stories often. I even played a small part in some of them. I've heard Bud and LeNora tell their stories while watching their many slides and home movies. I've listened while sitting around a campfire '50 miles from nowhere' in the Snag River country, and at Wolf Lake while hunters and camp personnel lingered in the cabin after a chilly day of moose hunting. I've always found the stories fascinating and entertaining, especially those about the polar bear years, already history by the time I joined the business.

The slides and home movies (8 and 16 mm) are family treasures that are brought out to show new friends on quiet evenings at The Ranch. Although we've seen them many times, and each time, we all enjoy them just as much. Many of Bud and LeNora's earlier slides and movies were destroyed in the early 60s. A fire gutted their rented house in Gakona. Out of everything lost in that fire, the slides and movies are missed the most.

Many hunters' names have been changed (some have not) in this book to protect their egos. All of the pilot/guides' names are real. It was not our intention to offend anyone. We told the stories the way we experienced them. No two can tell the same story from the same perspective.

The subject never dealt with in any of LeNora's works, is the amount of work the wives and companions of pilot/guides put into the business. When

211

I asked LeNora about this, she just shrugged and said, "Well . . . we just took care of things while they were gone." Boy, is that an understatement!

These women were, and still are, very important partners in the big game and fish guiding business. They frequently handle most, or all, of the written correspondence throughout the year. They generally do all of the business-related accounting, advertising, and banking. They stay home and raise the kids. They even go as far as to be home-teachers for their school-age children, and maintain the home-fires, which includes the power generators and/or huge woodpiles. They keep the other aircraft free of snow and protected from moose, caribou, and horses. They transport hunters and trophies, tons of groceries and barrels of gas and supplies hundreds of miles to/from the major transportation hubs. They entertain non hunting spouses and companions, sometimes for many days at a time. They feed the horses, water the dogs, sew the airplane covers, repair tents, repair saddles, sleeping bags and frequently the men themselves.

The women of these men, perform myriads of other little chores that help make a simple hunt possible, both for the pilot/guide and the hunter. These women were, and still are, paragons, models, of competence and patience—mostly patience. While the men were out having the wild and interesting adventures told about in these stories, the women were waiting at home, ready to handle any and every situation—but always waiting.

Yes, they took care of things while the men were gone with finesse, acceptance, perseverance, and endless patience. I take my hat off and bow to each and every one of them!

I met Bud and LeNora in the early 1970s when I was 16. I then worked for them as a general assistant in 1973. A tomboy all my life, I secretly thought "working for these old people will be a snap, I'll learn a lot and I'll be working outdoors. No more baby-sitting for me." It didn't take long, though, for me to realize those two old people were a lot tougher than I expected. They worked longer hours than anyone I had ever known. And they expected me to work just as hard. Very little of the work was easy! Just 2 weeks after I came to The Ranch, we went on a little hike. I made it one third of the way before I collapsed, out of breath with muscle cramps in both legs. They, and another couple, in their early 50s, darn-near ran up a rock-strewn creek bed to the small glacier at the top. I gained a new appreciation for the lifestyle they lived and changed my opinion about old people, while they hiked the rest of the way up and back!

In the years that followed, I watched and learned from both of them. They taught all of us youngsters, who they thought had the world by the tail. We weren't even classed as amateurs when compared to them. And we all learned far more than we thought we needed to know. Many of their horse-wranglers and assistant guides learned well and went on to become well-known fair-chase guides and/or pilots in their own right.

Bud and LeNora made me a part of their family that summer, then Colin and I married the following year. They loved and spoiled our children, Corri and Wes. It is the right of every grandparent. They taught them that there is no free ride. "It takes work and persistence to gain what you want," they said. They graciously kept me on as a family member, even after Colin and I parted in 1981. We've been good friends. I'm not sure what I would have done without them.

At the time of Bud's death in February 1985, I was serving as a volunteer Emergency Medical Technician with the ambulance service. I was based in Glennallen, 75 miles from The Ranch. Our unit responded to the call. They had just returned, the day before, from spending 4 months traveling Outside in their new diesel pickup truck and fifth-wheel travel trailer. Friends and family enjoyed their slides and movies. They picked up Bud's second, life-size, mountain-lion from the taxidermist while they were outside. They called and talked to Colin and the grandchildren, from a neighbor's home, then came home to a snowy, windblown driveway; a cold house with the water either drained or protected with antifreeze; and a cold generator. They traveled from the highway to the house via snowmobile, then started wood fires in the house and garage. The next morning, Bud was working on the D4 Cat, trying to get it started so he could plow the driveway and bring their vehicles all the way home.

We knew it must be very bad, if Bud was willing to let LeNora call for an ambulance. I figured he was too damned tough to just die. I was wrong. While in the car bringing them to meet the ambulance, Bud quietly died in LeNora's arms. And although we worked on him for another hour in the ambulance, and at the clinic, we couldn't bring him back. Life has never been the same for any of us.

Of all the memories I have, when I think of Bud, the mind-pictures which appear first are of his hands. They were strong hands, with thick fingers. No matter how hard he tried to clean them, there was always a little permanent black stains in the creases left from grime of repairing anything, and everything. He was always fixing something. Those

213

hands could easily turn bolts that made most people strain, even with a wrench. His hands could hold a chain-saw for hours. They were strong, and yet, they could gentle a cranky horse or fly the Cub as if it were a fragile butterfly. Those hands were always quick to pat a shoulder or shake a hand. Some of my favorite memories are of Bud, with two toddling grandchildren holding on to his thick fingers. One child on either side of him, going to help Grandpa check the oil in the generator, skin a fox or marten from the trapline, or just check the Cub's tie-downs.

LeNora and Bud were a pair. She is just as tough as Bud. In all these years, I've never seen her ill enough to stay in bed, and I've never seen her sit still for more than a few minutes. At 86, she's still doing 30 minutes of aerobic exercises every morning, and she tries to walk at least a mile each afternoon.

She slipped on an ice patch in April 1979, and shattered her ankle. She fell while helping Bud, with the D4 Cat, fall some trees on the homestead. Bud couldn't hear her call over the racket of the Cat's engine and the trees falling, so rather than risk having Bud back over her with the Cat, she started crawling home. She crawled nearly a half-mile in the cold, wet moss, before he shut off the Cat and could hear her calling. The day after we brought her home from the local hospital, encased in a hip-to-toe cast, I caught her mopping the kitchen floor. She'd throw the wet rag onto the floor, swipe it around with the end of a crutch, then flip it into the air, catch it and rinse for the next swipe. A few days later, she was climbing the stairs in the big house, by sitting then raising her backside a stair at a time, dragging the cast leg. She was supposed to stay off her feet for at least 3 weeks after leaving the hospital! "I'm 70 years old," she said. "There is too much to do to sit around and get old." In spite of frequently disobeying the doctor's orders, the ankle healed just fine!

LeNora still corresponds with many of their hunters and/or their wives, many other Alaska guides, and she still visits others each year. She's been very active in developing guaranteed access rights for Alaskans across national park lands. She is active in the local Republican party, and has served as a delegate to the Alaska Outdoor Council. She has been an active member of Slana Alaskans Unit for many years. There are always friends, family, and even strangers, dropping in to visit at The Ranch, and she stays busy regaling everyone with stories of their past. Homemade rhubarb or blueberry pies are always ready to serve her guests. Somehow, she's managed to write four books between those visitors and her winter trips to visit family and friends in Alaska and all over the Lower 48. She has toured Israel, South Africa, and the Grand Cayman Islands!

Often, I've wished I could have been there all of those years, maybe as a fly on the wall, or a mouse under the wood stove. I just can't imagine Bud dealing with 'Uncle Wilbur' for 3 whole weeks.

Cheri Conkle.

The National Park Service's latest "politically correct" ploy to keep people out of "their" parks is their contrived objection to noise and color pollution. I guess the thrumming sound of the engine of Bud's little red and white Super Cub taking hunters to the field would violate both noise and color pollution rules. Even a hunter's red hat or the discharge of his rifle is regulated to the past, and our children will never know *Hunting, the Way it Was in Our Changing Alaska.*   Evan Swensen, Editor, Alaska Outdoors magazine.

Bud & LeNora's son, Colin, lives with his wife, Patty, in North Pole, where they work for a local air charter service.

Cleo McMahan and his wife, Daphne, live in their comfortable home in Gakona. Cleo still flies and guides with their sons, Harley and Chuck. Both sons are renowned pilot/guides.

Bill Etchells still lives on his homestead/farm in Kenny Lake, raising horses and growing oats and hay.

Bill Ellis operates as a guide and outfitter with his wife, Lorene, out of Devil's Mountain Lodge, near Nabesna. Three of their sons are pilot/guides and expert aircraft mechanics.

Many other pilot/guides mentioned herein are gone, but never forgotten.